J. I. PACKER

& CAROLYN NYSTROM

PRAYING

Finding Our Way

Through Duty

to Delight

IVP Books

An imprint of InterVarsity Press
Downers Grove, Illinois

InterVarsity Press
P.O. Box 1400, Downers Grove, IL 60515-1426
World Wide Web: www.ivpress.com
E-mail: mail@ivpress.com

InterVarsity Press® is the book-publishing division of InterVarsity Christian Fellowship/USA®, a student movement active on campus at hundreds of universities, colleges and schools of nursing in the United States of America, and a member movement of the International Fellowship of Evangelical Students. For information about local and regional activities, write Public Relations Dept., InterVarsity Christian Fellowship/USA, 6400 Schroeder Rd., P.O. Box 7895, Madison, WI 53707-7895, or visit the IVCF website at <www.intervarsity.org>.

Thanks are due to Nathan Carson for creating the subject index.

Design: Cindy Kiple
Images: Bob Elsdale/Getty Images

ISBN-10: 0-8308-3345-5
ISBN-13: 978-0-8308-3345-0
Printed in the United States of America ∞

Library of Congress Cataloging-in-Publication Data

Packer, J. I. (James Innell)
Praying: finding our way through duty to delight / J.I. Packer and
Carolyn Nystrom.
    p. cm.
Includes bibliographical references.
ISBN-13: 978-0-8308-3345-0 (cloth: alk. paper)
ISBN-10: 0-8308-3345-5 (cloth: alk. paper)
1. Prayer—Christianity. I. Nystrom, Carolyn. II. Title.
BV215.P33 2006
248.3'2—dc22

                                                                    2006004128

P	18	17	16	15	14	13	12	11	10	9	8	7	6	5	4	3	2	1
Y	20	19	18	17	16	15	14	13	12	11	10	09	08	07	06			

CONTENTS

AUTHORS' NOTE

If you who pick up this book are as curious as we, you may have been intrigued to see that this book has two authors, and you may have wondered about our process of writing. The answer is that J. I. gave a set of talks on prayer that were taped, Carolyn worked on a transcript of what he said, and after a certain amount of to-ing and fro-ing, a text emerged that expressed the mind of both of us. Carolyn then wrote the exercises and devotional aids that follow each chapter; InterVarsity Press copyedited everything meticulously, as they always do, and the end product is what is now in your hands.

Because J. I.'s talks contained various personal references, and because in any case he has a style of his own, it was early agreed that the best course was to have it all read as if J. I. was speaking, even though we were doing a duet. So, whereas H. G. Wells wrote of the doings of the Invisible Man, here you have the sayings of a rather visible man and an almost invisible woman. J. I., however, wants it known that Carolyn contributed far more than might appear.

It is our hope that, though books on prayer abound, what we say here may be fresh and helpful to some. We do not ask our readers to take on board anything that we do not embrace ourselves, and to that extent we attempted to practice what is taught here before making it public. From our hearts this book comes; to others' hearts may it go; and for any good that it does, may God be praised.

J. I. Packer
Carolyn Nystrom

TO THE READER

This book has an activity title: *Praying.* That is precisely what it is about. It is a heart-to-heart affair in which two Christians who try to pray and wish they prayed better share thoughts about what they are doing with people whom they envisage as being like themselves. It was a challenge to write, and we hope it will be a challenge to read.

Praying is of the essence of Christian existence, and it involves beliefs, emotions, values, hopes and fears, certainties and uncertainties, knowledge and ignorance, so there is a good deal for us to write about. But the discussion will be practical as well as theoretical. Our aim is not just to clarify Christian understanding but to foster Christian living. In real praying, head, heart and hands go together. "I will pray with my spirit, but I will pray with my mind also," says Paul (1 Cor 14:15), and his words show the true path for the inner life. Then our hands must be ready to move, as God through our praying shows us that they should. We pray that in every case both spirit and mind will be fed, and prayerful Christian obedience advanced by what we have written.

The study of spiritual life as such is common these days, and that increases the ever-present danger that we will settle for exploring the theory and theology of prayer and go no further. All of us are inclined to kid ourselves that knowing about something is as good as doing it. Not so! J. I., for instance, knows a great deal about the English game of cricket and can talk cricket with other enthusiasts at the drop of a hat. But he is not a cricketer, for he has never actually played the game. Again, he loves classical music and knows a fair amount about it and can talk music with professionals, but he is not a musician, for he can neither compose music nor play an instrument. And if you get joyfully musty in a library researching prayer, yet end up with no time, energy or motivation to do more than mumble a few goodnight words to God at the end of the day before sleep sets in, you are not a praying person. We give warning that nonpractitioners will be left behind in the exploration of praying on which we now embark.

Let us continue on a personal note for a moment. As a Christian believer J. I. sees himself as a traveler on Bunyan's pilgrim path, and as a theologian (which is J. I.'s public identity) he sees himself as a catechist, one who teaches Christian basics to new believers and adult inquirers, seeking both viva voce and by writing to make and mature disciples of Jesus Christ. As a Christian pilgrim and a catechist theologian, he seems to himself to be very much a needy junior in God's school of prayer—a feeling that Carolyn shares about herself. Detective writer Martha Grimes likes to title each of her books after an unusually named English pub, and one such is *Help the Poor Struggler*. We gratefully borrow that phrase to make the point that in fact we are all, so we believe, poor strugglers in our experience of praying. So this book will look to God and search the Scriptures for the help we all need.

The paradox here is that while prayer is unquestionably natural, necessary and normal for Christian people, it constantly proves in practice to be the very opposite of plain sailing. Commands and encouragements to pray, with narratives of people doing it right and models for us to imitate and use, abound in the Bible from Genesis to Revelation, and the New Testament specifically is full of them. Jesus taught his disciples that "they ought always to pray and not lose heart" (Lk 18:1) and told the story of the persistent widow to make his point. "All prayer," says Paul, is part of the armor of God that every Christian must put on; all believers are to be "praying at all times in the Spirit, with all prayer and supplication"—that is, all appropriate forms of prayer in each situation (Eph 6:18). "In everything by prayer and supplication with thanksgiving let your requests be made known to God" (Phil 4:6). "Pray without ceasing"—in other words, keep on praying (1 Thess 5:17). When Jesus' disciples asked, "Lord, teach us to pray" (Lk 11:1), he replied: "When you pray, say: . . ." and gave them the Lord's Prayer, which he also gave as a model in the Sermon on the Mount after making three points about how not to pray, saying "Pray then like this: . . ." (Mt 6:9); that is, using the prayer not just as a formula but as a pattern. It all sounds so clear and straightforward. And yet . . .

Yet we end up struggling, and not just over making time for prayer or finding a place for it. Thoughts wander, hearts that ardently longed to be praying freeze once we start, and we dry up. We thought we knew what we had to say to God, but our minds lose focus as soon as we start to say it, our muddle reduces us to stumbling, using words that do not express our meaning, and finally our muddle descends into silence. If we try to use that silence as a time for listening to God, we find ourselves randomly dreaming. And if we recite set prayers or psalms at such a time, our words feel hollow and unreal; our heart does not seem to be in any of the things we are saying. Why these bewilderments, which we all know so well? To be told that they have something to do with sin, the anti-God allergy in our spiritual systems, that operates as a disruptive force in all of our communion with God is absolutely right, but this insight does not get us very far. What we want is help to pray properly, with reality and integrity and reverent concentration, here and now. Is such help available? That is the question to which we now address ourselves. Good praying is at once both duty and delight, but often we must begin where prayer is primarily duty. As we grow in the knowledge of prayer and in the practice of praying, however, God will sanctify our efforts and delight will come upon us. We urge you to please read on.

THE GOD WE PRAY TO

Now Jesus was praying, . . .
and when he finished,
one of his disciples said to him,
"Lord, teach us to pray." . . .
And he said to them,
"When you pray, say: Father, . . ."

LUKE 11:1-2

Lord, teach us how to pray aright,
With reverence and with fear;
Though dust and ashes in thy sight,
We may, we must draw near.
We perish if we cease from prayer;
O, grant us power to pray!
And when we meet thee we prepare,
Lord, meet us by the way.

JAMES MONTGOMERY
(1771-1854)

At the opening of this book, we invite our readers to pause a moment to ask yourselves honestly how you got on in prayer this week or first thing this morning. Our guess is that most of our readers are like us;

we want to get things right, but we are more than a little embarrassed to admit how far-reaching are the problems we have in praying. That being the case, the point from which we start is the universal Christian certainty, expressed by James Montgomery in the above lines penned two centuries ago: "we may, we must draw near. / We perish if we cease from prayer." We all *need* to pray, and we know it. We all are *told* to pray, and we do not argue against doing so. In our hearts we all *want* to pray, for we find in ourselves what we can only call an *instinct* to go to God for help and protection and comfort and encouragement, much as young children go to their parents for these things. Nor do any of us doubt that we are impoverished in all sorts of ways when we *don't* pray. So we keep on trying to pray, and we constantly look around for resources that will help us to pray better. Old Christians and young Christians, American Christians and African Christians, rich Christians and poor Christians, Christian intellectuals and Christian farm workers, healthy Christians and sick and disabled Christians, everywhere and at all times, we are all at one here. It was this solidarity of felt need here that became the trigger and launch pad for this book on praying—and on praying better.

THE VENTURE OF PRAYING

Patterns of personal prayer vary widely. Some of us use set forms. We borrow prayers from the Anglican Book of Common Prayer or draw on a wide range of devotional manuals. We use prayers that were composed by Celtic saints eons ago; we use prayers that come from the Middle Ages and prayers from Roman Catholics ancient and modern as well as prayers from Protestant sources. We make up our own prayers; we try to "formulate our souls," as P. T. Forsyth put it, by writing prayers for ourselves as a regular discipline. And many of us try to get on without using set prayers at all, some of us following the ACTS sequence (Adoration-Confession-Thanksgiving-Supplication), others not. But how happy are we with what we do?

Most Christians pray differently during different life stages. As young

Christians, enthusiastic about our newfound faith, we burble before the Lord about our lives in the way in which young children burble to their parents about all the things they see going on around them. But later we become less certain that such burbling alone is the essence of prayer. As children growing in their relationship with their parents cannot happily revert to baby ways of communication, so we reach out for a more mature and reverent prayer style, and we become less and less happy about the way we actually pray. We feel we are trudging along in a marsh, getting muddy and messed-up while going nowhere. We make requests to God and then we wonder whether they made any difference. We ask ourselves, *Is God answering my prayers? If not, why not? If he is, how is he doing it, because what's happening isn't quite what I asked for? Did I ask wrongly then?* The winter of our discontent at our experience of prayer seems to go on forever.

There are, of course, many pundits available who say, "I can help you; I will teach you a technique that works." Then they tell us about such things as listening prayer, centering prayer, labyrinth prayer, prayer in tongues, the prayer of silence, mental prayer, the prayer of union and how to get through the dark night of the soul. These phrases all have meaning, and they do in fact encourage fresh effort in praying. People sit gratefully through talks on these various techniques of prayer, and experiment with them, but they are soon found casting around for further help because their prayer difficulties have not yet been solved. Changed technique, alone, is not the remedy for their problems. Let us be realistic about where we are and where we are not in this matter of praying. Deep down all of us have found that prayer isn't as easy as some people make it sound, or as easy as we ourselves had hoped it would be once our technique was straightened out.

THE DANGER OF ROUTINE

When our praying seems to have run amuck, we wisely return to prayer as a duty. And so we establish a routine whereby we regularly pray at set times and in set ways—and this (like all the various techniques mentioned above) provides a measure of help. But here too we are wise to be wary. We must discern whether prayer has not become for us a mechanical routine we are able to carry out to our own satisfaction *just because* it is mechanical, something like the way we carry out the daily exercise of cleaning our teeth. We don't think about cleaning our teeth; we simply do it. If we routinize prayer in the same way, we don't have to think seriously about it at all, but we can go through the day with a nice warm feeling inside telling ourselves and God, "I've said my prayers; I've done it." Christians who routinize prayer as they attempt to make prayer a *genuine* exercise of communion with God are sometimes disappointed or perhaps encouraged, but for the wrong reasons.

Does routine work? For some, yes. For others their routine simply lines them up with the pagans of whom Jesus spoke, who thought they would be heard because of their many words (Mt 6:7). Routine prayer can actually come from a tired soul. It reduces prayer to an item to be ticked off in the checklist of things to do—preferably with as little mental and emotional engagement as possible. No one sets out to pray like that. But tired souls drop into the same semi-automatic mode of actions as tired bodies, and in that way prayer as a mechanical routine can become a mindless task that creates a sense of spiritual security that is false.

This pitfall is not to be equated, however, with having a specific time set aside for intentional communion with God. In that sense, our praying should be a regular routine, like eating meals. Good routine praying is not mechanical, a mere parroting of prayers, but is similar to the way that wise couples who live busy lives plan the time of day when they are going to talk about how the day has gone and just enjoy being together. Many who pray meaningfully have found it a wonderful help to schedule times with God and to plan in advance how they are going to use that time. It is like scheduling an afternoon where husband and wife will go for a walk together, where nobody will interfere, since there is a lot of stuff that they need to go over together and much they have to do for refreshing their relationship to each other. There is endless benefit to be gained from a regularly scheduled appointment for your time alone with your Lord and from planning ahead some of the ground that you will cover when you and he are alone together.

Married couples who plan such times of togetherness thus avoid the widespread trap for busy couples of living alongside each other and never talking in depth because they simply don't have time. For them, what started as love becomes a teeth-cleaning kind of relationship. Not good! And a person who plans prayer times with eager forethought will think (and perhaps say), *I don't want to break my appointments with God, for he certainly won't break his with me. I want to grow in grace, and my daily prayer time is essential for that.* Exactly! Christians are covenant partners with God, who will faithfully keep his covenant with us at all times. So, on the basis of the mutual covenant commitment, our friendship with God should grow deeper through having regular times set apart for meeting him in prayer. That at least is the ideal. But pitfalls remain.

Routine prayer, as we can now see, always brings the danger that the routine itself will become the goal and, once fulfilled, will become a source of false well-being. Routine prayer cannot of itself remove our feeling of perplexity about prayer. Faithful observance of routine may diminish the intensity of that feeling, but if we are honest we have to recognize that the perplexity itself remains. We are not sure of ourselves in prayer. We have known times when we felt that God had come very close to us as we prayed, and times too when we have brought problems to God and events have happened that we have been able to recognize as answers to our prayers and therefore as encouragements to go on praying. But on a day-to-day basis we are all still struggling, and we all need help.

THE STRUGGLE OF PRAYING

It seems, then, that *struggle* is the realistic word to describe the typical Christian experience of praying, and we are encouraged to note that when evangelical pietist and theologian Donald Bloesch wrote on our topic he titled his book *The Struggle of Prayer.*[1] We note too that in P. T. Forsyth's little book *The Soul of Prayer,* written almost a century ago, the reality of struggle is central.[2] Arguably, these are the men who have thought most seriously and written most deeply and weightily about prayer in our time. And certainly, the category of struggle will sound out as a kind of ground bass in our book.

John Charles Ryle, sometime Anglican bishop of Liverpool, England, wrote a tract that sold by the thousands under the title *Do You Pray?* (1852). It is now reprinted under the title *A Call to Prayer.*[3] Some extracts from it will help us forward as we seek to square up to the struggle of praying. Ryle's rhetoric is a century and a half old, but his points could not be more timely for us today.

> I ask . . . whether you pray, because *a habit of prayer is one of the surest marks of a true Christian.* All the children of God on earth are alike in this respect. From the moment there is any life and reality about their religion, they pray. Just as the first sign of life in an infant when born into the world is the act of breathing, so the first act of men and women when they are born again is *praying.* This is one of the common marks of all the elect of God. "They cry day and night unto him" (Luke 18:7). The Holy Spirit, who makes them new creatures, works in them the feeling of adoption, and makes them cry, "Abba, Father" (Romans 8:15). . . . . It is as much a part of their new nature to pray as it is of a child to cry. They see their need of mercy and grace. They feel their emptiness and weakness. They cannot do otherwise than they do. They *must* pray.
>
> I ask whether you pray because *there is no duty in religion so neglected*

---

[1]Donald Bloesch, *The Struggle of Prayer* (San Francisco: Harper & Row, 1980).

[2]P. T. Forsyth, *The Soul of Prayer* (1916; reprint, Vancouver, B.C.: Regent College Publishing, 1995).

[3]J. C. Ryle, *A Call to Prayer* (Laurel, Ms.: Audubon Press, 1996). Portions quoted are from pages 10-19, 26-31, 33. The whole tract is well worth reading, and the substance of it is incorporated in the chapter on prayer in J. C. Ryle's *Practical Religion* (1878; reprint, Edinburgh: Banner of Truth, 1998).

as private prayer. . . . I believe there are tens of thousands *whose prayers are nothing but a mere form,* a set of words repeated by rote without a thought about their meaning. . . . Many, even of those who use good forms, mutter their prayers after they have got into bed, or while they wash or dress in the morning. Men may think what they please, but they may depend upon it that in the sight of God *this is not praying.* Words said without heart are as utterly useless to our souls as the drumbeating of the poor heathen before their idols. Where there is *no heart,* there may be lip-work and tongue-work, but there is nothing that God listens to; there is *no prayer. . . .*

Have you forgotten that it is *not fashionable* to pray? It is one of the things that many would be rather ashamed to own. There are hundreds who would sooner storm a breach . . . than confess publicly that they make a habit of prayer. There are thousands who, if obliged to sleep in the same room with a stranger, would lie down in bed without a prayer. . . .

Praying and sinning will never live together in the same heart. Prayer will consume sin, or sin will choke prayer. I cannot forget this. I look at men's lives. I believe that few pray.

I ask whether you pray, because *diligence in prayer is the secret of eminent holiness.* Without controversy there is a vast difference among true Christians. . . . I believe the difference in nineteen cases out of twenty arises from different habits about private prayer. I believe that those who are not eminently holy pray *little,* and those who are eminently holy pray *much.*

Let me speak . . . to those who do pray. I trust that some who read this tract know well what prayer is, and have the Spirit of adoption. To all such, I offer a few words of brotherly counsel and exhortation. . . .

Brethren who pray, if I know anything of a Christian's heart, you are often sick of your own prayers. . . . There are few children of God who do not often find the season of prayer a season of conflict. The devil has special wrath against us when he sees us on our knees. . . .

It is essential to your soul's health to make praying a part of the business of every twenty-four hours of your life. . . . Whatever else you make a business of, make a business of prayer.

Never forget that you may tie together morning and evening devotions by an endless chain of short ejaculatory prayers throughout the day. Even in company, or business, or in the very streets, you may be silently sending up little winged messengers to God as Nehemiah did in the very presence of Artaxerxes (Neh 2:4). And never think that time is wasted which is given to God. . . . A Christian never finds he is a loser, in the long run, by persevering in prayer.

Tell me what a man's prayers are, and I will soon tell you the state of his soul. Prayer is the spiritual pulse. By this the spiritual health may be tested. . . . Oh, let us keep an eye continually upon our private devotions.

The wise Bishop Ryle makes us uncomfortable, and rightly so. He insists on the importance of prayer and chides any Christian who thinks otherwise. But he also encourages us as if good praying is a mountain that can be climbed. As a preacher he is being positive in order to make people aware that the problems and perplexities of prayer are not insolvable. And he is right, as we will now try to show.

In this book we contend that the key to heartfelt, meaningful, enriching realism in our prayers is threefold: clear realization of the reality of God, continual practice of the presence of God, and constant endeavor to please God every day of our lives. A word, now, about each.

Clear realization of the reality of God springs from knowing those facts about him that he himself has told us in holy Scripture. More of that in a moment.

Continual practice of the presence of God, in Brother Lawrence fashion, springs from awareness that one is always under God's eye and in God's hands, and as a Christian, is in the intimate company of God, whom we know as the holy Trinity—the holy Father, the holy Son and the Holy Spirit, the he who is they and the they who are he. Everybody's life on this earth is like a hike through scenic open country, which, with its ups and downs, smooth places and rough places, sets both difficulties and delights before each person who travels through it. The Christian's life has in it the same ups and downs that mark the lives of other people, but Christians hike in company with friends: and we are not thinking here of human friends, though ordinarily they are there too, but of these three divine Friends, who never leave one's side. As with human friends who come along with you when you go hiking, you rejoice in the fellowship of the holy Three and in what they bring that will help you along. You are glad of their company, and you do not forget for a single moment that they are there, which is what the practice of God's presence basically means. We will say more about this in the next chapter.

Constant endeavor to please God springs from love to God, called forth by wonder at the divine work of creation that surrounds us and by a greater wonder at the divine work of redemption that saves us. Each of us knows the love of the Father because, fully aware that it was not in us to love him, he nonetheless loved us to the point of sending his Son to be the propitiation for our sins (1 Jn 4:10). Each of us knows the love of the Son because he "loved me and gave himself for me," as truly as he did for Paul (Gal 2:20). And each of us knows the love of the Spirit be-cause, having renewed our hearts by uniting us to Christ our risen Sav-ior, he now indwells us to make us Christlike in character, and is grieved if we stray from the path of holiness (Eph 4:30). Jesus taught that the first commandment, the great and most important one, is "You shall love the Lord your God with all your heart and with all your soul and with all your mind and with all your strength" (Mk 12:30). Realizing the love of the holy Three, who in the unity of their being are the "Lord my God" to each of us, we are motivated supremely by what Isaac Watts called "the debt of love I owe" to love of the Three-in-One in response, and we find ourselves saying—praying!—with William Cowper:

Lord, it is my chief complaint
That my love is weak and faint;
Yet I love thee, and adore;
O for grace to love thee more!

How then should we express our love for God, such as it is? In a word, by seeking to please him. The best definition of love focuses on the purpose of making the loved one great in all appropriate ways. We cannot, of course, confer greatness on God, but we celebrate his greatness and so exalt him and render him homage by our praise, by our direct obedience, and by always trying to do that which, of all the options open to us, we calculate will please him most. Thus we glorify him. The three notions meld into one: loving God, pleasing God and glorifying God, the composite goal of the Christian's life. Following this track will lead us to a fruitful and fulfilling experience of the struggle of prayer rather than a frustrating one; that, we trust, will become increasingly clear as we proceed.

The way into the life of pleasing God is opened by realizing God's reality and practicing his presence, about both of which we have more to say. We give our attention now to the first of these, which we will write about at some length.

That the Bible tells us a great deal about God is hardly news, but we suspect that many Christians need to slap their own wrists rather sharply for neglecting it. (When did your church last mount a series of sermons or classes on the character qualities of God? When did you last make a study of them?) Certainly, the fuzziness of some Christians' ideas about our God is startling. Said a lady to a bishop, "But, bishop, surely we all believe in a sort of a something?" "A sort of a something" is as far, it seems, as some people's understanding goes. But we never "pray aright," as James Montgomery put it, until we are properly abreast of what the Bible displays to us regarding God.

In the remainder of this chapter we will set before you eight truths that the church's teachers have recognized over a period of nearly two thousand years that the Bible presents to us regarding the nature and action of God. It is surely a significant fact that from the age of the apostles to our own time the huge majority of those who receive the Bible as the Word of God have not had *any* serious doubts and uncertainties as to the Bible's view of God. Until very recently this has been an area of substantive agreement in all parts of the church in a very striking way. A lot of what Christians as a body once knew has, however, been forgotten in this era of biblical illiteracy, and we need now to spend a little time bringing it back.

Our first move must be to clear the ground by putting out of our minds the fantasies about God that the human imagination so readily comes up with. We hear people say, "I like to think of God in such-and-such a way . . ." Let it be said, loud and clear, that this "I like" mindset guarantees that all concepts of God that we form by our speculation and wishful thinking will be seriously wrong. Sin, the anti-God syndrome in our mental, moral and spiritual system, ensures that this will be so. Such ideas in fact lead only to a bottom line of uncertainty, so that people end up confused and bewildered about the God who is supposed to be the focus of their lives. We ask you, therefore, to turn your back deliberately on the world of theological guesswork and dreams, and to concentrate with us entirely on the Bible, where God himself bears witness about himself in order that we may begin to know him as he is. It has been facetiously said that the favorite flower of preachers must be the sweet pea, since the keywords in their sermon headings so often begin with the letter *p*. We ask to be taken seriously as we now delineate the God of the Bible under eight headings of which this is true. We hope that the alliteration will help to make these essential truths about God memorable and clear.

THIS IS YOUR GOD

Truth 1: God is personal. Personhood, or personality, is the highest category of existence that we know. C. S. Lewis tells the story of a young lady who was brought up by parents who saw themselves as exponents of advanced thought. They believed that the personal category was unworthy of God, and so they taught their daughter to think of him as "higher substance." When she got to years of discretion and unpacked the contents of her mind, she realized that all these years she had been thinking of God as an infinitely extended rice pudding. And since she wasn't a devotee of rice pudding, it was not in fact at all a helpful idea. In truth, impersonal ideas about God are radically inferior to his true being. Depersonalized deity is, thought wise, always a disaster.

In the Bible God is personal; that is to say, he is a being who speaks of himself as "I" and addresses us humans as "you." From Genesis to Revelation, not only do we find him speaking that way, but we see him relating to people, person to person, in a fully personal way. God is not an it, and we must not allow ourselves to think of God as an object, as if we could stand apart from him as observers watching him in the way that a biologist might watch the antics of a tadpole. No, no, no! God is always a subject, never a mere object. He is always above us, never below us. God presents himself to us in personal terms, and we must always think of him in personal terms as the God who is *here* and who confronts us and has his eye on us and takes an interest in us as persons just as we, being persons ourselves, take a personal interest in each other.

Since God is personal, it should come as no surprise to find that his relationship to humans involves two-way speech. God addresses Bible characters (and thereby us) using language, and we, like Bible characters, are called to converse with God, using language. There is no linguistic relationship between the biologist and his tadpole, but there is a linguistic relationship between you and me, and between us and God. Today, if we may put it so, God communicates with humankind in writing, as by letter (the written word of God), and humans in response communicate with God in direct speech, as by phone (prayer). But none of this would be possible if God were not personal.

Truth 2: God is plural. The first hint of this in the Bible is the mysterious *us* of Genesis 1:26, "Let *us* make man in *our* image" (emphasis added). In the creation story, the plurality of God isn't taken any further, but that mysterious *us* at the beginning of the Bible sticks in the mind as a pointer to what would later be made clear. Then in the New Testament, God is revealed as truly and personally plural. God is a Trinity, the Father, the Son and the Holy Spirit, three persons within the unity of God's being, three persons who relate to each other as persons, and who operate as a team for the salvation of God's people. Even though the word *Trinity* is not found in the Bible, the reality of the Trinity was there "in solution" all along. (The church's formulated doctrine of the Trinity was a third- and fourth-century development, focusing on this fact.) The three persons, Father, Son and Holy Spirit, are distinct in the New Testament, though it has no technical terms for expressing their shared life, nor do the writers ever pause to tell us that when they say "God" they are usually, like Jesus, speaking of the Father rather than of the three together, but they make it very clear that the three are one in both being and purpose, and they work together for our salvation. Whatever other aspects of the Trinity-in-unity are beyond our understanding, this united strategy of saving sinners is as clear as can be.

In John 3 Jesus introduced Nicodemus to the truth of the Trinity when he talked to him, first, about being born again by the Spirit in order to enter the kingdom of God the Father, and then about faith in Jesus himself as the one who would die for our salvation. "As Moses lifted up the serpent in the wilderness, so must the Son of Man be lifted up [on the cross], that whoever believes in him may have eternal life." (That is Jesus talking about himself.) "For God so loved the world, that he gave his only Son, that whoever believes in him should not perish but have eternal life" (Jn 3:14-16). There you have the truth of the Trinity—the Father giving us the Son to suffer for us, and the Spirit renovating us within to bring us into the Father's kingdom—and this truth runs all the way through the New Testament. The description of it as there "in solution" thus truly fits. Think of a liquid (tea or coffee, say) with sugar dissolved in it. The sugar is now in solution, but a chemist could crystallize it out. And similarly in the New Testament one can crystallize out the doctrine of the Trinity—the divine team working as one to bring us sinners into the fullness of eternal life.

Since the nature of the Trinity (one God in three persons) is beyond our understanding, we rightly call it a mystery. But since the fact of the Trinity is clear in the New Testament, with equal rightness we affirm it as a truth and a doctrine—that is, a truth to be taught. It is a foundational truth, without which the gospel itself cannot be stated. The gospel is the good news of God the Father planning our salvation, God the Son, the Mediator, achieving it for us, and God the Holy Spirit applying it to us as the gracious, willing guest who indwells us. Deny the Trinity, and consequently the incarnation and the personal ministry of the Holy Spirit who according the Nicene Creed is "the Lord and giver of life," and the gospel, like the deacon's fabled "one-horse shay," simply falls to pieces.

Truth 3: God is perfect. What this means is that God could not be better from any standpoint than in fact he is. He is not lacking anything or deficient in any way or needing any improvement. No, God is beyond all of that; he is already and eternally perfect, of his own kind, which is a kind that is unique to himself. In the book of Exodus, God tells Moses his name twice. A name, in the Bible world of thought, signifies the nature of the person whose name it is. God's first self-naming is at the burning bush, where God encounters Moses and sends him back to Egypt to bring his people out of slavery into a land of their own that God had promised to their ancestors long before. Moses thinks this a daunting assignment. After all he is not on the best of terms with either Pharaoh's people or his own at this point. He is, indeed, what we would call a refugee from Egypt. So Moses says, "If I come to the people of Israel and say to them, 'The God of your fathers has sent me to you,' and they ask me, 'What is your name?' what shall I say to them?" And in Exodus 3:14-15, we read how God answers that question. He says to Moses, "I AM

WHO I AM," which then becomes *Yahweh*, meaning "I AM," for short, as Bill is short for William and Bess for Elizabeth. "Say this to the people of Israel, 'The LORD [Yahweh, YHWH] . . . has sent me to you.' "

What, we ask, is going on here? *Yahweh*, the four-consonant Hebrew word which Christians used to render as "Jehovah," is the covenant name God gives himself to express his commitment to his people. In that far-off world, God would not be your God if he did not give you his name. For God's people to know his name was thus the sign and proof of his bonding with them, and by telling them God's name, Moses would be confirming that fact. But what did the name itself mean? The phrase, "I am who I am," can also be rendered, "*I will* be what *I will be*," or, "I am *what* I am." The thought expressed by this name was thus, in the first instance, an answer to the question "How does God exist?" He exists, it tells us, as the God of eternal and self-sustaining self-determination. He simply is and always was and ever will be, working out his will in sovereignty over his world. He is the God who is there, who is everywhere present and everywhere in control. He ordained what is now and ordains what will be. It is as if God, by giving himself that name, says to Moses and to us, "I am and I will be what I am and what I choose to be, forevermore. You are not in charge of things, but I am." Here we see the perfection of God's being—omnipotent, omniscient, omnipresent and omnicompetent—which in itself is matter for praise, as many of the Psalms show.

There is, however, a further question that we ask about God; namely, how does he behave? That question is answered by the second account of God telling Moses his name, which comes in Exodus 34, straight after the ugly business with the golden calf. Moses had gone up Mount Sinai to receive the laws of God, and while Moses was communing with God, his people in their impatience and unbelief had made the calf and plunged into a pagan orgy in front of it. When Moses had cleaned up the mess, breaking the tablets of the law in the process, he went up Sinai again to receive a replacement, and while he was there, "The LORD descended in the cloud and stood with him [Moses] there, and proclaimed the name of the LORD" (Ex 34:5). ("The LORD" in the Hebrew is "Yahweh." Every time you meet the word "LORD" in capitals in any version of the English Bible, it is a rendering of *Yahweh*.)

"The LORD passed before him and proclaimed, 'The LORD, the LORD, a God merciful and gracious, slow to anger, and abounding in steadfast love and faithfulness, keeping steadfast love for thousands, forgiving iniquity and transgression and sin, but who will by no means clear the guilty, visiting the iniquity of the fathers on the children and the children's children, to the third and the fourth generation'" (Ex 34:6-7).

God here declares that he acts toward humans in grace and mercy, which they need, yet also in holiness that will express itself in retribution toward those who do not take him seriously and do not respond in penitence for sin to his overtures of love. This is God's moral perfection, as manifested in all his dealings with the human race that he has made. The purity that sees lawless, self-aggrandizing action and loveless, self-seeking motivation as polluting defilements is integral to his perfection, and makes his grace to sinners endlessly amazing in the eyes of all who receive it.

God's moral perfection is constantly celebrated in the Psalms. In Psalm 86:5, for instance, the psalmist writes, "You, O Lord, are good." (*Good* in the Old Testament means generous and kind and gracious; it is a word of very broad meaning.) The sentence continues: "You, O Lord, are good and forgiving, / abounding in steadfast love to all who call upon you." This echo of Exodus 34 leads on to verse 10: "You are great and do wondrous things; / you alone are God." Yes, God is good, God is great, and all that he does is worthy of praise. God is perfect in every way.

Truth 4: God is powerful. Here we expand the hints we dropped a few pages back. Theologians express this truth by saying that God is *omnipotent,* meaning he is able to do everything that he chooses to do, just as Psalm 135:6 affirms, "Whatever the LORD pleases, he does, / in heaven and on earth." They amplify this by saying God is also *omnipresent.* He permeates every bit of his world, all the time as Psalm 139:1-6 shows. That is one of the dimensions of his power. And God is *omniscient*. He knows everything, literally everything that has been, is and shall be, and he knows us through and through. "O LORD, you have searched me and known me! . . . / you discern my thoughts . . . / and are acquainted with all my ways" (Ps 139:1-3). A series of declarations in the psalms including Psalms 93; 95:3; 96:10; 97; 98:6; 99 celebrate the fact that the Lord *reigns*. God is *king*. The image shown in these psalms is of a God of absolute monarchy, for all the kings of the ancient world were absolute monarchs in direct charge of everything within their kingdoms. The psalms are saying that God is that sort of king—and to a degree of absoluteness that no earthly monarch ever could match. He is always and everywhere on top; he is the absolute master in his own universe. "The LORD reigns." "The LORD is king forever and ever" (Ps 97:1; 10:16). Nothing escapes his cognizance and his control. This is a constantly stabilizing thought for the people of God.

Truth 5: God is purposeful. Here again, we expand hints already dropped. God has an end in view in all that he does. What is God's purpose in this world that he has made? It is twofold. On the one hand, it is the honoring and glorifying of his incarnate Son, the Lord Jesus Christ, who in turn glorifies the Father by his obedience. There is much in the New Testament highlighting these paired purposes. Scripture allows us, for instance, to listen in on Jesus' anguished prayer to his Father as he agonized over his forthcoming obedience in Gethsemane "to the point of death" (Phil 2:8). "My Father, if it be possible, let this cup pass from me; nevertheless, not as I will, but as you will." Then Jesus goes to his sleeping disciples and begs them, unavailingly, to share these moments of prayer with him, after which he returns to prayer and again expresses his resolve to obey his Father, "My Father, if this cannot pass unless I drink it, your will be done" (Mt 26:39-42). Jesus' actions in Gethsemane and after honored the purpose conceived by his Father from the beginning. He honored his Father through painful obedience "to the point of death, even death on a cross" (Phil 2:8). But the Father also honored and glorified the Son. We see this at his baptism, where the Spirit descended in the form of a dove and a voice (the Father's) from heaven announced, "This is my beloved Son, with whom I am well pleased" (Mt 3:17). And again at Jesus' transfiguration, when Moses and Elijah appeared with him while Peter, James and John watched: "A bright cloud overshadowed them, and a voice from the cloud said, 'This is my beloved Son, with whom I am well pleased; listen to him'" (Mt 17:5). Later, Jesus prayed, "Father, I desire that they also, whom you have given me, may be with me where I am, to see my glory that you have given me because you loved me from the foundation of the world" (Jn 17:24). Following his humiliation came his glorification, which remains an everlasting reality. The divine purposes were formed before time and extend to eternity. We, the followers of Jesus, are drawn into those purposes through Christ's love, death, risen life and ongoing intercession for us. No higher destiny can be imagined.

The truth is, however, that glorifying Jesus, who glorified the Father through his obedience, is only one side of God's purpose. The second aspect of it, bound up with the first, is the holiness and happiness of God's adopted family, which is the church, the people of God, millions of redeemed sinners including you and us. Then a third element of it is a consequence of, indeed an ingredient in, the second, namely, the church's grateful worship, which belongs to the happiness of which we are speaking. The way it works is that the Son, as the Father's agent and the mediator of his grace, gives the saints glory, that is, the blessing of a new inner life, a new heavenly hope and a new present joy, while the saints give the Son, along with the Father, the honor and praise that are jointly their due. The word *blessing* is used in two senses in Scripture to mark this, just as the word *glory* is. *Glory* in Scripture means both God on display (the glory God shows) and also people praising God (the glory we give). We give him glory for putting himself on display in our lives and for our eternal benefit. It is the same with *blessing*. God blesses us by his gifts. The Father blesses us by the gift of his Son, and the Son blesses us by his gift of salvation. Then we bless God by words of gratitude, devotion, thanksgiving and joy in his presence. The dual use of the words *glory* and *blessing* points to two aspects of the one divine purpose. The honor and glory of the Father's incarnate Son is the first, and the holiness and happiness of the Father's adopted family, including the church's praise for everything good, the second. This is the purpose of God.

Within this purpose the Lord Jesus comes to us through the Holy Spirit in a true personal approach as the Father's messenger and gift-bearer, and enters into an awesomely close relationship with us. He said to his disciples: "No longer do I call you servants; . . . but I have called you friends, for all that I have heard from my Father I have made known to you" (Jn 15:15). It was as if he said, "Understand that as of now, I keep nothing from you. I open my heart to you as friends do to their friends. Each of you must think of me as your friend, as I think of you as my friends." We who are Jesus' disciples should hear him as saying the same to us. The way of friends is to enjoy being together and as far as possible to have no secrets from each other. The Christian life is a matter of developing friendship with God, friendship that flows from the Father's gift to us of our Lord Jesus Christ, who on his own behalf, now makes friends with us in his own way. This too is an aspect of the purpose of God, namely, a transforming friendship with our glorified Savior whereby our life becomes a case of friend loving friend, friend serving friend, friend enjoying intimacy with friend, all along the line. We should think of ourselves that way as Christians; we are friends of Jesus Christ and of his Father, and we are to live out the reality of this friendship through prayer.

Truth 6: God is a promise-keeper. Before the words *promise keepers* were ever used for a contemporary men's movement, becoming a promise-keeper was a character quality that God established as his own. So the basis of all our asking in prayer, as of all of our trusting in God, is and must be knowing his promises, claiming them, relying on them and holding fast to them whatever happens, in the confidence that they will always be kept. Second Peter 1:4 speaks of the "precious and very great promises" that God has given us. Paul says: "All the promises of God find their Yes" in Christ (2 Cor 1:20). And, as we will see in due course, receiving God's promises and trusting those promises is an integral building block, a truly foundational activity in a Christian life. Promise-based prayer is the reality of which we will be speaking throughout this book. At the end of his life Joshua, reviewing the exodus from Egypt and the conquest of Canaan, affirmed to Israel's leaders: "Not one word has failed of all the good things that the LORD your God promised concerning you. All have come to pass for you, not one of them has failed" (Josh 23:14; see also Josh 21:45). The New Testament views Abraham as the classic model of saving faith, and Paul declares that trusting God's promise with praise was the essence of Abraham's prayer as he waited for the predicted son and heir. "No distrust made him waver concerning the promise of God, but he grew strong in his faith as he gave glory to God, fully convinced that God was able to do what he had promised. That is why his faith was 'counted to him as righteousness' " (Rom 4:20-22). Promise-trusting faith is indeed at the center of the biblical prayer pattern.

Truth 7: God is paternal. That is, in his perfection, God behaves toward those who are his in a fatherly way that, as such, is flawless. The biblical ideal of fatherhood blends authority, fidelity, affection, care, discipline, long-suffering and protection in a course of sustained love that aims always at the children's advance into strength, wisdom and maturity. God in his triunity relates to all his people according to this fatherly ideal, and more specifically, within that triunity, the first person of the holy Three does so. He, the eternal Father of Jesus the eternal Son, in whom we have been brought into our new life, adopts us sinners to be his sons and heirs with Jesus, who thus becomes our elder brother. Now by means of the ministry to us of the Son and the Spirit, our heavenly Father is leading us home to full Christlikeness and eternal glory.

In the Sermon on the Mount, to look no further, Jesus says much about how the Father relates to us. "Your *Father* who sees in secret will reward you" (Mt 6:4, 6, 18). "Your *Father* knows what you need before you ask him" (v. 8). "Our *Father* in heaven . . . give . . . forgive . . . deliver" (vv. 9-13). "The Gentiles seek after these things [material supplies], and your heavenly *Father* knows that you need them all. But seek first the kingdom of God and his righteousness, and all these things will be added to you" (vv. 32-33). "Ask, and it will be given to you. . . . If you then, who are evil, know how to give good gifts to your children, how much more will your *Father* who is in heaven give good things to those who ask him?" (7:7-11). In light of all this, and much more besides that the New Testament tells us about God's love for us his children, we can pray with perfect confidence to the Father as one who will never fail us. Human fathers may let us down, but not God. We can know with certainty that our praying will be heard and responded to in the way that is not only wisest in terms of God's own total purposes but also is best in the long run for us as the individuals we are. Thus we see that it is a truly wonderful thing to be in God's paternal hands.

Truth 8: God is praiseworthy. Our eight "sweet P's" have now shown us a series of key truths about God's character, his way of existing and his way of acting. God is *personal, plural, perfect, powerful, purposeful, promise-keeping, paternal* and, finally, in light of all that has preceded, a *praiseworthy* God. God merits all the adoration that we can give him, for the beauty, the goodness and the faithfulness that he shows us in so many different ways. It is helpful, in our praying, to make a distinction between praise and thanks, and to make sure we express both. Prayers of thanks focus to some extent on *us*. We thank God for particular gifts given to us and others personally, and for general gifts bestowed on all. Praise, on the other hand, focuses directly on God. We praise him because of who and what he is. It is the difference between one spouse saying to the other, "You are the most understanding person I know; that's one reason I love you so much" and "Thanks for the sandwich; I needed it." Both kinds of prayers are appropriate. But because we are naturally self-centered creatures, we tend to major on thanks, because God's gifts and mercies to us constantly fill our minds. Yet God himself is to be praised, for he is supremely praiseworthy.

> Praise the LORD!
> For it is good to sing praises to our God;
>   for he is beautiful,[4] and a song of praise is fitting. (Ps 147:1)

> Let everything that has breath praise the LORD. (Ps 150:6)

So it is good and right to occasionally wrestle our attention away from ourselves and turn it toward God in prayers of praise.

What this book offers, as you can now see, is less a "how to" than a "who to" (more grammatically, a "to whom") approach to praying. Realizing the reality of God, as we have described him, is the exercise of heart that sets prayer on the right footing. And now note what follows. In the light of this knowledge of who and what our God is, you and we have to be clear who we are when we come to God (the Father, the Son and the Holy Spirit) in our prayers. And that is a major matter.

To our everyday relations with people we respect—senior friends, acquaintances, interviewers, counselors, leaders, negotiators, teachers, whoever—we make a point of adjusting to what we know is their wavelength; we take care to be responsive and cooperative in light of who they are, and not pretend to be something other than what we are. Encountering them requires us to relate to them with realism, honesty and humility, every time and in every connection. So with God. When we ask God for an interview, requesting his attention (which is what we actually do when we pray), we need to be very clear in our own minds not only about who he is but also about who we are and what constitutes a humble, honest, realistic, reverent attitude toward him. That means remembering that we come to God as redeemed rebels, sinners saved by grace

---

[4]The ESV text reads "for it is pleasant," but a marginal note provides the alternative "for he is beautiful."

to be not just servants but adopted sons and daughters of God the Father, not just followers but friends of Jesus the Mediator, privileged persons therefore, now enjoying a fellowship and a destiny that are the opposite of what we deserved.

Thomas Goodwin, a Puritan, said somewhere that before beginning to pray he would "take a turn up and down" in his own past life, in order to make vivid to himself each time the depth of the mercy by which, as a new creation in Christ, he now lived. "Lord, teach us to pray," said the disciples. "When you pray, say: *Father*," was how Jesus' reply began. No one can call on God as *Father* with full Christian meaning who has not known the saving ministry of Jesus Christ. So approaching God as Father with a full realization of all that is involved not only in doing it but in being able to do it is where real, realistic Christian praying begins. And then the more we appreciate the holy love of our God in Christ, the more we will realize what sinners we are, and the more we realize what sinners we are, the more we will appreciate the holy love of the Father, the Son and the Spirit, and the more real our praying will then become.

❧ 2 ❧

THE PATH AND THE BY-PATHS

Teach me your way, O LORD,
that I may walk in your truth;
unite my heart to fear your name. . . .
Lead me in the path of your commandments,
for I delight in it.

PS 86:11; 119:35

Sheep farms are common in Britain, and that means that walkers in the English countryside become of necessity quite familiar with two kinds of trails. At the outset, they may look similar, but the outcome of following them is very different. A proper path takes you to a destination. It may be circuitous and it may lead you uphill, but it will certainly take you around the bog, and it will not walk you straight into the wall of a cliff. The second sort of trail, on the other hand, doesn't lead anywhere, at least not anywhere good. It may at first look as well traveled as the proper path, but its shape was carved by the feet of sheep on their way to lunch, not by human shoes walking on an errand, and it is set to peter out. Sheep paths are like that. Once you are on such a trail you cannot tell where you will wind up; perhaps it will just be in the company of squirrels. You move along thinking, maybe, that you are taking a shortcut and that it is going to be easy traveling, but you eventually find that your advance is blocked, the trail runs out and you can't get any farther. You are in fact on a by-path that has led you off track. By-paths might well display the sign: "Dead End, No Through Road," for that is the truth about them. Now, as in walking trails, there are by-paths in life and in prayer, and some Christians get onto them and find themselves stuck. In this chapter we will take note of how that happens so that we may by God's grace make sure that it doesn't happen to us.

The image of the by-path appears in a vivid episode in John Bunyan's *Pilgrim's Progress*, and it is helpful to travel with Christian (who of course represents ourselves) through these pages of Bunyan's powerful allegory to see how much damage following a by-path can do in one's attempt to live a Christian life. Christian and Hopeful have been walking along a path beside a river, and it has been very pleasant. They drink the sparkling water and eat luscious fruit drooping from trees watered by the river. Even the leaves taste wonderful. Shimmering through the trees is a sunny meadow laced with lilies and they lie down to sleep in perfect contentment. But after a nap they know they must travel on, and the path they have followed now bends away from the river alongside which they had hoped to continue. This is how Bunyan narrates what happened next:

> The way from the river was rough, and their feet tender by reason of their travels; so the souls of the pilgrims were much discouraged because of the way (Num. 21:4). Wherefore, still as they went on, they wished for a better way.
>
> Now, a little before them, there was on the left hand of the road a meadow, and a stile to go over into it, and that meadow is called By-path Meadow. Then said Christian to his fellow,
>
> CHR. If this meadow lieth along by our wayside, let's go over into it.
>
> Then he went to the stile to see and, behold, a path lay along by the way on the other side of the fence.
>
> CHR. It is according to my wish; here is the easiest going. Come, good Hopeful, and let's go over.
>
> When they were gone over, and were got into the path, they found it very easy for their feet. . . .

[And so they went on for quite some time until] night came on, and it grew very dark . . . and now it began to rain, and thunder, and lightning in a most dreadful manner. And the water [of the river] rose amain. Then Hopeful groaned in himself saying:

HOPE. Oh, that I had kept on my way!

CHR. Who could have thought that this path should have led us out of the way? . . .

By this time the waters were greatly risen, by reason of which the way of going back was very dangerous. (Then I thought that it is easier going out of the way when we are in than going in when we are out.) Yet they adventured to go back; but it was so dark, and the flood was so high that in their going back they had like to have been drowned nine or ten times.

Neither could they, with all the skill they had, get again to the stile that night.

So they slept under a tree, and Giant Despair caught them next morning and incarcerated them in Doubting Castle. Doubt, leading to hopelessness and despair, is what Bunyan here pictures as the result of taking a by-path and going out of the right way.[1]

Bunyan portrays by-paths as a threat to the larger Christian life, as indeed they are (more of that in a moment). The present point is that the danger and frustration of by-paths seems to apply in very specific ways to prayer. As we struggle to become men and women of prayer, we need to be wary of trails, however well worn, that lead us away from true praying. Along these by-paths weeds sprout in all directions, sending our attention off into fruitless and often painful distractions. We hope in this chapter to clear the ground for the life of prayer by getting rid of

---

[1]John Bunyan (1628-1688) was an English Puritan preacher and author who spent considerable time in prison for his faith. This extract from Pilgrim's Progress comes from pages 126-28 in an undated version published in Chicago by Moody Press. The full title is The Pilgrim's Progress: From This World to That Which Is to Come, Delivered Under the Similitude of a Dream. For more on the spiritual content of the allegory, see J. I. Packer's chapter on Pilgrim's Progress in The Devoted Life: An Invitation to the Puritan Classics, ed. Kelly M. Kapic and Randall C. Gleason (Downers Grove, Ill.: InterVarsity Press, 2004), pp. 183-99.

some of those weeds. True praying is an activity built on a theology, so we cannot look at either the work of prayer or the study of prayer in isolation from each other. We need to detect the ways and attitudes and beliefs in regard to prayer that undercut the reality of praying. Though praying ought to be a means of grace and of fulfillment to the heart, it doesn't always operate as such. Why not? Perhaps because we're doing it wrong.

AUTHENTIC PATHS

Counterfeits are always best identified by comparison with the genuine article. So before we look too closely at by-paths, we need to take a careful look at the authentic path of prayer. This covers three things. We distinguish them, though they belong together, because people tend to pray with any one of these in mind, often to the exclusion of the other two. Yet true praying involves a grasp of all three and is itself the fruit of taking all three to heart.

1. *The authentic path of prayer follows instruction from Scripture.* You see the word *way* used in Psalm 27:11 where the psalmist prays, "Teach me your way, O LORD, and lead me on a level path." "Teach me your way"; that is a plea for instruction. If we want to pray rightly, we must take instruction from God through his Word, the Scriptures. His path for us in prayer, as in the rest of our living, is not one we know by instinct but is a learned way, one he teaches. If we want to walk the true path, we will diligently receive that instruction and heed it. Otherwise, our calling on God will truly, and sadly, be by-path praying.

Where then in Scripture do we find our instruction? Do we really need to ask? Precepts and promises about praying abound in both Testaments. So do examples of authentic praying, among them no less than 150 psalms, all of which are models of praise and thanksgiving or of petition and intercession or of meditations that should lead straight into one of these modes of addressing God. But how many in our day have taken these prayer models seriously to heart? Not using the Psalter and

the great prayers of the Bible narrative as patterns for our own praying
is one reason why, when we pray, we stumble and fumble so badly.

2. *The authentic path of prayer expresses a God-taught commitment to a
way of life.* This is the way of *living* in accordance with the teaching that
Scripture presents. We learn in the book of Acts that the believers' path
of godliness in those first Christian years was called "the Way." Once you
put faith in Jesus Christ and began to live as his disciple, following his
teachings, you were on "the Way" (Acts 9:2; 19:9, 23; 24:14, 22). So in
Psalm 16:11, for instance, the psalmist says, "You made known to me the
path of life." That is, you made known to me the way of responsive,
grateful obedience, the way that I am going now. (The whole psalm celebrates the fact that David is now on track, by the grace of God.) "You
made known to me the path of life," and so my hope and my prospects
have become gloriously clear. "In your presence there is fullness of joy;
/ at your right hand are pleasures forevermore." That is the happy state
to which the authentic path leads, a happiness that I begin to enjoy from
the time I take my first steps on that true path, by my personal repentance of sin and faith in Christ as my sin-bearing Savior. As the path *to*
life is embracing God's instruction, so the path *of* life is living according
to that instruction, daily following "the Way." If our praying is authentic,
it will reflect throughout the fact that this is the constant direction of our
life. If not, it will truly and sadly be by-path praying.

3. *The authentic path of prayer requires purity of heart as we pray.* This
means a great deal more than might at first appear. In contemporary society, when we speak of the heart in the metaphorical sense, not as the
body's blood pump but as an aspect of our selfhood, we are likely to be
thinking of either a flood of emotional intensity ("I love you with all my
heart") or a flow of robust enthusiasm ("his *heart* is in what he is doing"),
and not of anything more. But in the consistent Bible view the heart is
nothing less than the taproot of the self, the deep source of our character
and purposes, of our attitudes and responses, of our self-image and self-
projection, in short, of the total human being that each of us is. The

Bible—which means, God, as revealed in the Bible—looks at us from a unitary perspective, and we are, according to the God's-eye view of us, good or bad according to our heart quality. Says Jesus: "What comes out of the mouth *proceeds from the heart,* and this defiles a person. For out of the heart come evil thoughts, murder, adultery, sexual immorality, theft, false witness, slander" (Mt 15:18-19, emphasis added). A bad-hearted person is like a bad tree producing bad fruit (Mt 12:33-35).

Conversely, in the parable of the sower, the seed sown in the good soil represents "those who, hearing the word, hold it fast *in an honest and good heart,* and bear fruit with patience" (Lk 8:15, emphasis added). We today assess people from the outside in grading them mainly by their skills, and we label them good *people,* despite their moral lapses, as long as they use their skills to do what we recognize as a good *job.* (Think of how we talk about frontline politicians, sports stars, entertainers, film actors and those who succeed in business.) God, however, assesses everyone from the inside out, measuring us entirely by the state of our hearts. It is with God's method of assessment, which digs so much deeper than ours, that we must all finally come to terms, as now we explore the nature of authentic prayer.

Authentic praying, as previously said, requires of us purity of heart. Now what is that? If in everyday speech we refer to pure hearts, we are likely only to be identifying some people as not inclined, as others are, to sexual shenanigans or to the underhand exploitation of others for personal advancement or to cruel abuse of them for some perverted self-gratification. But Kierkegaard put his finger on the deep truth of the matter when he titled one of his books *Purity of Heart Is to Will One Thing.*[2] Jesus spelled out that truth when he said, "You shall love the Lord your God with all your *heart* and with all your *soul* and with all your *mind.* This is the great and first commandment" (Mt 22:37-38, emphasis added). Heart, soul and mind here are words of overlapping meaning,

---

[2]Søren Kierkegaard, *Purity of Heart Is to Will One Thing* (New York: Harper & Row, 1948).

almost synonyms; Jesus is saying, as did Deuteronomy 6:5, which he is echoing, that we are to love our God with everything we have got. And in saying this he is effectively defining for us the purity of heart of which he had elsewhere said: "Blessed are the pure in heart, for they shall see God" (Mt 5:8). Purity of heart is indeed a matter of willing one thing, namely to live every day of one's life loving God.

How then should we spell out the dimensions of purity of heart? It is a matter of saying and meaning what originally the psalmist said: "Whom have I in heaven but you? / And there is nothing on earth that I desire besides you" (Ps 73:25)—nothing, that is, that I would not consent to lose if adhering to God required it. Thus, it is a matter of wanting and valuing "fellowship . . . with the Father and with his Son Jesus Christ" (1 Jn 1:3) more than I want or value anything else in this world. Again, it is a matter of developing, as Jonathan Edwards developed, "a God-entranced vision of all things,"[3] so that the thought of everything being God's property and in God's hands, and of God as in reality doing all things well, despite short-term appearances, brings unending joy. And it is a matter of making knowing and loving and pleasing and praising God my life task, and of seeking to lead others into the same God-glorifying life pattern. This is the motivational attitude that is reflected and expressed in all authentic prayer. Without it our calling on God, however regular and orderly, will truly and sadly be by-path praying.

But if that is so, who dare pray? Who of us dare think of ourselves as pure-hearted according to the above analysis? The answer is: every regenerate Christian, every born-again believer, without a single exception. For in the new birth God re-creates our disordered, egocentric, anti-God, anti-moral hearts in such a way that the personal disposition we have described and which we see perfectly embodied and expressed in the Lord Jesus' earthly life and ministry, has now become our personal disposition at the deepest level, natural and normal to us in the sense

---

[3]Title of a volume of essays celebrating the tercentenary of Edwards's birth; see *A God-Entranced Vision of All Things*, ed. John Piper and Justin Taylor (Wheaton, Ill.: Crossway, 2004).

that we only know joy, peace, and contentment as we act out what we now find our heart prompting us to do. And what is that? To behave in a Christlike way, forming habits of loving and serving God and neighbor, and resisting the promptings of sin in our spiritual system as it urges us to leave undone the active loving service that is now natural and normal to us, and to do what is now unnatural and abnormal to us, namely disobey God and go our way rather than his, just as we did before our hearts were changed. Many Christians, it seems, do not appreciate what has happened to them in their new birth and are careless about obeying and pleasing God; many more have desperate struggles against long-standing sinful habits that in effect have become addictions to unrighteousness, and they often lose the battles they fight, and there are many who evidently think it does not matter whether one strives to perfect holiness of life or not. But it does!—for without a purpose of holiness (purity of heart, that is)—there can be no authentic praying.

Praying that is really praying, then, presupposes an all-around commitment to Christian living—"love that issues from a pure heart and a good conscience and a sincere faith," as Paul expressed it to Timothy (1 Tim 1:5). By-paths in praying result primarily from lack of clear-headedness about this, as we have begun to see and will see more fully before this chapter ends. But as medical students need and are given a thorough grounding in physiology, that is the study of all aspects of the body's healthy functioning, before being introduced to pathology, the study of how and why and when the body malfunctions, so we propose to lay out a further, fuller picture of the path of Christian living before we say any more about Christian pathology, in other words by-path phenomena in both living and praying. This is the picture of what Scripture calls the *walk* and what we propose to set forth as the *hike*.

THE HIKE

J. I. has been a Christian for over sixty years, and in his youth he did a lot of hiking. Carolyn is not quite such a lengthy veteran in faith, but she too has hiked over a wide variety of terrain both spiritually and geographically. We speak from our own experiences, therefore, as we develop this illustration.

Hiking is walking over open country with its ups and downs, the clear spaces and tricky spots, forests and cliffs, the rough and the smooth. In rough country, hiking will have you clambering over rocks and scrambling under brush acquiring various scrapes and scratches along the way, but in smooth meadowland you can stride out with no more damage than an occasional foot blister. Our point is that the spiritual path of a Christian living for God is something like a hike in its various stages with its varied challenges.

To guide our thinking about what constitutes normal Christian experience we turn again to John Bunyan's *Pilgrim's Progress,* which provides a series of most illuminating pictures of stages in the Christian's long walk home.

J. I. has read this small book at least once a year for more than half a century because he finds it a classic above all other classics on the Christian life. *Pilgrim's Progress* (both parts) pictures the journey of life from the beginning of spiritual awareness right through to glory. Bunyan calls this journey a pilgrimage, but it could equally be called a hike. There is a constantly changing path, and Christian and his friends have to hike it. This hike, as Bunyan records it, divides into a number of separate episodes, each with its own motif. And each section ends with a little lyric. Granted, the lyric is mere doggerel, but Bunyan was very good at doggerel, and the spiritual message of these bits of semi-poetry is very telling—even to readers four hundred years later.

In the first section of the hike the person called Christian seeks and finds converting grace. Early in the book, having learned in the House of the Interpreter some initial truths about the real Christian life, he comes to the cross and finds his burden of guilt gone from his back. As he looks at the cross, he is conscious of being a new man in Christ; he takes three leaps for joy and goes on singing as follows:

Thus far did I come, laden with my sin;
Nor could aught ease the grief that I was in,
Till I came hither: what a place is this!
Must here be the beginning of my bliss?
Must here the burden fall from off my back?
Must here the strings that bound it to me crack?
Blest cross! Blest sepulcher! Blest rather be
The Man that there was put to shame for me![4]

Singing as he goes, and refusing to be daunted by the steepness of the hill Difficulty, Christian soon comes to House Beautiful, which is a picture of the church and its fellowship. There he learns many things that he needs to know. He goes on from there and conflict becomes the theme of the next episode. He fights successfully with the Devil, called Apollyon (that is, Destroyer), and soon thereafter travels through the Valley of the Shadow of Death, where all kinds of depressing, despairing thoughts crowd in upon him, and he wonders if he'll ever get through. But he resolutely makes his way through these two forms of conflict and eventually comes out of the Valley of the Shadow, and this is the song that he sings at that point.

O world of wonders (I can say no less),
That I should be preserved in that distress
That I have met with here! Oh, blessed be
That hand that from it hath delivered me!
Dangers in darkness, devils, Hell, and sin,
Did compass me while I this vale was in;
Yea, snares, and pits, and traps, and nets did lie
My path about, that worthless, silly I
Might have been caught, entangled, and cast down:
But since I live, let Jesus wear the crown![5]

---

[4] *Pilgrim's Progress*, (Chicago: Moody Press, n.d.), p. 41.
[5] Ibid., p. 74.

The theme changes in the next section. Companionship is the motif here. Christian catches up with Faithful, and they share their stories. Very soon Christian will lose Faithful, but then he will find another companion, a man named Hopeful, and they will travel the rest of their journey together. Living in fellowship and being sustained thereby is the thought behind each of these accounts of Christian's companions.

Every believer needs at least one fellow Christian with whom to walk closely, in full and frank openness about the ongoing experiences of both parties. Some speak of this as an accountability relationship, each one looking after the other spiritually and being quite intentional about it. In an accountability relationship, you pray for each other, you inquire of each other and care for each other, you speak honestly of your own spiritual challenges and shortcomings, and you strengthen each other's resolve to follow Christ. There is much to be said for the classic form of spiritual direction, in which the director's care for the counselee is a one-way street, but there is, we think, even more to be said for the Puritan Bunyanesque idea of the "bosom friendship," in which the care is mutual. And certainly, as Bunyan depicts it and as experience confirms, the Christian life is so incessantly taxing that all believers need all the counsel, help and encouragement that they can get today just as believers did in the Puritan age, 350 years ago. Faithful sings this song:

> The trials that those men do meet withal,
> That are obedient to the heavenly call,
> Are manifold, and suited to the flesh,
> And come, and come, and come again afresh:
> That now, or sometime else, we by them may
> Be taken, overcome and cast away.
> Oh, let the pilgrims, let the pilgrims then
> Be vigilant and quit themselves like men.[6]

---

[6]Ibid., p. 83.

Plenty of rough stuff breaks surface in this little song! And it is significant that Faithful sings of pilgrims in the plural; they are traveling together—which, as we said, is a great means of grace. But Faithful does not last long. He gets martyred in Vanity Fair, which represents the cruelty of the world to Christian people. Yet martyrdom for fidelity is in truth a spiritual victory, an overcoming of the world that thinks it has overcome its victim. A heavenly chariot takes Faithful straight to the Celestial City. As Christian, having escaped Vanity Fair, goes on, this is the song he sings.

> Well, Faithful, thou hast faithfully professed,
> Unto thy Lord, with whom thou shalt be blest,
> When faithless ones, with all their vain delights,
> Are crying out under their hellish plights;
> Sing, Faithful, sing, and let thy name survive,
> For though they killed thee, thou art yet alive.[7]

Yes, it is doggerel, but surely those last two lines are supremely thrilling doggerel. They proclaim the blessed hope of all Christ's redeemed people: "For though they killed thee, thou art yet alive."

Next, Christian—having linked up with Hopeful—passes through a long episode where the evil of moral and spiritual *compromise* is explored first through contact with a misleading man, an unprincipled worldling named By-ends from the City of Fair Speech, and some of his friends, and then through Demas, a silver miner who has a passion for worldly wealth. (Second Timothy 4:10 is being echoed here.) Both By-ends and Demas want Christian and Hopeful to join with them in what they are doing, but the pilgrims refuse and shake them off, and once again there is a little song Christian sings to mark the end of that episode.

> By-ends and silver Demas both agree;
> One calls, the other runs, that he may be

---

[7]Ibid., p. 111.

A sharer in his lucre; so these two
Take up in this world, and no further go.[8]

Spiritually, By-ends and Demas have got stuck, and the implication is
that they never get to the Celestial City. But on go the pilgrims, and the
curtain rises on a new episode, where the theme is carelessness leading
to collapse. That is the reality pictured in the story of Bypath Meadow
and Giant Despair, at which we have already looked. The pilgrims finally
escape Despair by using the "Key called Promise" to open all the doors
and gates of Doubting Castle, and are able to move forward again along
the true path, though somewhat scarred by their experience. As they go
on together they sing this song.

Out of the way we went, and then we found
What 'twas to tread upon forbidden ground:
And let them that come after have a care,
Lest heedlessness make them, as we, to fare,
Lest they for trespassing his prisoners are,
Whose castle's *Doubting* and whose name's *Despair.*[9]

We, Bunyan's readers, have now been warned! Failures in faithfulness dis-
solve assurance both of personal salvation and of the truth of the gospel itself.

Finally the pilgrims face the *crossing* of Jordan, in other words *dying*,
something for which all of us must prepare. Life is going to stop, and we
must be ready for it to stop whenever and in whatever way in the providence of God that happens. Here Bunyan paints in verse the glory to
which Christian and Hopeful finally come. This time the pilgrims do not
themselves sing the doggerel, but Bunyan prints it in his margin on their
behalf, and this is how it goes.

Now, now look how the holy pilgrims ride.
Clouds are their chariots, angels are their guide.

---

[8]Ibid., p. 124.
[9]Ibid., p. 137. By an oversight the fourth line is omitted.

Who would not here for him all hazards run,
That thus provides for his when this world's done.[10]

Authentic prayer, we said, issues from the authentically Christian heart of a born-again believer leading the authentic Christian life. Viewed from the outside the authentic Christian life is a many-sided affair, involving moral integrity, self-discipline, self-sacrifice, a quest for wisdom and much more. Viewed from the inside, however, it is essentially heart religion, first to last, a quest for more of God and more of life, both here and hereafter; and Bunyan's dramatizing of its trials and triumphs seems to us to ring as true today as ever it did—to be, in other words, totally realistic by biblical standards for any and every age. Neither the grace of God, nor the malice of Satan, nor the ways Christians are tempted to leave the right path, nor the way heart-to-heart fellowship refreshes, reenergizes, encourages and keeps us steady (to look no further) are any different now from what they were then. Bunyan's seventeenth-century idiom may strike us as quaint, but Bunyan's seventeenth-century wisdom strikes us as—well, simply wise. The life of trials and triumphs, dangers and deliverances that he describes is the hike on which all Christians have set out, and it constitutes the path from which so many by-paths beckon, on which so many pressures have to be resisted if we are not to go astray. Understanding this is basic to understanding what makes praying real, so let us explore the picture of the hike a bit further.

We are building up a picture of the Christian life in three stages. This procedure is comparable to painting a picture in the most literal sense. A painter is likely to start by laying down greens and blues, then blend in reds and golds, and finally add tints of pink and orange. Only at the end of the process does the full picture emerge. Presenting the Christian life as a hike, with ups and downs, rough and smooth, easy places and

---

[10]John Bunyan, *The Pilgrim's Progress* (Oxford: Oxford University Press, 1920), p. 192; not in the Moody edition.

hard ones, and a glorious home awaiting us at journey's end, is the green-and-blue stage: the colors are more bold, perhaps, than warm. Now we turn to celebrating the fact that God is with us in faithfulness throughout our journey: reds and golds, bright, warm colors here. Then we will complete our picture by saying more of the love of the "best friend," our Lord Jesus Christ, who is at our side throughout our journey. That will be the adding of pink and orange, the brightest colors of all, completing the picture.

THE GOOD COMPANIONS

J. B. Priestley wrote a once-famous novel titled *The Good Companions*. J. I. remembers receiving a copy as a prize at school. We now borrow Priestley's title and apply it to the Father, the Son and the Holy Spirit. All Christians hike in company with the holy Three—the Father beckoning us forward, the Son walking with us, alongside us always as he promised (see Mt 28:20), and the Spirit indwelling us to give clarity of thought and strength of heart, joy, hope, and love. Good Companions they are indeed. Traveling with the Trinity means that day by day we seek to please our Triune God, and day by day we receive help and pleasure and all kinds of good things from our God. He—the he who is they—is holy and he calls us to holiness, showing us the way and strengthening us to walk in it faithfully. When we speak about the three persons who are the one God as God above us (the Father), God within us (the Holy Spirit) and God beside us (the Lord Jesus), we are telling it like it is.

Now this holy triune God is pledged to Christians as a husband is pledged to his wife. That pledge is of total faithfulness within a bond that will not be broken. In the biblical teaching on marriage, a good husband expresses this faithfulness in loving care, in providing for his wife's needs, and in constant enriching of their relationship. Such is the ideal. This is also how the Father, the Son and the Holy Spirit care for us. Faithfulness to the covenant, loving oversight, providing what we really need and enriching our mutual relationship as we move on together is the essence of the divine action. Yet at the same time this holy, husbandlike Triune God is a God who hides, in the simple sense that we cannot always see what he is doing. Things happen that surprise, bewilder and grieve us, and God does not always tell us why this or that has taken place. He only reiterates, "I am with you always" and promises to keep us going through whatever the trouble is. There's a good deal in Scripture about God hiding himself in this sense, which we must not overlook.

The book of Psalms has often been described as Jesus' hymn book and prayer book. It consists of 150 poignant outpourings of praise, petition, thankfulness, complaint, testimony, celebration, meditation and intercession: prose poems from David and others, people whose horizon of thought and vision was totally filled with God, whose lives were ventures of faith and hope all the way, and whose passion to know, see, exalt, and enjoy God was unlimited. The Psalter has been called the little Bible because, despite the temporary and typical aspects of the Old Testament era under which it was produced, it covers the whole range of the spiritual experience of God's people in every age, ours as much as any. And though we Christians are ahead of the psalmists in our knowledge of God's triunity and of salvation through our Savior Jesus Christ, the incarnate mediator, substitutionary sin-bearer and reigning Lord, the psalmists remain far ahead of us in the integrity and intensity of their devotion. Psalm 86 contains the noteworthy plea, *"Unite my heart"*—integrate it, focus it, purify it and harness it—"to fear your name," followed by the equally noteworthy resolve, "I give thanks to you, O Lord my God, with my *whole* [united] heart, / and I will glorify your name forever" (vv. 11-12, emphasis added). The more we soak our souls in the psalms, the more we learn how great is the distance between us and these exemplars of mature pure-heartedness.

You would have thought these men would constantly enjoy God's smile of approval, but no. A recurring complaint in the psalms from

the lips of these people of God is that God is "hiding his face" from
them, so that (this is the picture) his worshiper no longer senses God's
presence, and it looks and feels as if God's regular care for the worshiper and for others in their current situation has simply stopped.
"Why do you hide your face? / Why do you forget our affliction and
oppression?" "Hide not your face from me. / Turn not your servant
away in anger, / O you who have been my help." "How long will you
hide your face from me?" (Ps 44:24; 27:9; 13:1).[11] This is not the place
to explore what reasons, disciplinary and nurturing, God may have for
hiding his face; the only point here is that sometimes he does it, even
from exemplary believers. As it happened to the psalmists, no doubt it
will happen to us too.

So we hike with our God. Sometimes we find that we are being taken
through strange and unwelcome country. Sometimes despite our knowledge of the permanence of God's covenant with us, we feel desolate and
desperate. But if we are Christians, we are all the time being led. Our
God is with us, he knows what he is doing, and you and I must learn to
walk with him and trust him, even when we cannot feel that he is near.
So, with this second layer of color applied to our painting, our image of
the Christian life becomes more solid. And there is more.

HIKING WITH JESUS CHRIST

The third layer of our painting of the Christian life is something at which
we have already hinted. Hiking with God is quite specifically hiking with
Jesus Christ, our Savior who calls us his *friends*. Friendship is a key term
for explaining the nature of the Christian life of fellowship with God. *Fellowship* today has become a rather colorless word. We Christians make a
great deal of it, but actually it is not a vivid word any more, if ever it was
one. The word *friendship,* however, has color and vividness and warmth.
Human friendships are precious enough, but this friendship is an-

---

[11]See also Ps 10:1; 69:17; 88:14; 89:46; 102:2; 143:7; Job 13:24.

nounced by no less a person than Christ himself. The Lord Jesus said to his first disciples, "No longer do I call you servants, . . . but I have called you friends" (Jn 15:15). Jesus used the term *friends* having just told them, "Greater love has no one than this, that someone lays down his life for his friends" (Jn 15:13). He wanted them to understand that on the cross he was serving and saving *them*—his friends. Them alone? No—all believers, which means us too.

The thought of friendship between God and believers was not new when Jesus spoke those words. Abraham, Israel's patriarch in the Old Testament, was called "a friend of God" (Jas 2:23, echoing 2 Chron 20:7; Is 41:8) and the New Testament cites him as a model for faith.[12] Clearly God values friendship with his people and builds that friendship on their faith. So we must take the category of friendship seriously and think of the Lord Jesus specifically as the special friend in whose company we make our progress as pilgrims and travelers. We speak of the three persons of the triune Godhead as our good companions on our journey, but now we are zooming in on the One who is to be the direct focus of all of our grateful attention and expectation—Jesus Christ our self-appointed friend. Jesus promises each of us his personal presence as long as life shall last—and beyond.

The apostle Paul is the supreme model of the Christ-centeredness in which the Christian's friendship with the Lord, responding to the Lord's declared friendship with us who believe, finds expression: "To me to live is Christ" and to "gain Christ and be found in him" is his goal (Phil 1:21; 3:8-9). "Christ . . . lives in me," said Paul, and Paul himself lives "by faith in the Son of God, who loved me and gave himself for me" (Gal 2:20). It is with Christ that he pleads for healing of the thorn in his flesh, and it is Christ who tells him, "My grace is sufficient for you, for my power is made perfect in weakness" (2 Cor 12:9). And it was of Christ that he was speaking when he wrote:

---

[12]See Rom 4:13-25; Gal 3:6-14; Heb 6:13-15; 11:8-19.

At my first defense [in Rome] no one came to stand by me, but all deserted me. . . . But the Lord stood by me and strengthened me, so that through me the message might be fully proclaimed and all the Gentiles might hear it. So I was rescued from the lion's mouth. The Lord will rescue me from every evil deed and bring me safely into his heavenly kingdom. To him be the glory forever and ever. Amen. (2 Tim 4:16-18)

Evidently what Paul means is that, standing unexpectedly alone in court, he prayed to Jesus for help and then found he had a telling answer ready for every question asked, so that he was dismissed with respect. Reliance for help is of course one of the privileges of friendship. It is clear that Paul hiked with Christ all of the time, in gratitude and dependence and with hope, and he found his Savior to be a trusty friend indeed. In this Paul serves as a model for us.

Some today have had little experience of real, deep friendship, so let us think for a moment of what friendship means at its best. It has been said that a friend is a push when you have stopped, a word when you are lonely, a guide when you are searching, a smile when you are sad and a song when you are glad; a friend is one who walks in when the rest of the world walks out. Friendship is more than mere acquaintanceship, however genial; it is a bond of intimacy built out of mutual trust, truthfulness, care and accountability. A human spiritual friend, writes James Houston, is "one who is loyal and has right motives, discretion, and patience in order to help his friend know God better. Since there is no end to the extent to which I can and do deceive myself, I need a spiritual guide to keep me honest. . . . A true friend in Christ will wake me up, help me to grow, and deepen my awareness of God."[13] When our Lord Jesus declares himself our heavenly friend, all this is implied and more.

---

[13]James M. Houston, "A Guide to Devotional Reading," appended to Juan de Valdes and Don Benedetto, *The Benefit of Christ,* ed. James Houston (Portland Ore.: Multnomah Press, 1984), pp. 181-82; echoing Aelred, *On Friendship,* in *The Love of God,* ed. James M. Houston (Portland Ore.: Multnomah Press, 1983), pp. 233-51.

The privilege of his friendship is overwhelming—and the benefit is too.

With all that, we have now painted our full three-layered image of the Christian life. Within that frame it is possible to think about by-paths as we try to identify and then remove blockages from the main path of prayer. Having shown what constitutes authentic Christian living from an inner-life standpoint, we can now move on to explore the nature of the authentic Christian praying in which that life finds expression.

HELP!

It has been said, with much truth, that the single word *help* is the best ingredient of prayer. Whatever else it is, prayer is always, at least implicitly and usually explicitly, a cry for help, an honest expression of need, predicated on the thought, *I can't get on the way I am.* A cry for help, with various adjuncts, is what prayer has always been throughout all the eras of human existence, in all the religions of which we have any knowledge, and is the formula for authentic Christian prayer as much as any other kind, as we will shortly see. But some other things need to be said before we get to that.

Here we need to draw a distinction. Some prayers for help emerge from ordinary human hearts, people praying as a result of *general revelation,* but other prayers for help come from believing Christian hearts and are based on God's *special revelation.* "General revelation" is the phrase used for that awareness of God's reality, which is inescapable and universal and comes through to everyone, although everywhere it gets falsified, to a greater or lesser degree, through the way it is processed in fallen minds and hearts. We hear about this in the first chapter of Romans, where Paul exposes the world's need for the gospel of Christ.

He declares that "the wrath of God is revealed" to people who "suppress the truth" (Rom 1:18). God's "eternal power and divine nature, have been clearly perceived, ever since the creation of the world, in the things that have been made" (v. 20). This evidence of God's character as revealed in his creation constitutes general revelation. All receive it, but fallen human beings refuse to accept it so as to worship God on the basis of it, and therefore "God gave them up" to their distorted notions and to their own faulty desires. As a result, they entered upon an accelerating downward spiral of sin with an ever-growing distance from God and a continued increase of guilt (vv. 24-32). If Paul were with us in the Western world today, he would diagnose our condition in exactly those terms.

Yet even those who have not acknowledged the general revelation of Romans 1 often have some inkling that there is "one above," as people say, who has it in his power to help. That sense seems universal to the human race. When people are in trouble—Christians and others too, right down to the most primitive cultists—they turn to God in sincere, though self-centered, pleas for help in their time of need. Donald Bloesch writes about this in relation to what he calls "primitive prayer" in tribal religions. He notes that it is egocentric, since the petitioner primarily seeks divine aid to insure his or her own prosperity and protection, and that the motivation is twofold: gain and fear.[14] Primitive people seek deliverance, not from sin but from misfortune and danger. Nor is it only primitive people who do this. The dictum that there are no atheists in the trenches points to the fact that just about everybody in trouble prays to whoever might be there to listen. They cry for help, thus verifying our basic definition of prayer. And sometimes, no doubt, they are helped as they asked to be. No limit can be set to God's goodness in particular cases.

Christians, however, have received and believed *special revelation*. This is the supernatural saving revelation from God that is set forth in Scripture and was embodied in Christ and is now proclaimed as the gospel of God. When we who believe the gospel pray for help, we have a God-given basis for our action. God, the promise-keeper, has declared that he will help his children, in his character as a prayer-answering God.

---

[14]Bloesch, *Struggle of Prayer,* p. 3.

There is no higher authority in matters of this kind than the Lord Jesus. Hear then some words from his Sermon on the Mount.

> Ask, and it will be given to you; seek, and you will find; knock, and it will be opened to you. For everyone who asks receives, and the one who seeks finds, and to the one who knocks it will be opened. Or which one of you [his disciples, those who believe in him already], if his son asks him for bread, will give him a stone? Or if he asks for a fish, will you give him a serpent? [No, of course not.] If you then, who are evil, know how to give good gifts to your children, how much more will your Father who is in heaven give good things to those who ask him! (Mt 7:7-11)

We can expect God to give help as a father would when his child asks for help. The Bible's picture of prayer is of asking the Father for help, asking him to supply the needs we express, and of Jesus giving us every encouragement to expect that our heavenly Father will do just that.

Unanswered Prayer

In this connection it is important for us frankly to recognize that there is no such thing as unanswered prayer from a child of God. That, of course, is a tremendous thing to say, and some would hesitate to say it; yet Jesus' words just quoted show that it would be sheer unbelief not to say it. But (and the *but* is rather significant) God, our heavenly Father, perfect as he is in wisdom, reserves the right to answer our pleas for help in the best way and at the best time. For example when Paul pleaded that his thorn in the flesh might be miraculously healed, and it wasn't, the Lord Jesus said to him, so he tells us, "My grace is sufficient for you, for my power is made perfect in weakness" (2 Cor 12:9). It was as if Jesus said, "You're to carry on, Paul, as you are. I promise you that you'll be kept going despite the thorn in your flesh. Your ministry won't suffer, though you'll live with the pain all your days. And that is truly my best answer to your prayer." Paul's comment as he narrates this to the Corinthians reveals a rare maturity: "Therefore I will boast all the more gladly of my weaknesses" (his pain and suffering), "so that the power of Christ may rest upon me." Paul got the message and saw that the Lord Jesus had truly answered his prayer, although not in the way he had asked.

Could Paul's way of praying for healing have been somehow faulty? Was Christ's response, positive as it was, meant to teach him that he had not been serious enough or reverent enough or kingdom-centered enough in his three prayer sessions about the thorn? None of the above, surely. Paul's motivation in his praying was certainly fear that his missionary ministry would suffer from his being physically disabled, and without doubt his praying was earnest, zealous and wholehearted, as all true prayer is. For God knows our hearts, and it is our hearts that he draws to himself in prayer. The "heart" means the center of our personal being. We can and should dare to put as much of our hearts as we know into our prayers, as we can be sure Paul did every time. When we read the psalms, we find that the psalmist is always intense and utterly uninhibited in the way that he expresses his thoughts, feelings, worries, love, worship, complaints, even hatreds. The kind of restraint that many associate with Western-type politeness and formality in church isn't at all in order when we pray. No, the models of praying in the Psalter show that it is for us to dig down as deeply into our own hearts as we can and put all of our heart into our praying. So proper praying will be always earnest, enthusiastic, serious, passionate; it will be prayer from the warm heart and not just prayer from the cool head. But here is a caution. What ought to make us passionate is not just the pressure of our own needs but our passion for the glory of God. Then all of our petitions for particular things, like Paul's for the healing of his thorn, are offered because we believe that it will bring glory to God for him to give what we are asking.

We must remind ourselves, however, that since our heavenly Father, who is as wise as he is loving, answers his children's prayers in the best way, what he does or fails to do in our immediate situation may look and feel at first as if he is saying a flat no to us. This is because of our slowness to realize that what we asked for, good and proper as it seemed, may not have been God's best. We are regularly less wise, more self-centered, even more pig-headed, and so less mature in our praying than we are aware, and again and again the divine answers are so crafted as to help us in these respects, where we have not realized our need for help, no less than in respect of the conscious need that prompted our petition in the first place.

Thus we may pray for the healing of loved ones, and God's answer is to heal them by taking them to heaven, which was not the mode of healing that we had in mind, and we find ourselves resenting this because the desire to have the invalid back in full bodily health for our own benefit had been so strong within us when we prayed. When this happens we are not always quick to grasp God's kindness. J. I. recalls a lady of perhaps seventy who told him she had given up on God because her Christian mother, aged ninety-one, had died, despite prayer for her recovery. Or we may pray, like Paul, for our own health to be restored and find, as Paul did, that God's way for us is that, upheld by his grace, we should learn to live with our complaint, and unlike Paul we are reluctant to accept this because we so much covet the experience of being well again. Or we forget Agur's wise prayer for "neither poverty nor riches; / . . . lest I be full and deny you / . . . or lest I be poor and steal" (Prov 30:8-9), and ask for wealth which never in fact comes, and we do not see that God is teaching us that we are better off as we are, and that contentment with a little and sustained reliance on our Father for daily bread are virtues of faith that it is his priority to strengthen in us through constant exercise.

In all of this our difficulties arise from our unawareness of the limits of our own spiritual wisdom, as well as our failure to realize that God does not limit himself by those limits of ours when he answers our prayers for help in time of need. When we pray, as now we can see, we must be submissive to our heavenly Father's wisdom and will, just as Jesus was in Gethsemane when he prayed, "Not my will, but yours, be done" (Lk 22:42). And we must be patient in the way that so many of the psalms model patience with their pained question, "how long?" (see Ps 13:1-2; 74:10; 79:5; 80:4; 89:46). "Lord, how long? How long do I have to wait for you to do something about this need that I'm bringing to you? This grisly mess about which I'm praying for your help?" Jesus tells the story of the unjust judge to teach that his people ought always to pray and never to give up. In this parable, the poor widow had to keep bothering the judge in order to get the justice that she was entitled to. The message of her story is that when we pray we may find that God takes longer than we expected to move in answer to our prayers. The unjust judge in the story said in so many words, "All right, just because she bothers me so much I'm going to do what she asks." But Jesus contrasts this lazy unjust judge with the righteous and just Father who loves us, and faithfully promotes our true interest. Jesus says in effect, "How much more will your heavenly Father answer your prayer not only in the best way but at the best time also, which may well mean your having to wait before he moves in response to your request." God's wisdom will appear in both how and when he answers his children's prayers.

When we speak of unanswered prayer, we often mean not answered according to the terms of our asking. But to call that "unanswered" is misleading and irreverent. We have seen this in the case of Paul's plea for his thorn to be taken away, and now look at the following.

> He asked for strength that he might achieve;
> he was made weak that he might obey.
> He asked for health that he might do greater things;
> he was given infirmity that he might do better things.
> He asked for riches that he might be happy;
> he was given poverty that he might be wise.
>
> He asked for power that he might have the praise of men;
> he was given weakness that he might feel the need of God.
> He asked for all things that he might enjoy life;

he was given life that he might enjoy all things.
He has received nothing that he asked for, but all that he hoped for.
His prayer is answered.[15]

We need to remember that we Christians (let alone others) are so mixed up and lacking in self-knowledge that we are not always aware what the real desires of our heart are. But when God answers prayer in his way, we are able again and again to say "Yes, I now realize that this satisfies me deep down, even more than the things I asked for would have done." The person pictured in the lines above was being remade in true godliness, to glorify God by being the person he was becoming. God was not being cruel to him, nor was God ignoring his petitions. God answered his prayers by granting the desires of his heart, which turned out, after all, not to have been expressed in his original words.

PRAYER BY-PATHS

It is very satisfying at the end of a climb to look back and see where you have come in your ascent, so let's do that before we go further. The ground we have covered in this chapter so far, and the point we have now reached, can be summed up thus. Authentic Christian prayer issues from authentic Christian living, and authentic Christian living, which we have pictured as our hike with the Trinity, expresses the converted and regenerate Christian heart. The regenerate Christian heart is the heart that is rooted in faith in our Lord Jesus Christ as our crucified sin-bearer and risen Lord; it is repentant, in the sense of an actual turning from sin and self-centeredness to obedience, righteousness, and God-centeredness; has a driving desire to please and glorify our God; and a confident, childlike humility that honors God as our loving heavenly Father who can be trusted to answer all our prayers for help and for the relief of our needs, even though not always in the terms of our initial re-

---

[15]Cited in ibid., pp. 92-93. There are many versions of this prose poem, all making the same point. Bloesch refers to Col. R. H. Fitzhugh, *The Paradox of Prayer,* as his source for it.

quest. This understanding of the nature of Christian heart religion is the basis on which everything else in this book rests, and if readers have found the assimilating of it a demanding task, as a hill-climb is often a demanding task, this is no surprise. With all of that in mind we move on now to look at some of the by-paths of prayer, those tempting side trails that finally take us nowhere. These by-paths are matters of failing to act on existing information and so missing truths about God and ourselves that should shape our praying as a life activity.

At this point we need to remind ourselves that one chronic symptom of our fallenness is confused thinking, a muddle in the mind, whereby we kid ourselves as to what we do in fact believe. We tell ourselves that we do not believe things that deep down we cannot doubt, and conversely we believe things of which we are really not sure. Professed atheism, whereby we deny the reality of someone else's God while ignoring inescapable inklings of God inside us, is a frequent instance of the former (the young C. S. Lewis is a case in point); and the professed embrace of the doctrine of a faithful, prayer-answering God, as presented in previous pages, is often an example of the latter. For again and again, when push comes to shove and our need for God to act is most urgent and we are most desperate for his help, and when the moment to pray has arrived, we find our hearts enmeshed in all sorts of doubts and uncertainties about the worthwhileness of praying, doubts that we thought we had long left behind us. Back they come—Satan sees to that—and they lead on to the first by-path we would mention, namely, petitioning God without deep-level certainty that he can be relied on to respond to our serious and specific calls to him to take action. Many who have prayed so are later found saying with bitterness: "Oh, yes, I prayed, but it didn't do any good. Nothing came of it." Perhaps they add: "I don't believe in prayer any more, so these days I don't pray at all." Temptation, unrecognized and yielded to? A scoring shot by Satan? Yes, but we don't help anyone off this by-path just by saying that. The confused thinking needs to be straightened out, and that is what we must now try to do.

It needs to be said with the greatest possible emphasis that God's promises, including those that relate to prayer, are utterly trustworthy, and uncertainty as to whether he will keep them in our own case, uncertainty that will of course keep our prayer half-hearted if it does not stop us praying entirely, is unbelief, and unbelief is sin. The diffidence we have described is not the reverence and humility that it imagines itself to be; it is in fact the lapse that James, talking about prayer for wisdom, calls double-mindedness and condemns as an offense to God that invalidates the petition. "Ask in faith, with no doubting, for the one who doubts is like a wave of the sea that is driven and tossed by the wind. For that person must not suppose that he will receive anything from the Lord; he is a double-minded man, unstable in all his ways" (Jas 1:6-8; cf. Jas 4:8). Attitudinally, secret suspicion that praying will do no good is at the opposite extreme from the cry, "I believe; help my unbelief" (Mk 9:24), which expresses strong faith distressed that it is not stronger and more wholehearted still. Skeptical suspicion that after all God may not be concerned to care for me will become in experience a self-fulfilling prophecy. God is to be petitioned on the basis of full trust in his love and his promises.

It will be helpful here to lay out in order all the relevant facts about our sovereign God who undertakes to hear and answer Christians' prayers. God is personal, plural (triune), purposeful and perfect. God calls us all to holiness, to worship and obedience, to trust as well as love Godward, and to love and good works manward. This is a picture of the truly God-centered, God-glorifying way of life. Believers who are answering this call may say, with John, "This is the confidence that we have toward him, that if we ask anything according to his will, he hears us. And if we know that he hears us in whatever we ask, we know that we have the requests that we have asked of him" (1 Jn 5:14-15; cf. Jesus' own words, Jn 15:7, 16; 16:23-24). When Christians are morally and spiritually astray, however, it is likely to be a different story. "If I had cherished iniquity in my heart, / the Lord would not have listened" (Ps 66:18). "You ask and do not receive, because you ask wrongly, to spend it on your passions" (Jas 4:3). Petition without devotion, seeking gifts from God though you are not living for God, will always be by-path praying.

The same applies to the praying of all who believe in God but are not Christians. Those who do not pray as disciples of Christ nonetheless beg someone they might term "the One above" to relieve their agonies, and God in mercy sometimes does so. But the double life of those who pray to him yet live for themselves does not honor him any more than does the praying of the double-minded Christian, and no one should infer that a person is fully in God's favor from the fact that his or her prayer has been fully answered in a particular case. The fact remains that a reconciled relationship to God only becomes real through single-hearted faith in our Lord Jesus Christ.

God's promise, however, entitles believers who are seeking God's will in their own lives to expect answers to their petitions, and it is here that the problems arise. The basic reason why is that it is beyond us to track all of God's answers to our prayers, since these do not always correspond in form to the original petitions. The prose-poem quoted earlier (pp. 58-59) shows this. God reserves the right to answer the prayer we *should* have made rather than the one we *did* make, in relation to a particular need. And we can be certain that there are many answers given, in the sense of things that would not have happened had Christians not prayed, which we simply fail to recognize for what they are. Part of the mystery—and it is indeed a mystery—of events that surround us is that, as we battle against rebel angelic forces, Satan's hosts, God pursues an agenda that, when seen in retrospect "from heavenly Jerusalem's towers," as a great Welsh hymn puts it, will be discerned as God maximizing good in this fallen world by means of the battle itself. The thought is staggering, but the reality is certain. And in this battle the prayers of God's people have a significance that to us is incalculable. "The prayer of a righteous person has great power as it is working," writes James (Jas 5:16). It has been truly said that more things are wrought by prayer than this world dreams of. As God's maximizing of good is a long-term business that may involve unexpected shapings of situations and unanticipated experiences for us all, so it certainly involves some correlation between faithful Christian intercession, often necessarily unspecific on how God will give the blessings sought, and the things that actually happen.

On J. I.'s eleventh birthday, he hoped (and had let it be known that he hoped) that his parents would give him a full-size bicycle—but he received a typewriter instead. His first reaction was disappointment, but soon the typewriter proved to be a superb present, as his parents knew it would. On his thirteenth birthday he finally received a bicycle, and as he began to appreciate the weightiness of the reasons why the bicycle had not been given earlier, he came to discern that what he had experienced was outstandingly good parenting, though it had not felt like that at first. A head injury at age seven meant he would be an unusually vulnerable cyclist (this was before the days of crash helmets), which was why his parents planned not to let him cycle until it was absolutely necessary, and typing (four fingers, self-taught) at a secretary's desk on Saturday afternoons had already, they knew, become a constant delight to him, so the gift of a typewriter of his own would be a sure-fire winner. In this series of gifts J. I. now sees a faint reflection of how God, all-wise regarding our present and future state and needs, and with his planned role for us as contributors to the world's good always in his mind, goes about the answering of our prayers. (Regarding God's planned role for his people, J. I. cannot forget that the head injury became a happy providence eleven years later, excluding him from conscripted military service so that he went to university at age eighteen and became a Christian there, which he thinks, would hardly have happened to him in the army.) To conclude that God is not answering our prayers unless he matches his answer precisely to the terms of our original request is another by-path; it does us no good to travel there.

A further by-path is too narrow a notion of prayer itself. This mistake takes more than one form. Some people think that petition is inappropriate, and their reason on the surface sounds quite respectful of God.

Why not bring requests to God? "Because God already knows what we need," they say—which of course he does. So the famous philosopher Immanuel Kant describes Christian petitionary prayer as "a superstitious illusion, for it is no more than a *stated wish* directed to a Being who needs no such information regarding the inner disposition of the wisher; therefore nothing is accomplished by it, and it discharges none of the duties to which as commands of God we are obligated; hence God is not really served."[16] Kant was one of the architects of the eighteenth-century rationalistic movement called the Enlightenment. The Enlightenment brought great progress in the areas of science, philosophy, logic, music, art, medicine. Yet, despite its name, it also brought much spiritual darkness into this world, and this is a case in point.

Granted, parents usually do know what their children need before their children ask. But nonetheless, for the building up of the parent-child relationship, they want the boy or the girl to come and tell them what they need. Then they do something about it in direct answer to the request for help. Two benefits are thus gained by a single action: real need is met, and a certainty is deepened in the child's mind that he or she is loved by Dad and Mom. So it is with God. In response to prayer (which God invites) God gives the gift that he has known all along that his child needed. The child of God shows love and dependence on God by expectantly expressing needs to God. And God responds to the child he loves by granting those desires—or by giving something different if in his fatherly wisdom he knows that that is better, just as an ordinary human parent will not give the two-year-old the shiny, sharp object (scissors or knife) he wants to play with but will instead give him a better, because safer, toy. It is a by-path, leading away from the very nature of prayer, to assume that God's knowledge makes petitionary prayer needless.

Another narrowing of prayer's nature is to limit its scope. Some peo-

[16]Immanuel Kant, *Religion Within the Limits of Reason Alone,* trans. Theodore M. Greene and Hoyt H. Hudson (New York: Harper & Row, 1960), p. 183, cited in Bloesch, *Struggle of Prayer,* p. 73.

ple seem to think petition and intercession for others is all that is needed, and they never get around to praise and thanks and celebration of God. These people miss much of the richness of fellowship with God in prayer as we see it in most of the biblical examples of praying. This weakness will be addressed throughout this book so there is no need to treat it at length here. Let the reader simply note that always to be making requests ("shopping-list" praying) is to ignore the many other forms of biblical praying, and this is one more impoverishing by-path.

Another by-path, much trodden today, is the pursuit of the idea that the best prayer is wordless. One source of this idea is the fact that when two people love each other there are times when they smilingly look at each other in silence, not needing to speak, simply enjoying their close rapport. A second source is the quite distinct belief, stemming from Asian religions and from gnostic and neo-Platonic aberrations among Christians, that God is to be realized and contemplated as an impersonal presence rather than a personal friend. Now it is certainly right to say that though prayer begins as words, it is not merely words; right to declare that when thoughts and words fail us, as they sometimes do, the Holy Spirit "intercedes for us with groanings too deep for words" (Rom 8:26); right to insist that there is a place for silence before God, listening and waiting, after we have spoken to him, while joy at God's love invades the soul. But there is no place for an unmediated flight of "the alone to the alone," bypassing Jesus Christ and the Bible in order to go straight to a noncognitive closeness to God in which the mind is emptied of all personal thoughts about him, and indeed of all thoughts whatsoever. This kind of New Age meditation (you can hardly call it prayer) proceeds along these lines at the present time, but New Age religion is essentially Hindu mysticism in Western dress, not Christianity. For Christians, however, wordless prayer is not the pinnacle of prayer achievement, but the periodic punctuation of verbal prayer, and we would be on a by-path if we rated it any differently.

One final by-path focuses on the effect of prayer. Some people suppose that when we pray, we are twisting God's arm, as if we are some-how getting onto the throne of the universe, so that we can say to God "*My* will be done." They think that because they are praying earnestly, whatever they ask for will happen, and that the only obstacle to it hap-pening would be if they were not praying earnestly enough. That, how-ever, is a superstitious and mistaken idea, a presumptuous interpreta-tion of Matthew 7:7-11, John 15:7 and similar passages. When Jesus says to his disciples, "Ask whatever you wish, and it will be done for you" (Jn 15:7), he qualifies his invitation by adding controls: they must be abiding in him and his words in them, the request must be "in his name," that is, one that he endorses, and "according to his will," that is, fitting in with the cosmic plan for the good of his people and others of which we spoke earlier (Jn 14:13; 15:16; 1 Jn 5:14). When we pray, it is not for us to suppose that we twist God's arm or are in any way managing the situation. We aren't. We should learn to think of our praying as less a means of getting from God what we want than as the means whereby God gives us the good things that he purposes to give but that we are not always in a fit condition to receive. God intends all along to give these good things, but he waits to be asked so that we will properly value the gift when it comes, and our hearts will be turned in gratitude and renewed trust to the One who gave. To imagine that our words move God to do something that otherwise he would not have cared to do, nor planned to do, is to misunderstand God's purpose in inviting us to pray. It is no accident that Christians down the centuries have typically prayed on their knees. In the position of kneeling, the body reminds the mind that God (not the person praying) is in charge. To think otherwise is to stray along a prayer by-path. Joseph Hart (1712-1768) understood this truth and created a hymn to express it.

> Prayer was appointed to convey
> the blessings God designs to give.
> Long as they live should Christians pray
> for only while they pray they live.

If pain afflict or wrongs oppress,
if cares distract or fears dismay,
if guilt deject, if sin distress,
the remedy's before thee, pray.

Depend on Christ, thou canst not fail.
Make all thy wants and wishes known.
Fear not, His merit must prevail.
Ask what thou wilt, it shall be done.

Prayer, like every aspect of the Christian life, should focus not on ourselves but on the staggering goodness of God. John Newton (1725-1807) said it well in words that are less familiar than his "Amazing Grace" but are nonetheless valuable reminders of God's love; words, therefore, which we do well still to sing.

Behold the throne of grace.
The promise calls me near.
There Jesus shows a smiling face
and waits to answer prayer.

My soul, ask what thou wilt;
thou canst not be too bold.
Since his own blood for thee was spilt,
what else can he withhold?

Beyond thy utmost wants
His love and power can bless.
To praying souls he always grants
more than they can express.

Teach me to live by faith;
conform my will to thine.
Let me victorious be in death,
and then in glory shine.

3

BROODING

Blessed Lord, who hast caused all holy Scriptures to be written for our
learning: Grant that we may in such wise hear them, read, mark, learn
and inwardly digest them, that by patience and comfort of thy holy Word
we may embrace and ever hold fast the blessed hope of everlasting life,
which thou hast given us in our Saviour Jesus Christ. Amen.

ANGLICAN BOOK OF COMMON PRAYER,
1549

Oh how I love your law!
It is my meditation all the day.

PSALM 119:97

Carolyn, who grew up in Midwestern farm country, remembers raising chickens. Brooding hens were both difficult and valuable. A brooding hen would sit for days, even weeks, on her eggs, barely moving except for brief respites to eat and drink. If you got a hand too near, she'd give you a sharp peck. If you tried to shoo her off the nest, she'd flap her wings in your face and scramble back onto her eggs. There she would sit, motionless, seeming to accomplish nothing at all. Yet at the appointed time (twenty-one days after fertilization) egg shells that she had kept warm through long days and nights began to jiggle and crack open, and tiny, soggy chicks emerged, soon to become the soft yellow peepers that Carolyn as a child loved to hold gently in her hands. Throughout the hen's time of brooding, it looked as if nothing was happening; it looked as if she was being lazy or indeed was asleep. But something important *was* going on beneath her. Her brooding was breeding; she was incubating new life.

Brooding prayer is a little like that. Christian brooding or meditating, as we call it, ripens, stabilizes and strengthens our renewed hearts. It is a vital, energizing element in our communion with God. What is it? In essence, it is directed thinking, which is a basic Christian discipline for all of our living and especially for our praying.

Brooding is a descriptive label for the discipline we have in view because it pictures the sort of activity involved. *Meditation,* the classic Christian word for it, is not a common term in ordinary speech. Today it most often refers to an exercise in Eastern and New Age religion that is very different from the spiritual discipline portrayed in this chapter. *Brooding,* on the other hand, is a familiar word for turning over in one's mind problems, strategies, choices to be made and difficulties to be overcome. All of us brood about everyday issues at some point or other. In one respect, however, this word also fails us: our ordinary brooding is inclined to be random, to lack focus and to leave us as confused as we were when we started, whereas meditation is essentially a matter of corralling random ideas about God in his presence and under his eye in order to form clear, orderly, vivid and nourishing thoughts about him. Again, the self-indulgent broodings into which we regularly fall are forms of moodiness that we could well do without, whereas if we want to be healthy Christians the discipline of celebratory thinking that we call meditation is something that we *cannot* well do without. It is an art that all praying people need to master.

"But I can't control my thoughts," people object, "my thoughts wander." Dear friends, you are not alone in that! We all moan about the way that our thoughts wander when we are trying to pray, but as a matter of fact they are wandering also a great deal of the time when we are on our own and just letting our minds run free. We think laterally by association rather than logically, to some purpose. We daydream, we fantasize, we reflect on experiences we've had which either delight or disgust us. We remember the impact of the emotion that brings these episodes back to our minds, and we dwell on them just because we felt so strongly at the time. *This was good, but that was a bad experience,* we say to ourselves as we mull over the events. We think of our joys, we think of our sorrows, we think of situations and perplexities that make us anxious. And so our minds run free, dwelling on these things: problems of relationships, puzzles about dead ends in the life we are living, doubts and uncertainties about particular activities in which we are engaged. *I'm not getting anywhere,* we fret and that thought brings on gloom and distress. Wandering thoughts of this sort constitute precisely the kind of brooding that does no good. J. I. recently read a detective story where a sentence with only five words jumped out at him. The detective was brooding on the crime, but "his thoughts were a blur." We all know what it is like when our thoughts are a blur. Our mind goes to and fro, restlessly traveling up and down and all around, but we aren't getting anywhere. The mind's flow is random, nothing gets sorted out, and we end up feeling deeply frustrated. Such is the constant human experience of wandering thoughts, and we cannot wonder that people assume nothing can be done about it.

But the apostle Paul seems to think that we can indeed exercise control over these blurred, aimless thoughts of ours and even tells us how to do it. "Finally, brothers," he writes, "whatever is true, whatever is honorable, whatever is just, whatever is pure, whatever is lovely, whatever is commendable, if there is any excellence, if there is anything worthy of praise, think about these things" (Phil 4:8). That is directed thinking. Paul clearly supposes that by practice and with our Lord's help we can learn to focus our thoughts and to keep them focused on things that are worth thinking about. As already indicated there is a name for this activity. It is called *med-*

itation. It has a history: Christians have been practicing it and writing about it for centuries, almost since Christianity was born. To repeat what was said a few paragraphs back: Meditation is an art that we must learn.

THE MEANING OF MEDITATION

Can we be more precise about the nature of Christian brooding or meditation? We have already described it as thinking in God's presence, thinking before the Lord, thinking about the Lord and our life in his world, by his grace, under his sway. To take another image from the farm, this kind of meditative brooding is comparable to a cow chewing the cud. A Christian who practices it brings things back to mind just as the cow brings back what she has taken into one of her stomachs. The Christian chews over these matters in the presence of the Lord, drawing from them nourishment, motivation, warnings and wisdom. It is a sort of talking but not in any sense is it a sign that you are losing your marbles; it is a sign, rather, that you are advancing in Christian sanity. Deliberately meditating in God's presence gets your thoughts into order before the Lord, and it is always progress when you manage to do that.

Among English-speaking evangelicals none thought and taught (and, without doubt, wrought) so much with regard to meditation as the Puritans. Some snippets from these masters of the art will help us forward at this point. Here first is John Owen, the supreme Puritan theologian.

> To be spiritually minded is . . . to have our minds really exercised with delight about heavenly things . . . especially Christ himself as at the right hand of God.[1]

Spiritual-mindedness is developed, exercised and reinforced by meditation.

> By . . . meditation, I intend the thought of some subject spiritual and divine, with the fixing, forcing, and ordering of our thoughts about it, with a design to affect our own hearts and souls with the mat-

---

[1]John Owen, *Works,* ed. W. Goold (London: Banner of Truth, 1965), 7:348.

ter of it. . . . In meditation our principal aim is the affecting of our own hearts and minds with love, delight, and humiliation.[2]

By meditation I intend meditating upon what respect and suitableness there is between the word and our own hearts, to this end, that they may be brought to a more exact conformity. . . . Because persons are generally at a great loss in this duty of meditation . . . I shall . . . give briefly two or three rules for the directing of believers to a right performance of this great duty, and they are these:

Meditate on God with God; that is, when we would undertake thoughts and meditations of God, his excellencies, his properties, his glory, his majesty, his love, his goodness, let it be done in a way of speaking to God, in a deep humiliation and abasement of our souls. . . .

Meditate on the word in the word; that is, in the reading of it, consider the sense in the particular passages, . . . looking to God for help, guidance, and direction, in the discovery of his mind and will therein, and then labour to have our hearts affected with it.

What we come short of in evenness and constancy in our thoughts . . . let it be made up . . . by frequent returns of the mind to the subject proposed to be meditated upon.[3]

Richard Baxter, the supreme Puritan pastor, understood meditation in the same way and urged that the hope of glory should be a regular theme. The task, he writes, is a "set and solemn acting of all the powers of the soul upon this most perfect object, rest, by meditation."[4] In this, Christians are "to use your understandings for warming of your affections, and to fire your hearts by the help of your heads."[5] Light must generate heat. "He is the best Christian who hath the readiest passage from the brain to the heart."[6] The meditative process consists of *consideration* (discursive thought) followed by *soliloquy* (talking to oneself in God's

---

[2]Ibid., p. 384
[3]Ibid., 6:224-25.
[4]Richard Baxter, *Practical Works,* ed. W. Orme (London: n.p., 1830), 23:310.
[5]Ibid., p. 338.
[6]Ibid., p. 340.

presence). Stage one is to bring the truth about our promised heavenly rest before our minds as clearly and fully as possible and then to awaken the affections—love, desire, hope, courage and joy—in appropriate responses, so that the hope of heaven becomes an object of delight and desire. Stage two is then "pleading the case with our own souls. . . . Soliloquy is a preaching to oneself."[7] Its aim is to move us to resolute Christian practice. What Baxter has in mind appears from the following:

> In thy meditations upon all these incentives . . . preach them over earnestly to thy heart, and expostulate and plead with it by way of soliloquy, till thou feel the fire begin to burn. . . . Dispute it out with thy conscience. . . . There is much more moving force in this earnest talking to ourselves, than in bare cognition, that breaks not out into mental words. Imitate the most powerful preacher that ever thou wast acquainted with. . . . It is a great part of a Christian's skill and duty, to be a good preacher to himself. . . . Two or three sermons a week from others, is a fair proportion; but two or three sermons a day from thyself, is ordinarily too little.[8]

Finally, one should move "from this speaking to ourselves, to speak with God" directly in prayer.[9] Earnest desire and hearty resolution, poured out in honest petition for help, strength and single-minded zeal in running the race of life will always secure God's blessing. The Puritans proved that in their own lives and so may we in ours.

Nor is it only Protestant pietists like the Puritans who have practiced this mode of brooding. There is also a noble tradition of directed and concentrated meditation on the other side of the Reformation divide, where it is commonly called contemplation or contemplative prayer. In the *Catechism of the Catholic Church,* signed by Pope John Paul II on October 11, 1992, we read:

---

[7]Ibid., p. 369.
[8]Ibid., 2:392.
[9]Ibid., 23:373.

Meditation engages thought, imagination, emotion, and desire. This mobilization of faculties is necessary in order to deepen our convictions of faith, prompt the conversion of our heart, and strengthen our will to follow Christ. . . . Contemplative prayer is also the pre-eminently *intense time* of prayer. In it the Father strengthens our inner being with power through his Spirit "that Christ may dwell in [our] hearts through faith" and we may be "grounded in love." . . . Contemplation is a *gaze* of faith, fixed on Jesus, "I look at him and he looks at me." . . . Contemplative prayer is *hearing* the Word of God. Far from being passive, such attentiveness is the obedience of faith, the unconditional acceptance of a servant, and the loving commitment of a child. It participates in the "Yes" of the Son become servant and the *Fiat* of God's lowly handmaid.[10]

The Catholic Church has a great deal of wisdom to share with Protestants about brooding as a way into prayer.

Thinking in God's presence is, as we have seen, the basic idea of Christian brooding, but what should we be thinking about? John Owen specified Jesus Christ in his glory. Richard Baxter insisted on the hope of heaven; which is right? The answer is that both are right, and there are many other topics to meditate on also. Proper Christian meditation is thinking about God and everything else in relation to God. It should include thinking about our own relationship to God, thinking about God's purposes and God's greatness and God's achievements and God's blessings, and thinking about what is involved in pleasing God, what it means to fully respond to God. It is thinking about our life under God, the life that chapter two pictured as hiking with the triune God as our resource, and the Lord Jesus as our self-identified Friend: life with its ups and downs, life with its immediate and long-term pressures, yet always life as hiking with the Lord. In meditative prayer we think about these things from all sorts of angles. The Puritans defined meditation as talking to oneself before addressing God, but in fact talking to God discursively

---

[10]United States Catholic Conference, *Catechism of the Catholic Church* (New York: Doubleday, 1994), pp. 713-16.

will include the thinking process that is meditation's essence, and there are many examples of precisely this in the Psalms. Where we have seen God solving our problems, we learn from the Psalms to say "Hallelujah!" Where problems still wait to be solved, we review their components and learn from the Psalms what it means to pray to God with the comprehensive word "Help!" In this way meditative thoughts easily and naturally move into prayer. Thinking in the presence of God becomes talking to the Lord directly, and talking to God leads back to further thinking in his presence. This is a natural transition, both ways.

The whole of a Christian's thought life should be bathed, or perhaps we should say housed, in prayer. When our hearts are changed at new birth, the thought life becomes permeated by thankful, joyful, trustful awareness of God. This awareness flows from a heart already given to Christ and inhabited by his Spirit. Thus the apostle Paul's command to the Christians at Thessalonica to "pray without ceasing" (1 Thess 5:17) becomes increasingly a habit of our minds. When this discipline has built into our inner being a habit of consciously turning our thoughts Godward, we will occasionally be overridden by floods of joy, also from the heart, and find ourselves moved to intense praise of God for all the wisdom that he has shown, all the things that he has made, all that he has taught us, and all the opportunities that he has given us. We thank God for the way he has enabled us to use our minds, and we thank him also for the link between heart and mind whereby gushes and gales of spiritual joy whirl us into spontaneous outbursts of worship. This is what happens when God, who inhabits both our hearts and our minds in the sense of our reasoning powers, enables his people to think and feel and move, in short to live, in a sustained attitude of prayer.

GOD'S VOICE

The autobiography of the late Lewis Smedes is full of wry touches.[11] One

---

[11]Lewis B. Smedes, *My God and I* (Grand Rapids: Eerdmans, 2003). The quotations that follow are from page 161.

chapter is titled "God and I, Almost Friends." There he writes, "[God] never, well, almost never, talks to me. I gather that he talks to other people," Smedes quotes a Latvian hymn: "My God and I go in the fields together. / We walk and talk as good friends should and do." Smedes might also have quoted the chorus: "He lives, He lives, Christ Jesus lives today! / He walks with me, and talks with me, along life's narrow way." The idea of prayer as "the great conversation"[12] belongs to Christianity everywhere. But Smedes, ever the honest realist, goes on to say, "When I am with God I do all the talking most of the time." He feels puzzled when people blithely say, "God talks with me," for this kind of two-way exchange had not been common in his own experience, and that is a condition that many of us share.

We are sure that there are some Christians to whom God speaks in ways that he doesn't speak to us, but we think hearing an audible voice from God is rather rare. Yet it remains a basic truth that God is a communicator, and he is going to speak his mind to his children one way or another. How will he do it? Meditation on biblical teachings and realities is one regular way. Meditation is a humble-hearted activity that again and again leaves us aware that God has guided our thinking and made some things clear to us thereby, and that in effect God is "speaking to me," telling me what I need to know. This is the united testimony of those who learn to meditate. God makes things clear through meditation, showing us things, telling us things, straightening out our thoughts on things. Many Christians have not acquired the habit of meditating, and so they miss this. We wouldn't want that to be the story of our lives or of yours.

MEDITATE ON GOD'S WORD

Scripture itself gives us many examples of meditative prayer, particularly the discipline of meditating on portions of God's Word. Here, at the start,

---

[12]"The Great Conversation" is the subtitle of an introduction to praying by the Roman Catholic philosopher Peter Kreeft, *Prayer: The Great Conversation* (San Francisco: Ignatius, 1991).

is an example of God himself directing this practice. Joshua, the new leader of the migratory Hebrews, is still shaking in his shoes trying to get over the fact that Moses is dead and that all the responsibility of leading Israel into the Promised Land now rests on his own shoulders. God comes to him and says:

> This Book of the Law shall not depart from your mouth, but you shall meditate on it day and night, so that you may be careful to do according to all that is written in it. For then you will make your way prosperous, and then you will have good success. Have not I commanded you? Be strong and courageous. Do not be frightened and do not be dismayed, for the LORD your God is with you wherever you go. (Josh 1:8-9)

God had already said, in a similar vein, through Moses that each future Israelite king should "write for himself in a book a copy of this law. . . . And it shall be with him, and he shall read in it all the days of his life, that he may learn to fear the LORD his God by keeping all the words of this law, . . . and that he may not turn aside from the commandment" (Deut 17:18-20). Those who lead (and we all lead others, one way or another) must be led by the Word of God, which we must absorb into head and heart as a lifetime project.

In Scripture we read of an experience recurring for the prophets whereby verbalized messages came into their minds and they knew that this was from God. But this is not the usual thing. The usual thing is that matters become clear after prayerful meditation, informed by praying over what we read in Scripture. Evidently this was how God meant it to be for Joshua, both as a man and as the manager of Israel's invasion of Canaan. "This book of the law shall not depart from your mouth." For Joshua that meant the five books of Moses, in whatever form he had them. In our day (as for the past 1,700 years), the acknowledged canon of Scripture includes sixty-one additional books, which together with the Pentateuch make the complete Bible. *That* is the book that is not to depart from our mouths but on which we are to meditate day and night. The English Bible, in almost any version, fills more than one thousand pages of fairly small print, and none of us will have exhausted the wisdom of those Scriptures by the time our life ends.

Within the Bible the Psalter highlights meditating on Scripture. The first psalm is in a sense the keynote of the whole book, and this is how it opens:

> Blessed is the man
>   who walks not in the counsel of the wicked,
> nor stands in the way of sinners,
>   nor sits in the seat of scoffers;
> but his delight is in the law of the LORD,
>   and on his law he meditates day and night. (Ps 1:1-2)

This is an echo of God's word to Joshua. It also reflects a spiritual reality that remains for today's Christians. When we come to a living faith in Christ and are born again, our inner being is changed in a number of ways, as we have already begun to see, and among them is the opening of our inner eyes to discern the self-evidencing divine origin of Scripture along with the divinity of the Christ who is set forth in its pages. John Calvin illustrated this from the immediacy of sight and tastes in the mouth, "Whence will we learn to distinguish light from darkness, white from black, sweet from bitter? Indeed, Scripture exhibits fully as clear evidence of its own truth as white and black things do of their color, or sweet and bitter things do of their taste."[13] As colors and tastes evidence themselves to be what they are, so does God's written Word. According to Calvin, the Scriptures, being fully human as they are, immediately impress the true believer as being divine in source and character. A believer who is reading meditatively knows, intuitively and undeniably, that these words are not merely human writing; they are from God. Calvin

---

[13]John Calvin *Institutes of the Christian Religion* 1.7.3, ed. John T. McNeill (Philadelphia: Westminster Press, 1960), p. 76.

illustrates this by the way sweet and sour affect the taste buds. If you have lemon juice in your mouth, you immediately know it is sour. If you have sugar in your mouth, you immediately know it is sweet. Similarly, the Word of God evidences itself as the Word of God. And so the spiritually hungry heart goes back to it again and again as the needle of a compass goes back to the magnetic north.

Carolyn tells of an unusual young man who at the age of twenty had already spent nearly a third of his life on a spiritual search. Raised in an Islamic country, in a nominally Muslim home, he first explored various Eastern religions and a variety of philosophies, sticking to each for a time, then leaving it to continue his search. Finally, as a college student in the United States he encountered a group of Christians and marveled at the loving ways they treated each other. Their religious explanations about a person named Jesus made little sense to him; still, he continued to admire the way these young Christians lived. Eventually one of them handed him a Bible and said, "Read Matthew, Mark, Luke and John; you will get to know this Jesus." This young man spent a weekend doing exactly that, reading and meditating on the person of Jesus as the four Gospels presented him. By the end of his reading the Spirit of God had done his work through the Scriptures. The young man's long spiritual search had reached its conclusion; his new spiritual journey as a Christian, trusting the Bible and worshiping its Christ, had begun. Reverend Mateen Elass has since served as a Christian minister of the gospel for more than two decades.[14]

The heart is drawn into loving trust in the God-given Scriptures in the same way that the heart is drawn into adoring fellowship with the Father and the Son, our Lord Jesus Christ. This is a basic fact about the born again. So the idea of meditating on the Scriptures day and night, the thought of the Bible or something from the Bible being in your mind as you rise in the morning and as you finish the day and close your eyes at night, isn't empty rhetoric (sermon talk!); it is neither hyperbole nor fan-

---

[14]For Mateen's story see Immanuel Presbyterian Church's website at <www.immanuel presbyterian.net> and click on "Church Leadership" and then "Mateen Elass."

tasy; it is not unreal; it is the natural way for things to be in the daily experience of the believer. Trustful thinking about God and his Word in tandem should be a constant each day of our lives.

But where does one begin? You can start by focusing on brief passages that have already meant a great deal to you and bring you joy every time you think back on them.

In recent years, I (Carolyn) have chosen a different sequence of Scripture for each new year, and then focused on a few lines each day of the week. It shapes a brooding sort of praying—beginning with God's words to me. A current sequence from Isaiah reads, Monday: "Fear not, for I have redeemed you; / I have called you by name, you are mine" (Is 43:1). Tuesday: "I am the LORD; I have called you in righteousness; / I will take you by the hand and keep you" (Is 42:6). Wednesday: "Sing to the LORD a new song, / his praise from the ends of the earth" (Is 42:10). Thursday: "A bruised reed he will not break, / and a faintly burning wick he will not quench; / he will faithfully bring forth justice" (Is 42:3). Friday: " 'I, I am the LORD, / and besides me there is no savior. . . . / [Y]ou are my witnesses,' / declares the LORD, 'and I am God' " (Is 43:11-12).

The Scripture itself invites prayerful meditation on all its length and breadth and envisages this as a work of true love. "Oh how I love your law! / It is my meditation all the day," says the psalmist (Ps 119:97). This love of the Word of God is evidently the overflow of love for the God of the Word; the two loves are one, and for us, as for all who went before us, it is either both or neither. Psalm 119, the longest psalm in the Psalter, celebrates the Word of God as an object of attention, trust, love, deep thought, obedience, desire and delight in all but one of its 176 verses. A person who focuses on Scripture as an object of study might lose sight of this, and also of the fact that much of Scripture is itself prayer—in written form, designed to give us models not only for petition but also for meditation. At a glance we can see that Psalm 119 is addressed to God throughout; it is all a prayer to God, recognizing the value of his Word.

But I'm just not a disciplined kind of person, and it is beyond me to pray and brood like that, we moderns might mutter. Yet look at Psalm 119:15-16:

> I will meditate on your precepts
>   and fix my eyes on your ways.
> I will delight in your statutes;
>   I will not forget your Word.

Here is an everyday constancy based on firm resolve; is such firm resolve really beyond you? Surely not.

But my life is full of anxiety, we might complain. *It is hard to give myself to meditation, even on Scripture, when I am constantly worried, which I am.* But turn to verses 23-24:

> Even though princes sit plotting against me,
>   your servant will meditate on your statutes.
> Your testimonies are my delight;
>   they are my counselors.

Come along, now! This is the way for you to go! Let the Scripture itself speak to you about your worries.

But meditation is hard, we might object; *I don't like sitting still and being passive.* You don't? Then look at verses 47-48:

> I find my delight in your commandments,
>   which I love.
> I will lift up my hands toward your commandments which I love,
>   and I will meditate on your statutes.

The psalmist pictures himself coming to meditative prayer with the same delight we express when a friend whom we love and weren't expecting to see suddenly comes toward us. Raising our hands is almost a reflex, an expression of exuberant joy. Are you making your restless body an excuse for evading serious meetings with God?

Why should I exert the effort necessary for meditation? we ask. Verses 97-99 declare:

Oh, how I love your law!
>   It is my meditation all the day.
Your commandment makes me wiser than my enemies,
>   for it is ever with me.
I have more understanding than all my teachers,
>   for your testimonies are my meditation.

Doesn't the prospect of gaining wisdom make meditation worth the effort? Sadly, there are couch-potato Christians just as there are couch-potato TV watchers, who look on at others' efforts but make no effort at anything themselves and so get nowhere. And yet energetic meditation on the content of God's written Word is no more than natural, just as it is no less than fulfilling at heart level, for the born again child of God.

MEDITATE ON GOD'S WORKS

The psalms encourage Christians to meditate not only on the Word of God but also on the works of God, the marvelous, mighty, merciful things that he has done and is doing even now. Such meditation is presented as a steadying, hope-creating activity for believers in distress. In Psalm 77 a man in trouble begins his prayer with that trouble:

I cry aloud to God,
>   aloud to God, and he will hear me.
In the day of my trouble I seek the Lord;
>   in the night my hand is stretched out without wearying;
my soul refuses to be comforted.
>   When I remember God, I moan;
when I meditate, my spirit faints. (Ps 77:1-3)

What is this psalmist meditating about? God in general, one supposes, but at first he cannot get his mind off his own terrible condition, so much so that he has to say "my spirit faints." But these sad thoughts do not remain the focus of his brooding. He forces his mind (John Owen's phrase) to "consider the days of old" (v. 5) and to recall when he sang "my song in the night" (v. 6), exulting in what God had done for him, and by verse 11 he is able to say:

> I will remember the deeds of the LORD;
>   yes, I will remember your wonders of old.
> I will ponder all your work,
>   and meditate on your mighty deeds. (Ps 77:11-12)

By controlling his thoughts, sending them into a channel toward God, focusing on the great things God has done—in creation, in providence and in grace—and thus thinking in a directed, disciplined way, so that God fills his whole horizon, this psalmist, though embattled by life's circumstances, is able to stabilize himself. He started in trouble and admits that trouble in prayer, but he then meditates with stubborn persistence on the mighty works of God and so gets steady and strong again. The wonders of the exodus and the passage through the Red Sea (corresponding for Christians to the wonders of their redemption through Christ, their regeneration in Christ and their subsequent experiences of God's goodness) are the mighty works that, as he reviews them, raise his mind above his present pain and renew his hope for the future. That kind of God-centered meditative prayer is an art that we need to learn from him.

There is nothing magical about the way meditation can change a mood. What happens is that the process of thought renews, at the conscious level, knowledge that Christians already have in their heart—knowledge that the God they trust is changeless and consistent, a faithful promise keeper who has undertaken to see his people through their life in this world, no matter how hard it may be, to the glory that is in store for them beyond. So reviewing what God has done in the past, both in the public history of world redemption and church renewal and in our own personal experience, naturally brings encouragement, refreshment, patience, stability and hope; for nothing in God's character or commitment has changed, and he can be trusted to keep his promises. Paul understood this, and so we find him writing of "God who raises the dead. He delivered us, . . . and he will deliver us. On him we have set our hope that he will deliver us again. . . . For all the promises of God find their Yes in [Christ]" (2 Cor 1:9-10, 20). It is conscious certainty about God's faithful consistency that explains how, by the time he ends his poem, the writer of Psalm 77 finds that joyful peace and confident expectation are becoming his again as he dwells on God's leading of his people in past days. And the same conscious certainty, breaking surface as we meditate, will enable us who, it may be, are traveling a troubled road as did the psalmist, to end up saying with Paul: "We rejoice in our sufferings, knowing that suffering produces endurance, and endurance produces character, and character produces hope, and hope does not put us to shame [disappoint, NLT], because God's love has been poured into our hearts through the Holy Spirit who has been give to us" (Rom 5:3-5).

The directed thinking modeled in Psalm 77 is self-directed, and the discipline of practicing it is self-discipline. As natural and joyful as thinking of God is to the born again, we often have to prime the pump of our hearts to focus on God's Word and works by wrenching our minds away from our immediate troubles, otherwise they will remain center stage indefinitely. Implicit in Psalm 77, this wrenching is implicit in Psalm 143 as well:

> My spirit faints within me;
>> my heart within me is appalled.
> I remember the days of old;
>> I meditate on all that you have done. (Ps 143:4-5)

And it becomes explicit in Psalm 42:6: "My soul is cast down within me; / *therefore*"—that is the wrench point—"I remember you." In all these passages the frazzled psalmist is renewing his confidence in God by focusing on God's Word and works in resolute meditation and thus he strengthens himself to go on crying "Help!" until help comes.

METHODS OF MEDITATION

What has been said so far boils down to this: meditating on what the Bible sets before us is a vital means both to a vivid grasp of God's revealed truth and to the energizing of faith during times of trial. From both standpoints meditation is equally a preliminary to prayer and an element of it. (So far we have spoken only of prayer as petition in times of need, but we will extend the definition before we are through.) So how are we to go about meditating?

The first point to make is that meditation is something that you can do well in more than one way. Different ways of meditating are right for different people at different times. As long ago as the fourteenth century, Walter Hilton, one of the great devotional teachers of the Middle Ages, said:

> You should recognize that in the matter of meditation there is no universal rule which can be established for everyone to keep in every situation. These things are by nature a gift of our Lord and are directed to the various dispositions of his chosen souls according to their particular state and condition. And according to each person's growth in virtue and spiritual estate, he increases opportunities of meditation, both for their spiritual knowledge and for their love of Himself.[15]

According to Hilton's wise perceptions, we must therefore take personal responsibility to find what form of Christian meditation is appropriate for us.

As tastes, skills, temperaments and powers of mind and body vary from individual to individual, so will styles of meditation vary. This is not a case of one size fits all. How you meditate most fruitfully depends on who you are and is something that you will discover by trying out the various ways of doing it, just as we find our preferred meal on a restaurant menu by trying out a range of dishes on successive visits. What is

---

[15]Walter Hilton, *Toward a Perfect Love,* ed. and trans. David L. Jeffrey (Portland, Ore.: Multnomah Press, 1985), p. 57.

merely good should never stand in the way of what is better, and what is best for us in this matter of meditating is something that we will discover, under God, through the experience of various experiments.

What then are our options in this matter? The Eastern way of meditation, which unhappily sometimes finds its way into Christian circles, is to concentrate on objects (for instance, stones) or abstract patterns or notions such as one hand clapping. But the Christian way, or ways rather (there are several), concentrate mind and heart, spiritual eyes and ears, we might say, on God as he has shown himself to us in holy Scripture. Here are some of the possibilities. The first two are preparatory to those that come after.

First, we should soak ourselves in the Bible, so that our minds are awash with it—or, as C. H. Spurgeon put it, till our blood is "bibline." J. I. has elsewhere urged that we should all become "Bible-moth" Christians; he has in mind the fact that the members of John Wesley's Holy Club in eighteenth-century Oxford were called "Bible-moths," as those who chewed through the Bible from cover to cover. John Owen said that every Christian should regularly read the Bible right through. Luther did this twice a year; the sixteenth-century Anglican Prayer Book set out a lectionary for daily use that took one through the Psalter monthly, the New Testament twice a year and the Old Testament once; Murray McCheyne, a nineteenth-century Scotsman, produced a plan for reading all Scripture once a year; T. C. Hammond, a twentieth-century Irish stalwart, read the whole Bible quarterly. Do not bite off more than you can chew, but make plans to read the Scriptures in their entirety on a regular basis.

Second (and this goes with the first) traverse the Bible in terms of overall images of its nature as God's communication to us, and of our due response as recipients of his messages. Images affect our imagination, and imagination is the midwife, if not the mother, of insight. We now suggest seven such images; you may be able to add to the list. (These seven start with the letter *l*. Yours may not, but they will be none the worse for that.)

See the Bible as a *library* of sixty-six books, of very different kinds, written over a period of something like a millennium and a half, yet meshing with each other to tell a single story about the words and deeds of the Creator-become-Redeemer as he formed a people for himself. Savor the flavor of the different books, and note how they fit together, with the history books as the backbone of the Bible and with the books of theology, wisdom, sermons and songs attached to the backbone in their proper place, like so many ribs. Get the hang of the Bible as a whole.

Explore the Bible as a *landscape* of human life in all its many modes and relationships, both with and without God. Bible characters are fascinating and will grow on you as models of how to and how not to order your existence. Make a point of appreciating each person you meet in the text, and try to see what makes each of them tick. They exemplify so much (which is, of course, why in the wisdom of God they are there). Learn more of God by watching him deal with them.

Read the Bible as a *letter* from its divine Author to every reader. When the biblical books were written, God had you and us in mind, and what has been written for all comes as a personal communication to each. The thought is mind-blowing, but it is true. As the nature of Scripture is essentially God bearing witness to himself in the form of and so by means of faithful human witness to him, so the message of Scripture to you and us is God elucidating to our minds and hearts, in an applicatory way, things that his servants wrote for people in their own day. Each of us, then, should read the Bible as God's love letter to us and labor to squeeze out of it every bit of meaning that is there, as we always do with love letters in this world because we know we are meant to. We should read the Bible as if the letters RSVP were written at the head of every page. A memorable misprint on the contents page of one of J. I.'s books long ago said: "RSVP means Revised Standard Version." But RSVP actually means, in French, *Répondez s'il vous plaît*—in English, "Reply, please!" It is as if God says to you and me, "Your Bible is my love letter to you—read carefully what I say there, and get back to me about it." All love letters call for answers, and the Bible is no exception.

Value the Bible as your *listening post* in enemy-occupied territory, which is what this world is, and tune in constantly for instructions, as spies do, setting up places for maintaining communication by radio with headquarters. This is an excellent picture of the discipline of reading the Bible with due attention, listening hard to all its teaching so as to live right in our constantly hostile world.

Rate all that Scripture says about living in faith and obedience as *law,* in the sense of the Hebrew word *torah*—not, that is, public legislation, at least in the first instance, but the kind of instruction, authoritative yet affectionate, that children in a good family receive from a parent: instruction that is meant to shape character and outlook, and to give understanding of what the family stands for and expects of its members. That is what *law* meant to the writer of Psalm 119 and what God's directives in Holy Scripture mean for us.

Reckon the Bible to be your *light* in a world of darkness surrounding you. "Your word is a lamp to my feet / and a light to my path" (Ps 119:105). The picture here is of a traveler—a hiker, we may say, recalling our imaging of the Christian life in these terms, or a camper, or a messenger—having to walk by night across open country, full of places where one could easily slip and fall and do oneself a major mischief. But there is a path, if only we can see to keep to it. Today, we would carry a flashlight to illuminate the terrain in front of us and show us the next bit of the path. In Bible times, people carried an oil lamp at night for the same purpose. In every age Scripture enables its readers to pick out the path of life, despite the intensity of the moral and spiritual darkness through which they often have to go.

Last, cling to your Bible as a *lifeline,* hold on like grim death to its promises and its assurances that almighty God always knows what he is doing on all those occasions (and for most of us there are any number of them) when you feel that grim death itself, in some shape or form, is precisely what you are up against. Lifeguards and the sometime devotees of

Baywatch (remember?) know well that people who think they are drowning grab and hang on to their rescuers like limpets, and they grip lifebelts and lifelines in the same almost convulsive way. That illustrates how intently we should take note of God's assurances to his people as we make our way through the holy Scriptures, and how we should further tighten our grip on those assurances in the toughest of times.

QUICK MARCH, SLOW MARCH

When military personnel are on parade, they perform a quick march and a slow march. So far, we have been assuming a discipline of Bible reading that corresponds to the quick march: namely, the following of a one-year or two-year plan, or a three- or four- or five-year program, as the case may be, that takes you by one route or another from Genesis to Revelation, after which you go back to the beginning and do it again—and again—and again, for as long as life lasts. We all need to do this, and we may well lose out badly if we do not do it, just as we may well lose out in health terms if we do not have a balanced diet of regular meals. Meditative reading of the whole Bible, whether in terms of our seven images or within a different frame of thought, is basic to everything that our life of praying should involve.

Francis Martin, a Roman Catholic, speaks of his early days in the Cistercian monastery where he learned the regular rhythm of soaking himself in the words of Scripture. There the brothers followed the Scripture in line with the church calendar so that nearly all of Scripture was read aloud during worship in the period of a year. In addition his order followed a typical monastic pattern of praying eight times a day beginning at 2:00 a.m. and ending at 7:00 p.m. During these daily periods of prayer they sang or prayed all 150 psalms in sequence each week so that they covered the entire Psalter fifty-two times in a year.[16]

Yet this is not the whole story with regard to meditation. Two long-

---

[16]Francis Martin, "Reading Scripture in the Catholic Tradition," in *Your Word Is Truth,* ed. Charles Colson and Richard John Neuhaus (Grand Rapids: Eerdmans, 2002), p. 168.

practiced procedures that correspond to the slow march must now be explored. First comes lectio divina, literally "divine reading," a technique of meditation that goes back at least to Benedict of Nursia (480-547), a monastic pioneer and composer of the Benedictine *Rule* for monastery life. Kathleen Norris, a Presbyterian laywoman who over a period of twelve months spent a great deal of time in a monastery, writes of this procedure as follows:

> I've been a devoted reader since childhood, and I have been surprised to discover that what Benedict termed *lectio divina,* and what many contemporary Benedictines call "spiritual reading," has given me a new appreciation for the contemplative potential of the reading process. *Lectio* is an attempt to read more with the heart than with the head. One doesn't try to "cover" a certain amount of material so much as surrender to whatever word or phrase catches the attention. A slow meditative reading . . . of the Scriptures, *lectio* respects the power of words to resonate with the full range of human experience.[17]

In the Benedictine tradition, lectio divina has to do first and foremost with one's inner attitude in all reading of Scripture; among today's Roman Catholics and those evangelicals who have adopted this practice, the usual first move is to select a brief passage and stay with it.

A typical lectio meditation today might involve the following four steps. First, *lectio:* reading aloud a sentence or two of biblical text. It will be read slowly, savored, perhaps read several times aloud with changing emphasis on each word. Second, *meditatio:* prayerfully pondering the words, asking yourself such questions as, How is my life touched by this passage? What does it show God doing? What is it inviting me to do? How do I react to it in full honesty, deep within? Third, *oratio:* responding verbally to God, praying the passage or praying what the text inspires us to pray. Finally, *contemplatio:* a time of peacefully resting in God, waiting in silence in the divine presence

---

[17]Kathleen Norris, *The Cloister Walk* (New York: Berkley Publishing, 1996), p. xx.

with alert, hopeful expectancy.[18] A new sharpness of focus on something may not be given, but then again it may. Practicing lectio divina takes time, perhaps thirty minutes to an hour for a single verse. But this slow prayerful reading of God's Word engages the mind and the heart with a refreshing force that the brisk march would easily miss.

Surely there is wisdom in both ways of traveling through the Bible: the steady march—two, three or four chapters a day, showing you the great contours of God's grand design—and also the slow march, where you read only one or two verses but some biblical picture settles into the core of your being and you consciously nestle into your own place in the palm of God's hand. This slow meditative reading of a small text again and again may lead to an experience like being in a dark room when suddenly someone releases the blinds. The blinds fly up, the light rushes in, and you see all sorts of things that you didn't see before. Carolyn has found, though, that often lectio divina isn't spectacular in the way that this illustration might suggest, but quiet. That image, that picture, that single thought in the passage read becomes fruitful for today, thrills the heart today, gives a needed orientation for living today. And one is left breathing with heartfelt gratitude, *Thank you, Lord.*

Another technique of slow-march meditation was first worked out for use with Gospel narratives, episode by episode, but in fact it fits all biblical stories of specific events. You could call it the "fly on the wall" procedure. You use your imagination to put yourself into the scene as an observer, watching and listening, focusing your attention on the words and acts of God (in the case of Gospel stories, on the words and acts of Jesus, God incarnate). You overhear, for instance, what Jesus said to the woman at the well in John 4, and what God said to Moses at the burning bush in Exodus 3, and to Elijah on Mount Horeb in 1 Kings 19. Then you ask yourself, *If that was what God said to that person then, what has he to say to me now?* And then, *What truth, or insight, or promise* (what some call a

---

[18]Jan Johnson, *Savoring God's Word* (Colorado Springs: NavPress, 2004), pp. 87-91.

"best thought") *should I take with me from the passage to keep ruminating on for the rest of this day, if not indeed longer?* How naturally all this will lead into prayer of various kinds is easy to see.

The knowledge—indeed, the experience—of God by his Spirit applying biblical truths to our own consciences as we meditate on them will, if we are not careful, tempt us to an attitude of self-importance that is utterly ungodly. We must remember that God (not self) is the true center of our universe. Certainly God does make Scripture speak as from his own mouth to all who seek his face, but that does not mean that we are at the center of his universe or that we, rather than he, constitute the center of our own little world. God is great, and we are small; we exist for him, not he for us, although he has freely loved us, saved us and pledged himself to us; and one sign of our maturing spiritually is a more and more vivid sense of the contrast between us and him. A version of the meditative technique just described that helps to ward off self-importance is always to ask of every passage two prior questions—what does it say and show regarding the triune God, and what does it say and show about life in this world in general—before we turn to the question, what has this passage to say to me in particular about myself, my living, my sins, my tasks, my heart, my preparation for things to come? J. I. testifies to the value of this three-question routine, which he has followed for many years.

Another variant of this heart-healthy brooding on Scripture sets you on an exhaustive interrogation of the biblical text. You ask questions of every paragraph that you read. This process is sometimes called inductive Bible study, the discipline out of which grows its first cousin, expository preaching. A reader following this form of meditation would ask three sets of questions. First, what information does this passage convey? (For example, note or mark characters, places, actions, events, lines of argument and how all of these relate to each other.) Second, what is the meaning of these related bits of information and how does that meaning connect with the larger teachings of canonical Scripture? (For example, in John 4:24 you might ask: What does Jesus mean by saying, "God is spirit, and those who worship him must worship in spirit and truth?") Third, ask, what are the implications of this passage for me? (For example, how might I better worship God in spirit? in truth?) Thousands of Bible study guides (some written by Carolyn) and millions of biblical sermons (some preached by J. I.) have grown from this inductive method that begins with thoughtful, prayerful meditation on a particular section of Scripture.

There is yet one more way of meditating on Scripture that we would like to mention. It is topical meditation such as Owen and Baxter recommended. You select one theme and allow your mind to dwell on it, exploring its various ramifications, reflecting on various passages of Scripture that build up an account of it. For example, you may meditate on the wisdom of God, the glory of Christ (Owen's choice), the scope of salvation or the hope of heaven (Baxter's choice). You must, of course, know Bible truths about these things before you can meditate on them. Here a concordance or a topical or thematic Bible will come in handy for discovering appropriate biblical passages. At the end you must ask yourself, *How then should I respond to this reality? What should I pray for, give thanks for, and resolve to do and not do?* All of our meditating, whatever our method, should lead us to this point.

One final path of meditative and postmeditation praying is so obvious as to be easily overlooked. Simply pray the prayers of the Bible! There are hundreds of them, some of the greatest prayers ever written, almost all of them starting with a meditative celebration of some truth about God's being and action that lays a foundation for the petition that follows. What better way to pray than to pray God's own words back to him? You can personalize the prayer by inserting personal pronouns or names. For example, from Psalm 9:9-10, we might pray, "LORD, you are a stronghold for the oppressed, a stronghold in time of trouble. All those who know your name put their trust in you, for you, O LORD, have not forsaken those who seek you. This is the situation of _____. Please be a refuge to him/her in this time of trouble."

Many great prayers of the Bible invite us to this sort of praying very directly. Leaving the psalms aside, samples include Hannah's prayer of thanksgiving in 1 Samuel 2:1-10, David's prayer for his people and his son Solomon in 1 Chronicles 29:10-19, Solomon's prayer of dedication in 2 Chronicles 6:14-42, Daniel's prayer of corporate confession in Daniel 9:4-19, Habakkuk's prayer of commitment during suffering in Habakkuk 3:17-19, Mary's prayer of praise in Luke 1:68-79, Paul's prayer of blessing in Ephesians 3:14-21, his prayer of thanksgiving for Christian friends in Philippians 1:3-11, and his prayer for the spiritual advance of Christians he had never met in Colossians 1:9-12, Jude's prayer of benediction in Jude 24-25, and, of course, our Lord's model prayer in Matthew 6:9-13. With the Bible as our prayer book, we will never be short of broodings and beacons to shape our praying.

MEDITATION AS MENTORING

Meditation mentors us. Meditation operates as a kind of spiritual workout because in it God applies his Word to us through prompting us to apply it to ourselves. Meditation matures us by sharpening our vision of God, and it leaves us having to face maturing questions like: In light of what I've read, what should I do, and what should I stop doing? What attitudes on my part are right, and what attitudes on my part are wrong? How have I slipped into the wrong ones, and how am I to develop the right ones? What does Christlike godliness involve for me, and how am I to pursue that goal? What renewing of hope and strength do I need from my God right now? What help do I need to be more Christlike than I have been? Meditative questions like these move us into prayer, and so they should.

Meditation operates as food and exercise for the soul, a food and exercise that are necessary for growth. Some Christians are spiritually anorexic, because they fail to "eat" enough, through not having learned to meditate. Stunted Christians are as they are because they don't meditate.

Some Christians suffer from arrested development and remain infantile, because they have not been meditating as Christians should. Out of meditation comes increased knowledge of God, the world, ourselves, Jesus Christ and the promises of God given for our encouragement and steadier reliance on God's guidance. Out of meditation comes ripe wisdom for facing the world's value systems and behavior patterns that are contrary to the way of Christ. We must not be seduced by them, so we need to clearly see what is wrong with them. Meditation will give us that clear vision. And meditation will give us at every point a deeper understanding of petitioning God when we say "Help," of praising God when we say "Hallelujah," and of pleasing God when we say "Hallowed be thy name."

Mary, sister of Martha, is found in Luke 10:38-42 sitting at Jesus' feet, listening to him and learning from him. Martha thought Mary was being lazy and complained to Jesus that she was not being helpful. "Martha, Martha," Jesus replied, "you are anxious and troubled about many things"—all quite right in their place, be it said. Hungry travelers needed to eat, and someone had to prepare the food. Hostess Martha was right to be tackling this as her immediate task. But food preparation was not at that moment Mary's priority. We guess that she knew Martha could manage without her; certainly, she now heard Jesus say to her exasperated sister, "Mary has chosen the good portion, which will not be taken from her." Mary models the prioritizing of learning from the Lord, which we do by meditation, and Jesus justifies her for so doing.

The lesson for us is not that domestic work is not important but that we must each be Martha and Mary by turn. Martha did indeed get her turn at Jesus' feet when he met her at Lazarus's tomb and told her, "I am the resurrection and the life. Whoever believes in me, though he die, yet shall he live, and everyone who lives and believes in me shall never die." And then, no doubt after a long and weighted pause to let his words sink in, Jesus asked Martha eye to eye, "Do you believe this?" She had heard and thought, and her mind had become clear in that extended moment, and her answer is the best that anyone could ever give, "Yes, Lord; I believe that you are the Christ, the Son of God who is coming into the world" (Jn 11:25-27). Dealing with all the practicalities of Christian life is a high priority, but listening to the Lord by meditating on his Word is an even higher priority for us. First things first, yet the ideal is both things together! It should be a case of both-and, being Martha and Mary by turns, for all of us. May God help us then not only to *behave* but also to *brood* to his glory, so that we learn to pray better, more heartily, more wisely, more humbly, more thankfully and in greater faithfulness to the holy Three, who in their divine unity are so wonderfully faithful to us. This is the way we must go.

❦ 4 ❧

PRAISING

Praise the LORD, O my soul;
all my inmost being, praise his holy name. . . .
Praise the LORD, you his angels,
you mighty ones who do his bidding,
who obey his word.
Praise the LORD, all his heavenly hosts,
you his servants who do his will.
Praise the LORD, all his works
everywhere in his dominion.
Praise the LORD, O my soul.

PSALM 103:1, 20-22 (NIV)

I'll praise my Maker while I've breath,
And when my voice is lost in death,
Praise shall employ my nobler powers.
My days of praise shall ne'er he past
While life and thought and being last,
Or immortality endures.

ISAAC WATTS (1674-1748)

C. S. Lewis, writer of the Narnia books and of a string of stellar exposi-
tions of Christianity, was a praying man. Some of this he shows us in his
final book, *Letters to Malcolm: Chiefly on Prayer;* and his practice

matched what he said of himself there. He attended his parish church regularly on Sundays and his college chapel regularly on weekdays, diligently praying his way into and through the liturgy of the Anglican Prayer Book. Then, so his friend and biographer George Sayer tells us, when taking a train journey Lewis would go to the station very early "and walk up and down the platform saying his prayers." Also, when he stayed at the Sayers's home, Lewis would retreat to his room each evening about six with a Bible "and say his prayers." Also, when Sayer brought Lewis morning tea in bed, "he was already awake, and . . . usually praying." He also liked a quick walk before breakfast, "drinking in the beauty of the morning, thanking God for the weather, the roses, the song of the birds, and anything else he could find to enjoy."[1] Lewis always knew that prayer is integral to life with God, as witness his words about the day in 1929 when "I gave in, and admitted that God was God, and knelt and prayed; perhaps, that night, the most dejected and reluctant convert in all of England."[2] Prayer was big in his life pattern as a believer from the start.

But early on, so he tells us, he had a problem: why does God, the God of the Bible, the God of Christianity, call on us to praise him?[3] Lewis's experience, like our own, with humans who seek compliments had not been pleasant. "We all despise the man who demands continual assurance of his own virtue, intelligence or delightfulness." Why should God insist on being praised? Did he want praise (as is so often true of humans) so that he could feel good about himself? Why did so many of the psalms seem to bargain with God about this, as if to say: "You like praise? Do this for me, and you shall have some." Was this the way of real religion? Was such praising really necessary?

Many devout Christians follow the well-used outline of ACTS (Ado-

---

[1]George Sayer, *Jack,* 2nd ed. (Wheaton, Ill.: Crossway, 1994), pp. 340, 342, 344.

[2]C. S. Lewis, *Surprised by Joy* (London: Fontana, 1959), p. 182.

[3]C. S. Lewis, "A Word About Praising," in *Reflections on the Psalms* (San Diego: Harcourt, 1958). The quotations that follow are all from this nine-page chapter 9.

ration, Confession, Thanksgiving, Supplication) when they pray, and so begin with words of praise, often half-heartedly, plodding their way through the preliminary exercises until they can get to what's really on their hearts, namely need in its various forms. Only then do their prayers warm up. They wonder, as they go along, *why the preliminaries?* Confession of sins and thanksgiving for good things enjoyed, they understand, after a fashion, but adoring God for who and what he is feels like a routine of burdensome flattery. So why praise God first—or indeed at all?

THE PRAISE DILEMMA

So we must ask: Is the prayer of praise—praise prayer, we will call it— anything more than a bargaining counter directed toward God? Why does God ask for it? What is the true point of it? Should humans bargain with God by attempting to trade gain for praise? The psalms, usually our guide for good praying, do not provide much help with these questions. They give us many examples of different kinds of prayers but little analysis as to why we are to pray in the ways that are modeled there, and that is certainly the case with regard to our present concern. Thus David appears to offer praise in exchange for battle victory when he opens Psalm 54 with the request, "O God, save me, by your name, / and vindicate me by your might," and then promises in verse 6, "With a freewill offering I will sacrifice to you; / I will give thanks to your name, O LORD, for it is good." Another psalmist, Heman, appears to offer praise as a bargain for life in Psalm 88:10 when he asks, "Do you work wonders for the dead? / Do the departed rise up to praise you?" What kind of God trades protection for compliments? Or does he? Are we, perhaps, missing something?

Lewis, for one, became quite sure that we who think in these terms are indeed missing something. This appears from his account of how he resolved his own original problem. He began by reflecting on what it means to say that a work of art "demands" appreciation:

Admiration is the correct, adequate or appropriate response to it, . . . if we do not admire we shall be stupid, insensible, and great losers, we shall have missed something.

He applied this idea to God:

[God] is that Object to admire which (or, if you like, to appreciate which) is simply to be awake, to have entered the real world; not to appreciate which is to have lost the greatest experience. . . . The incomplete and crippled lives of those who are tone-deaf, have never been in love, never known true friendship, never cared for a good book . . . are faint images of it.

And then Lewis discerned he had got hold of the wrong end of the stick altogether with regard to praise.

I thought of it in terms of compliment, approval, or the giving of honor. I had never noticed that all enjoyment spontaneously overflows into praise. . . . I had not noticed how the humblest, and at the same time most balanced and capacious, minds, praised most, while the cranks, misfits and malcontents praised least.

I think we delight to praise what we enjoy because the praise not merely expresses but completes the enjoyment. . . . [T]he delight is incomplete until it is expressed.[4]

So praise of the God whose truth, beauty, grace, mercy, greatness and faithfulness we appreciate is the most natural thing in the world, and can be the most joyful too, as well as the most health-giving. "Praise almost seems to be inner health made audible."[5]

Lewis's wisdom helps us see two things. First, that what looked like bargaining with God is simply honest anticipation of glorifying him through active enjoyment of a renewed display of his active love. Second, that the corporate praise to which the psalms constantly call us,

---

[4]Ibid., pp. 92-95.
[5]Ibid., p. 94.

and which we seek to achieve in church every Lord's Day as we sing out together our shared appreciation of God and his ways, brings him close to us. Writes Lewis: "I did not see that it is in the process of being worshipped that God communicates His presence to men. It is not of course the only way. But for many people at many times the 'fair beauty of the Lord' is revealed chiefly or only while they worship Him together."[6] Psalmists anticipate this experience in the temple through the sacrifices; Christians seek it in what are nowadays called their "worship spaces" (church buildings, that is), as they look to the Savior's promise, "Where two or three come together in my name, there am I with them" (Mt 18:20).

For clarity now, since all this may be coming to us as new thinking, let us formalize the essence of what we have said before we go further. Six alliterative words, linked in three pairs, will help us here.

Praise as declaring and distancing. One function of praise prayer is that our spoken words declare who God is and our relationship to him. Why does God invite our praise? In part it is because as we praise God in prayer, we verbally declare and inwardly realize, every time, that, as it has been put, "He is God, and we are not." To hear words of praise to God from our own lips helps us to recognize our distance from God. Yet paradoxically these prayers of praise also take us into his presence. As we proclaim both to God and to each other how far he is above us and beyond us in his wisdom, power and purity, a sense of his closeness to us is repeatedly given.

Psalm 95 illustrates this. It starts by celebrating God as our Creator, "the Rock of our salvation," whose hand holds "the depths of the earth," the "mountain peaks" and the sea, "for he made it," and the entire landscape since "his hands formed the dry land" (vv. 1-5). What is the appropriate response to such a God? It is not only to declare these things; it is also for us to draw near, but not with any sense of pride. We are to "sing

---

[6]C. S. Lewis, *Reflections on the Psalms* (Orlando: Harvest Books, 1958), p. 93.

for joy to the LORD" (v. 1), but how? The psalmist calls for a praise shaped by humility, so that we acknowledge even with our bodies our great distance from this almighty Creator God.

> Come, let us bow down in worship,
>   let us kneel before the LORD our Maker!
> For he is our God
>   and we are the people of his pasture
> the flock under his care. (Ps 95:1-7)

Come? Bow down? Kneel in reverent humility? To bow and to kneel are universal, time-honored gestures of acknowledging greatness in some form. Praise prayer acknowledges our dependence on the God who is great in power and wisdom, when we are neither. We approach him in prayer and thus draw near to him because he invites us to do that. But our mental attitude, our posture, our very words must ever declare the difference and distance between God and us.

So who gains from praise prayer? Is it God who has his ego stroked? Or is it praying humans to whom God communicates (in and through their humble praise) some new revelation of his own greatness? C. S. Lewis settled for the latter position. The Jewish sacrificial system, he observed, was not designed to sate a bloodthirsty God. No! "The sacrifice was not really that men gave bulls and goats to God, but that by their so doing God gave himself to men." Lewis compares the Old Testament sacrifices with the Christian obligation to go to church (never one of Lewis's favorite disciplines, though he was exemplary in his regularity at church and college chapel). He asserts that corporate praise, as in a church worship service, is not merely given to gratify God. "It is in the process of being worshipped that God communicates his presence to men."[7] So we praise God in prayer. We declare his greatness to his face while on our knees, and in this act God bridges the distance between us and reveals himself to us. As we declare him to be very far above us, so we find him

---

[7]Ibid., p. 93.

to be very close to us. He receives our praise; we receive his love. That is how praise prayer works.

Praise as discipline and diet. In matters of health, discipline and diet ordinarily go together. A disciplined person will take regular exercise and be careful to eat and sleep enough—not too little, nor too much. It is diet, however, (the food we take in) that actually nourishes us, keeping us alive and strong. Praise prayer is both discipline and diet. As C. S. Lewis sorted through his questions about this activity, he began to notice the kinds of people who praised (anything) and those who simply didn't. He observed that "cranks, misfits, and malcontents praised least," while the "humblest, and at the same time most balanced and capacious minds, praised most."[8] He noticed that lovers seemed to praise most of all, and to delight in drawing others into their praise of the beloved one.

We see this in Psalm 96:1 where the psalmist invites all creation to "sing to the LORD a new song; / sing to the LORD, all the earth!" He calls on the seas to roar, the heavens to be glad, the fields to exult, the trees to sing for joy, the earth to tremble and rejoice, and all people to "declare his glory among the nations" (v. 3). What a chorus of praise! We would have to be spiritually deaf not to want to join in such a symphony. We may never have thought of what we call the natural order, the created world around us, as our partner in praise; maybe it is time we did. The fact is that in this, as in other matters, companionship quells inhibitions and creates incentives. As the discipline of bodily exercise becomes easier to give your heart to in a gym, where you are surrounded by a whole crowd of people exercising already, and as sticking to a prescribed diet becomes easier when everyone at the table is on the diet with you, so you are swept up into personal praise much more quickly and powerfully when you realize that praise—from angels, from glorified saints, and from all creation—is going on all around you. And we have already heard Lewis describing praise as "inner health made audible."[9]

---

[8]Ibid., p. 94.
[9]Ibid.

If praise prayer is both discipline and diet, we who want to pray well have great reason to give ourselves to it in a big way. We are to tackle praising as we would any discipline. Having made up our minds to do it, we just do it, both privately and in church, as best we can, knowing that the more we do it the better we will be able to do it. If our God asks all the earth to sing his praises, who are we to refuse? To do so would bring spiritual harm in the form of defective development. And if praise prayer is part of our proper diet, to neglect this kind of praying will signal, even trigger, spiritual starvation, with lack of energy and lowering of morale. We will then be in danger of becoming the cranks, misfits and malcontents that Lewis so rightly characterized as unable to give praise. Learning to praise is necessary from every standpoint if we are to grow in grace.

Praise as duty and delight. By now it is surely clear that praise and thanksgiving belong together, and meld into each other. In idea they are distinct, praise centering on what God is, and thanksgiving on what he does, as a comparison of Psalms 135 and 136 clearly shows; but in practice, sooner or later, the two ideas come together, since God lets us see what he *is* precisely by what he *does*. So Psalm 106 begins:

> *Praise* the LORD!
>   *Give thanks* to the LORD, for he *is* good;
> his steadfast love endures forever!
>   Who can proclaim the *mighty acts* of the LORD,
> or fully declare his *praise?* (Ps 106:1-2, emphasis added)

The words in italics illustrate the melding to which we referred.

Glory is a key biblical word that expresses the composite notion of weight or weightiness, wealth and whatever else belongs to the state of being wonderful. God, we are told, *shows* his glory (who and what he is) by what he does; then his rational creatures, angels and humans, *give* him glory (praise and thanks) for what he has done (and does, and is going to do); thus we glorify him ("the one who offers thanksgiving as his sacrifice glorifies me," [Ps 50:23]); and thus God gets himself glory and glorifies himself by moving us to give him glory in this way. This, fundamentally, is what the angels were made for:

Ascribe to the LORD, O heavenly beings,
    ascribe to the LORD glory and strength.
Ascribe to the LORD the glory *due his name.* (Ps 29:1-2)

And it is what we humans were made and redeemed for: "Whatever you do, do all to the glory of God" (1 Cor 10:31). Praise is not an option; it is a vocation and a duty. Psalm after psalm expresses this.

Here is another example. "Give thanks to the LORD, for he is good," begins Psalm 136. In this chorus song of praise, each verse recites a praiseworthy deed of the Lord, and then comes the repeated refrain giving the reason *why* we are to praise: "for his steadfast love endures forever," and each deed done is a fruit of that steadfast love. Clearly the praise of Psalm 136 is not simply a suggestion. It is a divine order complete with warrant justifying that order in every line. Praise for God's manifold praiseworthiness is a duty, and it will be a sign of something wrong with us if we do not thus give God his due.

Psalm 42 takes us in a similar direction but goes further. This delightfully structured psalm begins with a beautiful prayer of longing for God:

As a deer pants for flowing streams,
    so pants my soul for you O God.
My soul thirsts for God,
    for the living God.
When shall I come and appear before God? (Ps 42:1-2)

But longing leads the psalmist to questioning, not questioning of God but questioning of himself. Twice he writes "Why are you cast down, O my soul, / and why are you in turmoil within me?" (vv. 5, 11). Moments and moods of distress and desperation come to us all, and for whatever reason the psalmist is bogged down in such a mood as he writes. Where does this sacred longing take him? Against the background of his knowl-

edge that the steadfast love of God endures forever, he lets the ache in
his heart direct him to the duty (and wisdom!) of remembering. "My
soul is cast down within me; *therefore* I remember you" (v. 6, emphasis
added). What does the psalmist remember? He remembers delight.

> These things I remember
>   as I pour out my soul:
> how I would go with the throng
>   and lead them in procession to the house of God. (Ps 42:4)

It is this pattern of longing, leading to the duty of remembering, leading to remembered delight, which in turn leads the psalmist to tell himself to hope, and actually to begin hoping once more. Twice he repeats:
"Hope in God: for I shall again praise him, / my salvation and my God"
(vv. 5, 11). Thus this lovely psalm shows us the link between the duty of
praise and its delight—here, the combined delights of remembering, celebrating and looking ahead to more great things.

One of the greatest joys of delight is to share it, and one of the con-
trasting frustrations is to lack that opportunity. Here is Lewis again,
quoted more fully this time.

> I think we delight to praise what we enjoy because the praise not
> merely expresses but completes the enjoyment; . . . the delight is in-
> complete until it is expressed. . . . It is frustrating to . . . come sud-
> denly, at the turn of the road, upon some mountain valley of
> unexpected grandeur and then have to keep silent because the people
> with you care for it no more than a tin can in a ditch.[10]

We would do well to remember Lewis's poignant illustration of unsee-
ing eyes whenever we participate in a worship service where the music
is obviously someone else's favorite—but not ours.

While I (Carolyn) was teaching a youth communicant class last spring,
we discussed this very issue. The class had already spent some time

---

[10]Ibid., p. 95.

thinking together about the implications of 1 Corinthians 12 where Paul defines the church as "the body of Christ," with Christ as its head. We had talked about what it means to be connected within a single body of Christians not much like ourselves, to serve God together as a single unit, to praise God together in corporate worship. So I posed a tense question for teenagers. "What about music? What would you do in a worship service where *nothing* there was your kind of music?" It got a little quiet for a moment. I could see wishful mental images of drums and guitars and fast-paced music on a screen (which is rare in our church). I could see their mental images of organ, strings and hymnals (more common here). Then Leslie, age fifteen, said with a shrug and a bright smile. "Stand up and sing!" I laughed at her generous concession, spoken with such full energy—and I wondered how many mature Christians, facing the question in the opposite form, could have done the same. It is this kind of generosity toward each other that makes authentic corporate praise a reality.

In Psalm 66 we see the psalmist both praising God with delight and delighting to involve others in that praise:

> Shout for joy to God, all the earth,
>> Sing the glory of his name;
>> give to him glorious praise!
> Say to God, "How awesome are your deeds!" . . .
> Bless our God, O peoples,
>> Let the sound of his praise be heard, . . .
> Come and hear, all you who fear God,
>> And I will tell what he has done for my soul. (Ps 66:1-2, 8, 16)

Here again, praise appears both as a duty and also as an expression of joy and delight. The importance of understanding this conjunction is great, so we will spend a little more time exploring it.

In everyday life, the word *duty* regularly signifies an unwelcome obligation, like paying taxes and, before that, filling out our tax forms, so our delight is ordinarily found in something other than what we think of as the doing of our duty. But why is this? In the sense that everyone feels this way, the separating of duty and delight in our minds is entirely natural, but in relation to the way God made us to be we are all at this point in a profoundly unnatural state—for we are fallen creatures. The anti-God allergy called original sin resides and marauds in our moral and spiritual system, leading us to deeply egocentric motivation, moral corner-cutting and worse, callousness and cruelty, undervaluing and exploiting others, constant self-admiration and self-pity, playing God while evading the real God, loving ourselves but not loving him, wanting to be praised while declining inwardly to praise or admire others, and many other self-centered vices. For sinners as such, duty, which is first God-centered and then others-centered, can never be a delight. And since, in Christians, sin—though dethroned—is not yet destroyed and still leaves its finger marks more or less obtrusively on everything that we think, wish, plan and do, it is understandable that the thought of praise as both duty and delight hardly seems real at first. And to the extent that original sin still shapes us, praise, though an acknowledged duty, will not be a delight.

But Christians, believers in Jesus Christ, are regenerate—born again, new creatures, dead and risen with Christ, alive to God in Christ (the New Testament has many ways of expressing this). That means that we have been changed, supernaturally renovated in the core of our personal being, what Scripture calls the *heart;* and the nature of this change, which has been brought about through union with the risen Christ, is that now our hearts have become in a decisive way a transcript of his. In the days of his flesh, as the Gospel stories show, the incarnate Lord was controlled—we might even say, driven—by the life-unifying desire to please, honor, exalt and glorify his heavenly Father in all things by obedient service, and his joy was to do his Father's will and magnify his Father's name always and everywhere—in other words, to live a life that expressed worship and adoration of the One who had sent him to earth. That same desire, with the Son and the Spirit joined to the Father as its object, is now implanted in Christian hearts. At motivational level, and perhaps in outward conduct too, original sin will hit back and fight the new heart, producing conflict, tension and less-than-perfect performance, with consequent frustration and distress at our own continuing sinfulness. But for all that, the desires of the renewed heart are now dominant within, and that means that the duty of praise will increasingly become a delight—indeed, the supreme delight—of our life.

Once again, C. S. Lewis helps us to grasp what is involved here, this time by his idea of heaven: "a state" he says "in which angels now, and men hereafter, are perpetually employed in praising God." To conceive this,

> we must suppose ourselves to be in a perfect love with God—drunk with, drowned in, dissolved by, that delight which, far from remaining pent up within ourselves as incommunicable, hence hardly tolerable, bliss, flows out from us incessantly again in effortless and perfect expression, our joy no more separable from the praise in which it liberates and utters itself than the brightness a mirror receives is separable from the brightness it sheds. The Scotch [i.e., Westminster Shorter] Catechism says that man's chief end is "to glorify God and enjoy him forever." But we shall then know that these are the same thing. . . . In commanding us to glorify him, God is inviting us to enjoy him.[11]

Here then we have the final answer to Lewis's own question: why does God so constantly and insistently require us to praise him? The answer is: So that we may get into the habit of doing what in heaven we will do spontaneously and wholeheartedly in and from and for enjoyment of God. God's joy and our joy in our praising will then coincide. Lewis knew that performing the duty of praise may for the moment bring us little or no delight, just as the five-finger exercises prescribed to budding

---

[11]Ibid., pp. 96-97. Lewis's use of *Scotch* for Scottish is a strange lapse. *Scotch* is an outdated word applied nowadays only to whisky, mist, terriers, eggs, tape, broth and broom. Scottish people resent the word as pejorative in other contexts.

pianists are ordinarily felt as a joyless bore. Nonetheless, he says, "the duty exists for the delight. . . . [W]e are like people digging channels in a waterless land, in order that when at last the water comes, it may find them ready." And "there are happy moments, even now, when a trickle creeps along the dry beds; and happy the souls to whom this happens often."[12] Indeed, the number of praising psalms in which these trickles already find expression (trickles, by comparison with what awaits us; floods, in relation to where we are now) show that already, in this life, heartfelt adoration will again and again bring heartfelt joy. This thought takes us straight to our next point.

ALL TOGETHER, NOW

There is a great difference between being a solo instrumentalist or singer and playing in an orchestra or being part of a choir. In both cases you concentrate just as hard on the notes and on the quality of your own sound, but being in the orchestra or choir when things go right gives you a kind of lift that you do not ordinarily get as a soloist. Why is that? The exhilaration is a spinoff from the awareness of being in a harmonious fellowship, every member of which is at each moment concentrating with you on making music happen with fullest beauty and power. (J. I. is here remembering an efficient but uninspired British orchestra director of whom the players said that when he conducted "nothing ever *happened*.") In the praising of God, something of the same principle operates. But when God's people praise him together with their whole hearts, it is safe to say that something *always* happens.

We are created to praise God as individuals, but not always as solo instruments. The Scriptures are full of corporate praise and encouragement to find delight in praising God with other believers, backed as we saw by all of his creation, and in joining with the mighty throng of heavenly beings, angels and perfected saints in their ongoing praise. It is hard

---

[12]Ibid., p. 97.

to imagine our mumbled, whispered, tentative praises as part of such a grand scene, but over and over Scripture portrays our praise praying as one ingredient in this massive chorus of adoration and expects it to take the form of song. (Many of the psalms have their original, now lost, Hebrew tunes included in their headings.) Paul tells Christians to "be filled with the Spirit, . . . singing and making melody to the Lord with all your heart" (Eph 5:18-19). Singing, it seems, is of the essence of corporate praise.

A certain eagerness grows from the prospect of conjoined praise. The psalmist in one of his songs of ascents (ascent to the temple, the place of such praise) declares, "I was glad when they said to me, 'Let us go to the house of the LORD!' " (Ps 122:1). Jonah, the rebellious prophet, prayed longingly about corporate praise as he lay in the belly of a fish, his custom-designed time-out zone.

> I shall again look
> > upon your holy temple. . . .
> I with the voice of thanksgiving
> > will sacrifice to you. (Jon 2:4, 9)

Psalm 84 opens with similar longing to be part of the temple's corporate praise:

> How lovely is your dwelling place,
> > O LORD of hosts!
> My soul longs, yes, faints
> > for the courts of the LORD. . . .
> my heart and flesh sing for joy
> > to the living God. . . .
> For a day in your courts is better
> > than a thousand elsewhere. (Ps 84:1-2, 10)

The writer of Psalm 96 breathes enthusiasm as he exhorts us to join existing praise and draw others into that worship, ever enlarging the chorus of those who praise God:

Oh sing to the LORD a new song;
   sing to the LORD all the earth!
Sing to the LORD, bless his name;
   tell of his salvation from day to day.
Declare his glory among the nations,
   his marvelous works among all the peoples!
For great is the LORD, and greatly to be praised. (Ps 96:1-4)

The New Testament brings an added dimension to corporate praise. Here we encounter praise united and sustained as a way of life in the context of the church, a living multipeopled organism headed by Christ, of which every congregation was (and is) called to be a credible microscopic sample. Paul, as we saw a moment ago, called on the church at Ephesus to live a Spirit-filled life full of musical praise—using "psalms and hymns and spiritual songs, singing and making melody to the Lord with all your heart, giving thanks always for everything to God the Father in the name of our Lord Jesus Christ" (Eph 5:19-20). Paul's vision— his dream, we may call it—in this letter is of Christians living in sustained mutual love (v. 2), always submitting to each other out of reverence for Christ their Lord (v. 21) and singing as they go, with the music of praise prayer constantly on their lips because it is constantly in their hearts, a vision that fifteen-year-old Leslie was already beginning to live out. It is true that for centuries we Western Christians, at least, have for the most part been a pretty quiet lot—but does Paul's vision have to remain a dream forever?

It is observable that periods and movements of vitality in the church have always been marked by fresh outbreaks of Christian praise songs in one form or another: praise prayer, that is, in the sense we have given to this phrase. Some forty years ago the charismatic movement rediscovered and emphasized the importance of praise songs in worship, and has contributed both an abundance of folk and rock-type lyrics and the now widespread pattern of a half-hour of musical praise by the whole congregation at the start of any worship gathering. The unfamiliarity of both idiom and layout has made this a controversial development in the eyes of some, but the fact remains that we can hardly attend a contemporary Christian worship service without witnessing a high degree of delight in praising God, and feeling drawn joyfully to join in. It would be a happy thing if all those congregations that maintain older styles of corporate praise would make their own patterns of song equally potent and attractive.

Evangelism, meaning what evangelicals have always meant by the word, that is, invitatory presentation of the historical facts, divine promises, and living Savior, that together constitute the substance of the gospel, is much discussed these days, and various forms of seeker-friendly gatherings, distinct from regular patterns of congregational worship are proposed. One point sometimes missed in these discussions is that the robust and exuberant praises uttered by God's people, as they celebrate their certainties in Christ, has great drawing power for individuals who are spiritually adrift. Whether in the form of old hymns, therefore, or modern songs, whether led by a traditional church organ or a keyboard-guitar-and-drums praise band, much praise prayer should surround the preaching of the Word of God, both when that is being done in a focused evangelistic way and more pastorally, in the ordinary ongoing weekly worship of believers. Experience seems to show that wherever the Word is preached in an enlivening way, and everyone sings the praises of God from the heart, individuals will come in from outside and be affected by God, thus fulfilling within a Christian frame the psalmists' anticipation of Israel's magnetic outreach.

Praise and evangelism (missions, outreach) do indeed come together in the biblical vision of present kingdom life, so Christians rightly see praise prayer as having a direct relationship to sharing the love of God with those who do not yet know it.

The same psalm that begins "Oh sing to the LORD a new song" continues:

> Ascribe to the LORD, O families of the peoples,
>   ascribe to the LORD glory and strength!
> Ascribe to the LORD the glory due his name! . . .
> Say among the nations, "The LORD reigns!" . . .
> He will judge the world in righteousness,
>   and the peoples in his faithfulness. (Ps 96:7-8, 10, 13)

When praise prayer becomes corporate, God invites the world to the party, and each group of those who are already at the party should be as compelling an advertisement for what goes on there as possible. It is rightly urged that evangelism should convey a clear invitation to repentance and faith in Jesus Christ for salvation; it should equally be urged that the invitation involves linking up with those who worship God already, and joining in their life together. And when that community is marked by biblically faithful preaching and wholehearted praise prayer, people will constantly be drawn into the church as God's first step in drawing them to Christ. Praise prayer, we may truly say, is contagious with a contagion that we can hardly have too much of at the present time.

Psalm 66 is a recounting of God's "awesome deeds" which also includes an invitation:

> Shout for joy to God, all the earth;
> sing the glory of his name;
>   give to him glorious praise!
> Say to God, "How awesome are your deeds! . . .
> All the earth worships you
>   and sings praises to you;
>   they sing praises to your name."
> Come and see what God has done:
> he is awesome in his deeds toward the children of man. . . .
>
> Bless our God, O peoples,
>   let the sound of his praise be heard. . . .

Come and hear all you who fear God,
and I will tell what he has done for my soul. (Ps 66:1-3, 4-5, 8, 16)

Praise and proclamation join hands in this psalm. In our own church worship services, at their best, the same will happen.

The New Testament speaks with similar clarity about Christian identity and Christian vocation and makes the same connection between corporate praise and evangelism.

You are a chosen race, a royal priesthood, a holy nation, a people for [God's] own possession, *that you may proclaim* the excellencies of him who called you out of darkness into his marvelous light. Once you were not a people, but now you are God's people; once you had not received mercy, but now you have received mercy. (1 Pet 2:9-10, emphasis added)

The people who have received God's mercy must remember that they themselves needed that mercy and so be willing to "proclaim the excellencies of him who called you out of darkness into his marvelous light." Is the proclamation that Peter had in mind Godward in praise or manward in witness? Commentaries divide, so the only safe (and probably correct) thing is to say that it is both, though most certainly the second. Praise and proclamation once again join, therefore, this time so that others may be drawn to become "God's people," along with those who are such already.

PRAISE AS PREPARATION

On March 23, 1631, knowing he was on his deathbed (his life ended eight days later), John Donne, dean of St. Paul's, London, wrote "Hymn to God My God, in My Sickness," which began thus:

Since I am coming to that Holy room
Where, with thy Quire of Saints for evermore,
I shall be made thy Music; As I come
I tune the Instrument here at the door,
And what I must do then, think here before.

Donne's image is of an Elizabethan or Jacobean banqueting hall, where musicians would be brought in to play for as long as the feast lasted. Tuning their instruments at the door is what they would do just prior to their entry. Donne's thought is that the music will all be praise for God's pleasure and that he himself is the instrument that, in company with countless other such instruments, will be playing that praise. C. S. Lewis echoes Donne's phrase and Donne's thought, as he reflects, realistically enough, on the often difficult and daunting character of our experiences in the school of prayer, including our attempts at praise. ("Irksome . . . humiliating . . . frustrating . . . time-wasting—the worse one is praying, the longer one's prayers take.")[13] But one day the tuning of the instrument will be done, and we, in Donne's sense, as ourselves both instrumentalist and instrument, will start really to play. We will round off the present chapter by briefly reflecting on this.

Is heaven like an eternal church service? This is another question that troubled the young Lewis, who never developed a great love of church services—in spite of thirty-four years of faithful attendance, following his conversion to theism in 1929. For him, church was a discipline, and a difficult one. "No," he decided, "Our 'services' both in their conduct and in our power to participate, are merely attempts at worship; never fully successful, often 99.9 per cent failures, sometimes total failures." But these puny services of corporate praise prepare us, however dimly, for an eternal future where praise and delight come together. Lewis elaborates on this as he dwells on the fact that praying, here and now, is a Christian duty.

> If we were perfected, prayer would not be a duty, it would be delight. Some day, please God, it will be. The same is true of many other behaviors which now appear as duties. . . . To practice them spontaneously and delightfully is not yet possible. This situation creates the category of duty, the whole specifically *moral* realm. . . . But . . . there

---

[13]C. S. Lewis, *Letters to Malcolm: Chiefly on Prayer* (London: Geoffrey Bles, 1964), pp. 147-50.

is no morality in heaven. The angels never knew (from within) the meaning of the word *ought,* and the blessed dead have long since gladly forgotten it. . . . This is why Dante's Heaven is so right. . . . This also explains . . . why we have to picture that world in terms which almost seem frivolous. . . . We can picture unimpeded, and therefore delighted, action only by the analogy of our present play and leisure.[14]

Lewis's breathtaking point is surely undeniable. When we are resurrected in our finally perfect state, *duty* will be a word that we will not need. Thoroughgoing love (admiration, appreciation, valuation, gratitude, goodwill), both to our triune God and to all our glorified fellow sinners, will be the spontaneous, wholehearted, unqualified and indefatigable expression of what we now are. All the thoughts that pass through and come from our minds will have at their center praise to God, all the time and all the way. And it will be *fun!*—pure, celestial, transcendent, glorious fun. We will never have enjoyed anything so much. We are not there yet, but we are rehearsing for heaven, nothing less, every time we give ourselves to praise. We are tuning ourselves up to be the instruments making the music with which heaven will be filled. Thank you, John Donne, for your gift to us of the perfect analogy.

Now we see why at many Christians' funerals joy blends with grief as we glimpse for a moment this eternal view, perhaps with the uttering of the words "Precious in the sight of the LORD / is the death of his saints" (Ps 116:15) or perhaps with the often used quote from the King James Version of Revelation: "I heard a voice from heaven saying unto me, Write, Blessed are the dead which die in the Lord: Yea, saith the Spirit, that they rest from their labors" (Rev 14:13). Far from demeaning this life, a Christian's eternal perspective makes that life (and death) precious—even to God. Our loved ones go, as we ourselves will one day go, simply, safely and with utter satisfaction to be part of God's praise music

---

[14]Ibid., pp. 147-48. Dante, following Thomas Aquinas, conceived heaven as the endless joy of contemplating the evermoving changelessness of God, as when we watch a waterfall or the ocean.

forever and ever. In heaven the song has already started, and in the book of Revelation God briefly draws the curtain so that we can form some idea of what is happening:

> Day and night they never cease to say,
>> "Holy, holy, holy, is the Lord God Almighty,
>> who was and is and is to come!" . . .
> They cast their crowns before the throne, saying,
>> "Worthy are you, our Lord and God,
>>> to receive glory and honor and power,
>> for you created all things,
>>> and by your will they existed and were created." . . .

> After this I looked, and behold, a great multitude that no one could number, from every nation, from all tribes and peoples and languages, standing before the throne and before the Lamb, clothed in white robes, and palm branches in their hands, and crying out with a loud voice, "Salvation belongs to our God who sits on the throne, and to the Lamb!" And all the angels were standing around the throne and around the elders and the four living creatures, and they fell on their faces before the throne and worshiped God, saying, "Amen! Blessing and glory and wisdom and thanksgiving and honor and power and might be to our God forever and ever! Amen." (Rev 4:8, 10-11; 7:9-12)

Some of these thoughts were in Carolyn's mind as recently she sat through the night with a dying believer of eighty-eight, reading Scripture, singing to her and praying for her until God took her home. Some of them were in J. I.'s mind as not too long ago he recited Scripture and prayed for his comatose sister during the last four hours of her earthly life. Some of them were certainly in the mind of another eighty-eight-year-old, John Wesley, who the day before his death sang with great effort the first two verses of Isaac Watts great hymn, sparked by Psalms 146 and 148, "I'll praise my Maker while I've breath," the opening stanza of which we used as an epigraph for this chapter. Through the night that followed, Wesley kept repeating "I'll praise—I'll praise" (all he could now manage to say) until his heart finally stopped beating. A non-Western student once memorably said, "Wouldn't it be wonderful if Dr. Packer died preaching." Maybe so, but to die praising, while at rehearsal, as one might express it, would surely be even more wonderful. For Watts is exactly right in the way he expresses the central contented confidence of every regenerate heart:

> My days of praise shall ne'er be past
> While life and thought and being last
> Or immortality endures.

We, Carolyn and J. I., can think of nothing better than that when our time comes we should be enabled to depart this world praising, and it is our hope and prayer that the same will be true for everyone who reads these pages.

5

PRAYER CHECKUP

Search me, O God, and know my heart!
Try me and know my thoughts!
And see if there be any grievous way in me,
and lead me in the way everlasting!

PSALM 139:23-24

Checkups in the interests of well-being are familiar features of modern life. The servicing patterns of new cars specify periodic checkups that must be done, and would-be buyers of secondhand models are told never, never to close the deal until a trusty expert has carried out a checkup of everything under the steed's shining hood. Middle-aged and elderly people are urged to have a physical checkup annually; and indeed checkup is defined in the *Canadian Oxford Dictionary* (1998) as "a thorough examination, especially of a person's general medical condition." Now the starting point for everything we will say in this chapter is our belief that the Christian's spiritual condition needs a regular checkup too, and that this is part of God's will for all his children. For, in particular, our praying cannot be healthier than is our spiritual life as a whole.

Have you ever thought of that? Have you ever had a spiritual checkup? Have you ever asked for one? Is this a new idea for you? As the Lord Jesus once pointed out (Lk 5:39), there is a principle of inertia in human nature that defies us to be open to new things when we feel we are doing comfortably with what we have already; a defiant insistence on feeling we are all right makes many who have never had a physical checkup resent the idea that they might need one. In the same way, you may find the idea of a spiritual checkup repellent. Even if so, however, please stay with us, and let us put you in what we are convinced is the biblical picture on this matter.

It is more than fourteen hundred years since Pope Gregory the Great wrote *Pastoral Care,* his insightful guide to pastors about their spiritual responsibility to those in their flock. In the third section of that book Gregory guides pastors, for well over a hundred pages, through such topics as "How to Admonish the Humble and the Haughty," "How to Admonish Those Who Sin on Sudden Impulse, and Those Who Sin Willfully," "How to Admonish Those Who Do Evil Secretly and Good Openly." After all of this advice to pastors on how to challenge their parishioners, Gregory then wrote a short but deeply cutting (and curing) final chapter directed entirely to the pastor: "How the Preacher When He Has Done Everything as Required, Should Return to Himself, to Prevent His Life of Preaching from Making Him Proud."[1] More than four hundred years ago Puritan teachers took a path like Gregory's and spoke of pastors as "physicians of the soul" whom we should allow to examine us, probing our personal weaknesses and shortcomings and prescribing remedies for the restoring of our spiritual health (or, of course, the establishing of it, in cases where believers have yet never been in good condition). More than 250 years ago, John Wesley institutionalized mutual pastoral care of this kind in the band meetings (regular gatherings of between five and ten committed persons) that were the human building blocks of the Methodist societies;[2] at about the same time Welsh revival

---

[1]St. Gregory the Great, *Pastoral Care,* trans. Henry Davis, in *The Works of the Fathers in Translation* 11, ed. Johannes Quasten and Joseph C. Plumpe (Westminster, Md.: Newman Press, 1955). Pope Gregory the Great lived from 540-604 and served as pope the last fourteen years of his life.

[2]On the bands see John Wesley, *A Plain Account of the People Called Methodists* (1748), in *Works,* ed. T. Jackson, 3rd ed. (1872; reprint, Grand Rapids: Baker, 1986), 8:248-74, esp. 257-59. The full rules for the bands are given on pp. 272-74.

leader William Williams wrote *The Experience Meeting* to guide leaders of larger mutual-help groups of the same kind.[3]

In many of today's practices of Christianity this pastoral structure is largely lost. Some Bible study groups center on the biblical text but avoid any personal response to that text. Some Christian sharing groups meet for mutual support in facing life's pressures and problems but shy away from specific directions for spiritual growth. And some spiritual directors (a breed almost extinct among Protestants until very recently) listen to people and counsel them in a therapeutic way in relation to what they themselves say about themselves, but do not press diagnostic questions about their life with God that might put them on the spot. To be sure, other writers, small group leaders, pastors and spiritual directors walk in the strong footprints of our spiritual forbears and challenge those in their care to let Scripture shape their lives, to examine their motives for hints of self-serving, and to seek connection (and correction) from the living God.[4] The fact remains, however, that all Christian believers, both those who are making growth in grace their priority and those who are not, need spiritual checkups from time to time, and that is something we need to face.

This book is an exploration of the universal Christian experience of struggling in prayer, in face of all the difficulties and distractions that the world, the flesh and the devil put in our way to stop us praying to any good purpose. We have already identified with our readers as fellow strugglers, sharing what helps us in hope that it will help them too. So far, we have dwelled on what we may call God's I.D.; we have pictured

---

[3]William Williams, *The Experience Meeting* (Vancouver, B.C.: Regent College Publishing, 1995).
[4]For example InterVarsity Press publishes more than 150 Bible study guides for personal and group use, all of them emphasizing a combination of studying the biblical text and testing oneself to live, think, and pray accordingly. And Richard Foster, for instance, makes valuable contributions in the area of small group and personal spiritual formation as he draws from Scripture and from the whole history of Christianity in *Renovaré's Spiritual Formation Workbook: Small Group Resources for Nurturing Christian Growth; Devotional Classics;* and *Spiritual Classics,* all published by HarperSanFrancisco.

Christian living as a lifelong hike in our Savior's company; we have looked at how Bible-based meditation helps to form prayer; and we have hinted—hardly more—at the way the God-exalting, self-deflating, soul-expanding activity of praise lightens our path and rejoices our heart as our thoughts go forward to heaven. These themes together establish our overall landscape (or, as we put it earlier, they form the basic colors on our canvas) and so make up the big picture into which everything else that we have to say will be fitted, and of which all those items will be so many details.

But before moving on we must pause to note the need for regular checkups in relation to the ground we have so far covered, and to the praying that is truly the lifeline for all our Christian living. Why must we do this? Because admonitory checkups are a stated concern of our triune God, and if we have no time for them and give them no place, we will inevitably lose out. Many modern Christians seem unaware of this; some have very obviously come to grief as a result. The fact is that we will all pray more honestly and live more safely when we learn to regard checkup as a necessary spiritual discipline, and give it its proper place in our lives. So let us look at it now.

God calls all his people to be holy, that is, consciously, conscientiously and continuously set apart to live in his company and for his glory, with all that this involves. Nothing in Scripture, surely, is clearer than that! In Old Testament times God, having through Moses given Israel his laws, sent prophets (messengers, spokesmen) to rub those laws into the hearts of the Israelites by declaring to them what God thought of their lawless behavior and how they needed to change, and what would happen if they went on as before. So God through Jeremiah bewails false prophets, who said, professedly in God's name, that all was well when in fact it was not:

I did not send the prophets,
   yet they ran;
I did not speak to them,

yet they prophesied.
But if they had stood in my council,
   then they would have proclaimed my words to my people,
and they would have turned them from their evil way,
   and from the evil of their deeds. (Jer 23:21-22; see also
     2 Kings 17:13-15)

And Daniel bewails failure to heed the words of true prophets: "We have sinned against you. . . . [A]nd have not obeyed the voice of the LORD our God by walking in his laws, which he set before us by his servants the prophets" (Dan 9:8, 10).

Then in the New Testament we find our glorified Lord Jesus Christ, the incarnate Son of God, commandeering John as his amanuensis (we would say, secretary) to write seven business letters in the same standard format to seven Asian churches. The letters tell each church what Christ had seen in his checkup of them and what changes they must make in order to encompass the vital, forthright, fearless, faithful, trustful holiness that was his will for them, and would bring them all the grandeur promised to those who overcome. (The modern counterpart would be the employer who checks up on the performance of his employees and tells them that while some have done well, most of them need to pull their socks up, and adds that there is a terrific bonus awaiting those who do.) It is clear that the God whose eye is always on us, just as it is on the sparrow, is constantly checking up on the quality of our Christian lives, and we have to keep pace with him in this. That is why the best Christian teachers of all times make much of the discipline of self-examination.

For centuries exponents of Christian devotion—Patristic, Reformational, Puritan, Wesleyan, Roman Catholic and Eastern Orthodox— were in agreement on the importance of regular self-examination as a necessity for spiritual health. What they had in view was a measuring of ourselves, morally and spiritually, positively in terms of things done and negatively in terms of things left undone, by the behavioral ideals that God sets before us in his Word—that is in the Ten Commandments, the sermons of the prophets, the personal poems of the psalmists, the grave counsels of the books of Proverbs and Ecclesiastes, the life and teaching of Jesus, and the practical exhortations of the New Testament letters. Whereas introspection, whether it ends in euphoria or in the gloom of self-pity and self-despair, can become an expression of self-absorbed pride, self-examination is the fruit of God-centered humility, ever seeking to shake free of all that displeases the Father, dishonors the Son and grieves the Holy Spirit, so as to honor God more. Thus self-examination is a fundamentally healthy process, leading into repentance, where mere introspection can leave us just feeling sorry for ourselves. The distinction between the two activities is clear, and it is a bad sign that so many evangelical Christians today seem unable to practice spiritual self-examination. That introspection, without intent to change, is basically unhealthy is generally agreed without a struggle, but the claim that spiritual self-examination is truly health-giving often has to be fought for, at least (sadly) among those who see themselves as Bible believers, and it becomes all too apparent that the practice of this discipline is rare.

Self-examination is so called in echo of Paul's words to the arrogant Corinthians: "Examine yourselves, to see whether you are in the faith. Test yourselves" (2 Cor 13:5). This command indicates that examining ourself is something that we sometimes have to do but conceals a possible misunderstanding as to how it is done. For the paradoxical truth is that we do it precisely by asking God to do it, and laying ourselves open to him for that purpose. At school we do not grade ourselves but are graded by our instructors, and we do not perform our own medical checkups but arrange for our physician to do them; and in this case we go to God to admit our lack of self-knowledge and to have him show us and tell us how we are doing spiritually. Thus our praying in this process begins with submitting and ends with listening. Let us see how it all works out.

GOD THE PHYSICIAN

Think for a moment of your annual physical checkup. A medical practitioner, one who has studied both physiology and pathology and so can recognize both normal and defective processes in the human organism, takes notice of everything in your body that functions: your breathing, your blood pressure, your heart, your circulation, whether your eyes, ears and digestive system work properly, whether there is any particular malfunction of which you are conscious, whether there are any malfunctions of which you are not conscious, and whether there are any puzzling symptoms that need to be further investigated. That is how a thorough physical checkup goes. Now when God puts us through a spiritual checkup, a similar thoroughness is in evidence. He takes notice of all aspects of our inner life, the life about which only we and he know. Here are some examples of diagnostic procedures that he follows.

God checks up on our faith. Do we really know what we should know about God, and do we trust in Christ as we should? Do we look out for and take careful note of God's promises found in Scripture, and do we claim them in our prayers and rely on him to keep them? Does our faith bring us peace of heart—peace with God through forgiveness, peace with circumstances through leaning on the Lord, peace with people because through faith we love them? Or is that which we call our faith no better than superstition, groundless fancying, that is, about God and his ways, that leaves us fearful and frantic? Does our faith hold up in crises or give way under pressure? These are some of the main angles from which God checks up on our faith.

God checks up on our repentance. One of the beauties of worship services in the Anglican Prayer Book is the regular acknowledgment of sin and call to repentance. Over and over we see that repentance is more than a matter of regret and remorse for what has gone wrong; it is a matter of mounting resistance to the impulse to go wrong again. It is, in other words, a change of life that we are constantly seeking to make; a matter essentially of the will rather than the feelings. A life of repentance is, in reality, a life of self-denial. When Jesus talked about self-denial he was, as Richard Baxter the Puritan neatly put it, telling us that we have to say no to "carnal self," that is, to our inner selfhood that has been shaped by sin into the mold of an ugly, self-serving egocentricity. This misshapen carnal self seeks to lead us along its own path, the path of self-centered self-indulgence, always reaching out to grasp and use power, position, privilege and possessions for purposes of pleasure and pride. Jesus warned that saying no to its specific urges may feel like gouging out our eye or cutting off our hand or foot—saying goodbye, that is, to something you feel you cannot live without—yet it has to be done, and God checks up on us to see whether or not we are doing it. For that, and nothing less than that, is the reality of our repentance.

J. I. recalls a conversation with a clergyman, at the end of which the cleric said abruptly, "Well, you must excuse me; I must go. I see I have some repenting to do." So he went and spent the next hour doing it. Have you ever said anything like that to yourself? To a spiritual friend? What, really, do you know of personal repentance? Real Christianity is serious about penitently tracking down and turning from all the false steps of the past—and God checks up on our repentance.

God checks up on our love. The greatest command, according to Jesus, is a love for God with all our heart, mind, soul and strength, and alongside that, the next greatest requirement is a love for our neighbor—a love as wholehearted as the love we shower on ourselves. What is love? Whether directed to God, to a fellow human or to ourself, the purpose of love is to make the loved one *great*—God, by worship and service that exalts him; other persons, by care and help that meets their true needs; and ourself, by never aiming at less than the best. But sin in our system enslaves our natural self-love to unnatural pride, so as to keep us from loving God and others. So God exposes to our consciences, our self-absorption and self-centeredness, our tendency to focus entirely on ourselves and our own concerns. God knows that inordinate love of self keeps us from loving him enough to practice any form of self-sacrifice for him. He also knows that love of self keeps us from loving our neighbor in the ordinary sense of showing imaginative humanity, helping people who need help—when it involves our own inconvenience. Christians are not always distinguished at either of those points. And love that is focused on self rather than on God and on others restricts and indeed strangles our praying in profound ways. As a test, bring to mind your last attempts to pray. Approximately what percentage of that prayer had to do with your own well-being as compared with the glory of God and the welfare of others? God presses upon us this kind of soul-searching. It is part of his loving checkup.

God checks up on our humility. The pride of which we have been speaking is one element in original sin; indeed, if Augustine and Thomas Aquinas and C. S. Lewis are to be believed, it is the essence of it. Pride is the passion always to be and to feel yourself to be number one in power and importance. The wily serpent in the Garden of Eden tempted wide-eyed Eve with the words, "You will be like God, knowing good and evil" (Gen 3:5). He was luring her toward the world's first gesture of pride, and she took his bait. In yielding to Satan's deceptive ploy, Eve and Adam let pride anchor itself within, and human nature was from then on permanently distorted. So pride is still there in our hearts, engendering self-confidence and self-reliance at points where no such attitude ought to enter so that we don't depend on our God as we should; engendering self-aggrandizement so that pleasing God as a life goal is excluded; and engendering also conceit and self-satisfaction of a spiritually killing kind. To be puffed up with pride at our own achievements is to be very sick in one's soul.

Pope Gregory the Great in his classic *Pastoral Care* warned that pastors are vulnerable to pride. In his final chapter of admonitions to pastors he speaks to them about the sensitive moment just after preaching a fine sermon: "When a sermon is delivered with due propriety and with a fruitful message, the mind of the speaker is exalted by joy all his own over his performance, . . . he must not disregard his own [spiritual] health and develop tumours of pride."[5] The ancient and medieval theo-

---

[5] Gregory the Great, *Pastoral Care,* trans. Henry Davis (New York: Newman Press, 1955), p. 234.

logians who sought to categorize mankind's major lapses constantly named pride as one of the seven deadly sins, and many spiritual leaders have defined pride as the root sin from which all other sins sprang. Thomas Aquinas, for example, spoke of pride as "contempt of God" outmatching all other sins in turning away from God.[6] It is likely that much of our difficulty in obeying God's command to love him with our whole being and our neighbors as ourselves is rooted in the sin of pride: we want self to look good, especially to ourselves, and so we concentrate on serving ourselves, thus putting ourselves first, ahead of other people, even ahead of God. Pride has evil effects on the lives of others and pride brings pharisaic hypocrisy, the self-deception of self-righteousness, into our relationship with God. To combat the great evil of pride, we have to learn humility, and God regularly checks up on us on how we are doing at this point.

What then is humility? It is honest realism and realistic honesty. Whereas pride is all parading, play-acting and pretending, humility is rooted in facing facts. What facts? The fact of our smallness and sinfulness before God; the fact of our weakness and inability to shape and control the future, whether our own or anyone else's, just because we are all in the hands of a sovereign God; the fact of our stupidity and silliness that lurks behind every pose of being smart and savvy that our pride prompts us to adopt; the fact of our inborn fascination with ourselves and constant concentration on being happy, fulfilled, and a success; the fact of being habitually self-conscious, concerned about what others think of us, when we ought to be God conscious in a way that takes us beyond ourselves. Facing these facts cuts us down to size, and humility grows out of being thus cut down.

Genuine humility is not only Godward in direction, it also colors all relationships with other humans. To detect whether it is growing in us we

---

[6]Thomas Aquinas *Summa Theologiae* 44 (New York: McGraw-Hill, 1963), p. 139.

can prayerfully invite God's help in self-examination as we ask ourselves such questions as: Am I able to joyfully perform tasks in my church that have little or no visibility? Do I regularly credit others for their labor? Can I value and enjoy people who are not normally considered respectable? Are my thoughts toward the difficult people in my life infused with grace? Do I give my spouse first choice of TV channel, room temperature or vacation? Are my prayers usually on behalf of other people? Is it relatively easy for me to give my time or my money—and tell no one about it? Do I see every opportunity not as an earned right but as a gift from God? Do I cut short thoughts of comparing myself favorably with others? Do I honor others with my thoughts, words and actions? To the extent that we can honestly say yes to questions like these, we are beginning to learn humility toward others—and so to conquer the sin of pride. It will help us to note that both pride and humility begin in the heart and in the mind. Pride is not at the outset a sin of action, nor is humility a virtue of action, which is why we often deceive ourselves about their presence within. Pride and humility are attitudes of heart that find expression in action, and actions of true humility toward others grow from a heart that is already humbled before God.

Humility cannot be fully detected or measured by direct inspection, for trying to inspect our own humility is itself a yielding to pride (which is why it was so grotesque when a listener said after a talk: "I'm so glad you spoke on humility; that's my strong point, you know!"). The most we can ever do is concentrate on negating and mortifying the various expressions of pride we are already aware of, and on asking our Lord to show us what more negating and mortifying needs to be done. That is a request that the God who watches us even as he watches over us, and who maintains his perfect knowledge of us in all matters where we do not truly know ourselves (that means, in every matter without exception all our lives!) is fully equipped to answer.

God checks up on us in the matter of wisdom. The compiler of Proverbs tells us:

Blessed is the one who finds wisdom,
    and the one who gets understanding,
for the gain from her is better than gain from silver
    and her profit better than gold. (Prov 3:13)

We are all much more inclined to foolishness than we know, and God constantly has to be peeling off of us layer after layer of supposed wisdom so that we may face the reality of our foolishness and then find out from him what real wisdom really amounts to. Only then will we be able to reckon with him and with the consequences of what we say and do in the way that Christians should.

What does the Bible mean by wisdom? How does God teach us to think of it? Wisdom in the Bible is essentially a matter of knowing the way through life: knowing what to aim at and how to get there, knowing what life itself is like and how to cope with it. First and foremost, wisdom is a matter of knowing what God is like and how to relate to him: wisdom is rooted, we are told, in the "fear" of the Lord (Ps 111:10; Prov 1:7; Job 28:28), that is, in the reverence that recognizes God's hand in all things, that responds to all of his teaching in his Word and that relies on his faithfulness in all situations, even the darkest of them. And then, within that frame, wisdom is a matter of knowing what people are like and how to deal with them and shape relationships with them most prudently. Wisdom is a gift from God that is found through being sought; those who think they have it already and those who are not interested in acquiring it (sadly, there are such, including some Christians) do not seek it from God by the appropriate means (learning it from Bible writers and Bible characters who embody it), and thus they fail to find it. "If any of you lacks wisdom," says James, the classic New Testament wisdom writer, "let him ask God, who gives generously to all without reproach, and it will be given him." (Jas 1:5). Do we do this? We pray *with* wisdom when we pray *for* wisdom to see what hopes, expectations, petitions to God and plans for ourselves and others wisdom now suggests. Is that the perspective of our praying? It should be; it needs to be. Wisdom forms strategies, calculates consequences, channels passion, sustains sobriety, discerns and avoids foolishness, and cherishes peace and harmony at all times. Without wisdom there is no God-pleasing life. We may be sure that as God checks up on us, Christlike, Holy Spirit wisdom is one of the things he looks for and rejoices to see.

Summarizing the thrust of what we have surveyed, then, we may now say that *God checks up on our focus:* how far our faith, repentance, love, humility and wisdom, such as they are, have combined to make us clear-sighted about our goal in life, and the priorities that it imposes. God wants us, in other words, to discern whether we've got life together or whether, as yet, we haven't. There is an old fable that tells of a donkey who saw good oats in two opposite corners of a field and could never make up his mind which corner to go to. So there he stood in one spot, half-way between the corners, until he starved to death. Often we are too much like that donkey. We are torn apart by alternative options and desires, and we seem not to have what it takes to decide between the options. God checks up on us at that point. Are we sufficiently integrated in Christ to know how to make those decisions? Are we clearheaded enough in Christ to determine our own priorities, both overall and in making particular choices? Have we got our life into proper focus? Will we be ready to cope with death when it comes?

We find a good model of a Christian who had got his life together in the apostle Paul, who wrote, "One thing I do: forgetting what lies behind and straining forward to what lies ahead, I press on toward the goal for the prize of the upward call of God in Christ Jesus" (Phil 3:13-14). Of course, from one standpoint, even in prison, let alone at other times, Paul was multitasking: doing 50, 60, 100, 120 different things every day. So are you, so are we, so is everyone. But Paul was able to say "One thing I do" because he had got it all together. Each specific thing he did was integrated into the one Christ-centered thing he was doing all the time.

Paul was following up in practice his own inference of the Christian's priority that he draws from the Christian's identity. "If then you have been raised with Christ, seek the things that are above, where Christ is. . . . Set your minds on things that are above, not on things that are on earth" (Col 3:1-2). He was enjoying what he prayed that the Colossians might also enjoy—"knowledge of [God's] will in all spiritual wisdom and understanding, so as to walk in a manner worthy of the Lord" (Col 1:9-10). Paul knew what was most important and how all of those 101 other tasks and actions fit under the one most important goal. God checks on us to see whether we are like Paul and like Paul's Master, because this single-mindedness is what we also see, and see supremely, in the Lord Jesus. Thus the divine physician probes us, and his probing goes on all the time.

GOD THE SEARCHER

We have been exploring aspects of our life that our omniscient God, who knows us through and through, always has his eye on, and it is very good for us to remind ourselves and be made sensitive about them. But the exploration has for the moment taken us out of the personal checkup situation that we began thinking about, and we need now to get back to it. The thesis we put forward was that we need spiritual checkups for spiritual health just as we need physical checkups for bodily health. It follows from this that as wise persons will initiate each physical checkup by making an appointment with their physician, and just as they will then look to their physician to tell them what he or she has discovered and advise them accordingly, so, if we are wise Christians, we will initiate regular spiritual checkups by asking our God to survey us thoroughly and tell us what we should do and be willing to let him do in relation to whatever negative things he may find. Granted, praying is the topic of this book, and it is not a general treatise on the Christian life, but any weakness of faith, any neglect of repentance or, actually, refusal to repent of and forsake particular bad habits and paths of sin, any cherishing of

unloving and unhumbled attitudes, and any failure of focus—any lack
of clearheaded wholeheartedness, that is—in our personal discipleship
to the Lord Jesus, will constantly drain the life out of our praying. So as
we explore the theme of requesting and receiving God's checkup, we
must cast our net wide and ask him to tell us of anything—yes, anything—that he sees in us that is draining life, energy and joy out of our
communion with him. This seems to follow from the nature of the case,
and the Bible hammers it home anyway by setting before us a prayer
psalm (a model prayer, that is there for us to use) in which the psalmist
works up from his celebration of God's closeness and awesomeness to
doing precisely what we have said. This is Psalm 139.

Here we have one of the many psalms in which the psalmist speaks
in the first person singular. This kind of psalm is meant to be read in a
very personal way. The *I* of the psalm is both an individual and an inclusive *I*. It is I, the psalmist, and I, each reader and reciter of the psalm.
Every single person who hears or reads this kind of psalm is individual-
ized by it, for God asks us all, personally and directly, every time: Is this
your prayer? These psalms are models of praise and prayer for us to enter
into, and we can only enter into them one person at a time. Since Psalm
139 is a personal prayer addressed to God, its full import is best absorbed by reading it aloud, so that it is both read and heard simultaneously. We now invite the reader to do just that, and to this end the entire psalm (six stanzas, the fourth, fifth and sixth shorter than the first
three) is reproduced below. Please make it your own prayer as you speak
the words.

> O LORD, you have searched me and known me!
> You know when I sit down and when I rise up;
>   you discern my thoughts from afar.
> You search my path and my lying down
>   and are acquainted with all my ways.
> Even before a word is on my tongue,
>   behold, O, LORD, you know it altogether.

You hem me in, behind and before,
    and lay your hand upon me.
Such knowledge is too wonderful for me;
    it is high; I cannot attain it.

Where shall I go from your Spirit?
    Or where shall I flee from your presence?
If I ascend to heaven you are there!
    If I make my bed in Sheol you are there!
If I take the wings of the morning
    and dwell in the uttermost parts of the sea,
even there your hand shall lead me,
    and your right hand shall hold me.
If I say, "Surely the darkness shall cover me,
    and the light about me be night,"
even the darkness is not dark to you;
    the night is as bright as the day,
    for darkness is as light with you.

For you formed my inward parts;
    you knitted me together in my mother's womb.
I praise you for I am fearfully and wonderfully made.
Wonderful are your works;
    my soul knows it very well.
My frame was not hidden from you,
when I was being made in secret,
    intricately woven in the depths of the earth.
Your eyes saw my unformed substance;
in your book were written, every one of them,
    the days that were formed for me,
when as yet there were none of them.

How precious to me are your thoughts, O God!
    How vast is the sum of them!
If I would count them, they are more than the sand.

I awake, and I am still with you.

Oh that you would slay the wicked, O God!
   O, men of blood, depart from me!
They speak against you with malicious intent;
   your enemies take your name in vain.
Do I not hate those who hate you, O LORD?
   And do I not loathe those who rise up against you?
I hate them with complete hatred;
   I count them my enemies.

Search me, O God, and know my heart!
   Try me and know my thoughts!
And see if there be any grievous way in me,
   and lead me in the way everlasting!

If you have just now prayed aloud this psalm to God, you will have appreciated and entered into its great emotional honesty and intensity and transparency. You will have recognized that this prayer psalm is on the borderline between what the previous chapter called brooding (thinking about God in God's presence) and what in the ordinary sense we call prayer (talking directly to God about himself and oneself, and about life). The psalmist takes us to and fro over that borderline, and so in fact will all honest prayers of self-examination and worship.

In the first three stanzas we find ourselves practicing God's presence and admiring God's greatness. What we are admiring in stanza one is God's omniscience, and here the key words are *you know*. "Oh, Lord, you have . . . *known* me! / You *know* when I sit down and rise up" (vv. 1-2). "Before a word is on my tongue, / O LORD, . . . you *know* it altogether" (v. 4). "Such *knowledge* is too wonderful for me; / . . . I cannot attain it" (v. 6). But you, Lord, have it. You know me through and through. This is breathtaking! At one time or another, nearly everyone has wished to read the thoughts of someone else, but of course, we cannot do so, and maybe that is a good thing. Certainly there are moments when we have reason to be grateful that no other person can read our own minds—except God! Even that may feel a little unnerving. That the God who knows every square inch of the faintest star in the universe, who understands the most complex philosophy (both its flaws and its wisdom) and who counts the exact number of hairs on our heads also reads our thoughts and desires, our motives, our dreams, might make us uneasy— yet to believers it brings enormous comfort. God *knows* us—in the most thorough sense of that word—and whatever weird and unworthy things he finds inside us, he loves us still.

In stanza two, the psalmist celebrates God's omnipresence and here the key words are *you are there.* Where? Everywhere. "If I ascend to heaven, you are *there!* / If I make my bed in Sheol, you are *there!* If I take the wings of the morning / and dwell in the uttermost parts of the sea, / even *there* your hand will lead me, / and your right hand shall hold me" (vv. 8-10). We can never get away from God's presence, never escape it or shake free of it; we are never outside of his upholding hand. That's the omnipresence of God. In the words of C. S. Lewis, "We may ignore, but we can nowhere evade, the presence of God. The world is crowded with him. He walks everywhere *incognito.* And the *incognito* is not always hard to penetrate. The real labor is to remember, to attend . . . in fact to come awake. Still more, to remain awake."[7]

Just as with his omniscience, God's omnipresence too can bring either unease or comfort. Fleeing from God is futile—as the prophet Jonah so drastically discovered. How we, as the people of God, respond to his divine omnipresence depends in part on our spiritual health. If we are uneasy in welcoming God's constant presence, maybe this reveals a spiritual sickness, some cherished private perversity perhaps, for which we need to invite God's forgiveness and healing. The prayer of Psalm 139 shows us how to do that.

Stanza three of Psalm 139 (vv. 13-16) speaks of the omnipotence of

---

[7]C. S. Lewis, *Letters to Malcolm: Chiefly on Prayer* (London: Geoffrey Bles, 1964), pp. 100-101.

God, which accompanies his omniscience and omnipresence. Here the key phrase is *you formed*. Fiat creation, purposive design and artistic craftsmanship are all brought together in that verb. God by his power formed me, my circumstances, my hours, my days, everything about me and everything about everybody else as well. "You *formed* my inward parts," says verse 13; "Your eye saw my *unformed* substance," says verse 16. Here we are being told that long before the technology of ultrasound, whereby we can see embryos in the womb and admire a thumb, a nose, a toe, as it grows there, God could see that baby being formed, God knew him or her, God was actually shaping stomach and heart and hair and fingernails and personality. God knew us, each one, even when our own mother knew only a swelling in her belly and a fluttering movement that set her imagining who might be growing inside.

God's power, blended with his knowledge, has sobering implications. "In your book were written, every one of them, / the days that were *formed* for me, / when as yet there were none of them" (v. 16). I (Carolyn) remember well the day when I sat down and calculated the days that my own firstborn child had lived: a mere 8,175 days until a car crash on the way to work ended Sheri's life as well as that of her own unborn child. At age seven, Sheri had completed nearly a third of her lifetime—and God knew. He had counted the days. When Sheri danced at her senior prom, she had completed more than three quarters of it—and God knew. He had counted the days. At college graduation, she had completed all but seventy-one days. God had already counted them. I am grateful that those counted days were in God's knowledge, not mine. It is comforting to know that the length of Sheri's life did not somehow escape the knowledge and the power of God, that her life (far too short by human measure), continues to this day in his presence. God the Creator shapes—conceives, constructs, connects, controls—all that he brings into any mode of being, and this shaping is his omnipotence in action.

Having surveyed the greatness of God, the psalmist next puts himself into mental review for stanza four and says understandably, as he looks back at what he has surveyed, "How precious to me are your thoughts, O God! / How vast is the sum of them! / If I would count them, they are more than the sand" (vv. 17-18). It is possible to count sand (or of course, sheep) in an attempt to fall asleep. God's thoughts, because they are beyond number, might be even more soporific. Perhaps the psalmist really did put himself to sleep by trying to focus and count them. But he wakes up, and, joy of joys, he can say with the startled comprehension of any newlywed, "I awake, and I am still with you" (v. 18).

Now suddenly there is a shift in this prayer psalm, such a startling shift that in public reading the next paragraph is often omitted. It seems to break completely with the comforting joyful tone of the psalm so far. It speaks of hatred and killing—and it is directed at the enemies of God. Stanza five (vv. 19-22) shows the psalmist moving from admiring God to desiring peace with justice in the world. "Oh that you would slay the wicked, O God! . . . / your enemies who take your name in vain!" (vv. 19-20). What is going on here? Bear in mind, first, the uninhibited intensity of this psalm: if Jonathan Edwards merited the description of being a God-intoxicated man, much more does this psalmist. We spoke of his intensity before and hope that our readers are by now entering into it. In moments of great intensity the human mind may jump abruptly from one thing to another, as surely your own experience has shown you, and that is what we see happening here, without any reduction of intensity in the way the new thought is expressed. Second, bear in mind that the psalmists, like the prophets, long with a huge aching passion (of which, alas, we today know very little) to see God, their God, the rightful Lord of all, triumph over all the anti-God forces that surround them and dishonor him. God has enemies!—"men of blood" who, because they are totally against him, are indiscriminately hostile to all who in any measure are aligned on his side. The psalmist voices his personal abhorrence of God's and his enemies as a class in the way that we ourselves might execrate today's urban terrorists and suicide bombers.

Christians, however, taking the words of these verses on their lips, and similar words from other psalms, should direct them against the devil and his demons, "the spiritual forces of evil in the heavenly places" (Eph 6:12), against which spiritual warfare must go on without end. (We can never hate the devil too much!) The prescribed path for Christ's disciples, however, is always to ask God to bless *persons* opposing us (Mt 5:44; Lk 6:27-28, 33-34; Acts 7:60), and our imperfectly sanctified hearts are not pure enough to pray for God to vindicate himself against his human foes without personal animosities invading and corrupting our motives. The purifying of the heart, however, is the next reality of which the psalmist speaks.

SEARCH ME, O GOD

And so we come to stanza six (vv. 23-24). "Search me, O God, and know my heart! / Try me and know my thoughts!" That is said against the background of what is recognized in the first verse: "O LORD, you have searched me and known me!" But now the psalmist prays that out of the searching, which God is actually doing all the time in him as in every other person, God will let him see any shortcoming that God himself sees. In other words, having celebrated God's greatness and goodness as his sovereign Maker, permanent environment, and constant x-ray monitor, he now turns to God for his checkup. He wants it to be thorough, and because he knows so well who and what God is, he expects it to be thorough. And he is ready if need be, for the knife.

> Search me, O God, and know my heart!
>   Try me and know my thoughts!
> And see if there be any grievous way in me.
>   and lead me in the way everlasting!

He is saying to God: If you see anything wrong, tell me so that I may put it behind me. Thus you will "lead me in the way everlasting." It is only as we see the power of the vision of God in his greatness and glory in the first eighteen verses of Psalm 139 that we can appreciate the force of the prayer "Search me, O God."

There is a hymn that spells out in detail the significance of that final prayer. It is a poignant plea for the gift of spiritual honesty through having God tell us what he sees in us when he searches us.

Search me, O God! My actions try,
And let my life appear
As seen by thine all searching eye—
To mine, my ways make clear.

Search all my sense, and know my heart,
Who only canst make known;
And let the deep, the hidden part
To me be fully shown.

Throw light into the darkened cells,
Where passion reigns within;
Quicken my conscience till it feels
The loathsomeness of sin.

Search, till thy fiery glance has cast
Its holy light through all,
And I by grace am brought at last
Before thy face to fall.

Thus prostrate I shall learn of thee,
What now I feebly prove,
That God alone in Christ can be
Unutterable love![8]

This hymn fleshes out for us some part, at least, of the desiring in Psalm 139:23-24 that grows out of the admiring in its verses 1-18. The psalmist is a very genuine believer; he has a heart for God; he would surely say what Psalm 73:25-26 says—"Whom have I in heaven but you? / And there is nothing on earth that I desire besides you. . . . / God

---

[8]Francis Bottome, "Search Me, O God" (1823).

is the strength of my heart and my portion forever." He wants closeness to God more than he wants anything else in the world, as, deep down, all regenerate persons do. In verses 1-18 he has been brooding, with joy as great as his wonder and admiration, on how close his God (Yahweh, the Lord, God-in-covenant, v. 1) actually is to him at all times. Now he begs for his checkup, to ensure that nothing in him will get in the way of him being close to God at all times. The two-way street of fellowship with God is what this psalm is basically about, and the full-scale checkup is now being sought in order to deepen that fellowship. God's searching of the heart, the psalmist knows, besides any matter for renewed repentance that it may uncover, will operate as a spiritual tonic, toning him up in two particular qualities that mark all men and women of God: *emptiness* (because God is constantly emptying us of ourselves so that he may fill us with himself) and *eagerness* (because eagerness for more of God is the measure of what you have of God already: the more you have, the more you want). The eager desire with which the psalm closes, "lead me in the way everlasting," can never be too passionate, too zealous, too intense; some things can be overdone, but not this. We should constantly be praying with all our heart, from the depths of our being, "Lord, at all costs, whatever it takes, in your love and faithfulness and wisdom, lead me in the way everlasting—keep me running, as fast as I can—get me safely home." The psalmist's great longing should be ours too.

How does God search us? It is a two-tone affair. On the one hand, he applies Bible teaching on standards and ideals for godly living to our consciences, judging us, to start with, regarding the realities we discussed—faith, repentance, love, humility, focus—and going on from there. He does this by prompting us through the indwelling Holy Spirit actually to judge ourselves. The General Confession of the historic Anglican Prayer Book states what we always find: "We have followed too much the devices and desires of our own hearts. We have offended against thy holy laws. We have left undone those things which we ought to have done, and we have done those things which we ought not to have done, and there is no health in us." Then, on the other hand, God the Spirit forms questions in our minds that we have to answer, questions about goals, motives and attitudes, and what really goes on in our heart's secret places.

As those in the various counseling professions know well, questioning the motives and exposing the inward reasons for actions taken or not taken is a direct means of getting people to face themselves, become more realistic about themselves, and reprogram themselves as necessary, and that is God's way with us too. *Search* implies all of this. T. S. Eliot was right to say that we humans cannot bear much reality, but each time God searches us he will confront us with as much reality as we can handle at that moment in order to change us for the better, according to his purpose of totally remaking us in the image of our Lord Jesus Christ. In this he is (let us never forget) both loving and wise, and both qualities are in action when his search is on.

As we let God thus work us over, examining ourselves in the knowledge that hereby he is examining us, the requested salutary searching and exposure of wicked ways (all ways that are less than the best come under that heading) actually takes place. It is by these means that the checkup is effected. How often should we ask for it? Once a year may be often enough for a medical checkup, but once a week at a preset time (the Puritans opted for Saturday night), is a good routine for God's checkup of our behavior and our heart. Experience—the experience of Catholic, Orthodox and evangelical saints, past and present—has decided.

MISTAKEN IDENTITY

Should we expect that after such a checkup, praying will become easy? No. Though prayer will then, we may hope, be more honest and go deeper, *easy* is never the word that fits real praying (as distinct, be it said, from unconsidered burbling or mechanical recitation in God's presence).

We are here up against one of the realities of spiritual life that we do not always recognize, namely, that there is a great deal of make-believe about us. Again and again we think that we are being honest with ourselves and with God when, in fact, make-believe is as far as we've got. Almost four centuries ago Francis DeSales, a Catholic pioneer in teaching the path of prayer, laid it down that the first step in meditation and praying is "to place oneself in the presence of God." But that's easier said than done, because our make-believe gets in the way.

C. S. Lewis points out this problem, which was his no less than it is ours. We all have superficial and inadequate ideas about ourselves, often amounting to real self-deception. We have mistaken imaginations of ourselves. We carry around a public identity that becomes a mask hiding us from ourselves, and it is beyond us to remove that mask. So, left to ourselves, we are hidden from ourselves, and we need God to unmask us to ourselves just as we need God to unveil himself to us in revelation and to open our spiritual eyes to see his glory. So whenever we try to pray, we must look to the Spirit of God to strip away our fantasies and delusions and enable each of us to put the real *me* in the presence of the real God. "In prayer," writes Lewis, "this real I struggles to speak, for once, from his real being. . . . The prayer preceding all prayers is 'May it be the real I who speaks. May it be the real Thou that I speak to.' . . . Only God himself can let the bucket down to the depths in us. And, on the other side, he must constantly work as the iconoclast. Every idea of him we form, he must in mercy shatter."[9] And many of our ideas about ourselves have to be shattered too. It thus appears that only through the help of the Holy Spirit can we ever achieve reality in our prayers.

About this, however, P. T. Forsyth gives us good direction to start us on the track.

Go into your chamber, shut the door, and cultivate the habit of praying audibly. Write prayers and burn them. Formulate yourself. Read a

---

[9]Lewis, *Letters to Malcolm*, pp. 81-82.

passage of Scripture and then sit down and turn it into a prayer, written or spoken. Learn to be particular, specific and detailed in your prayer so long as you are not trivial. General prayers, literary prayers and stately prayers are, for private prayer, traps and sops to the soul. To formulate your soul is the best means to escape formalizing it. This is the best, the wholesome kind of self-examination through which God puts us. We find ourselves, we come to ourselves in the Spirit. So face your special weaknesses and sins before God. Force yourself to say to God exactly where you are wrong. When anything goes wrong, don't ask to have it set right without asking in prayer what it was in you that made it go wrong, and ask that that be put right also. Let prayer be concrete, factual, a direct result of life's real experiences.[10]

Without the Spirit of God, this realism and the reality to which it leads will not happen. Forsyth wrote these words in 1916, nearly a century ago, but they are as timely today as when he first put them on paper and will continue so as long as the world lasts.

Again we ask, as we close this chapter: what, in positive terms, is the relevance of all of this to our actual daily praying? In a word, it helps us to pray healthily, by keeping us in good shape in God's sight. Spiritual health means being alert and energetic for works of love and obedience; the alternative is degenerating into insensitivity and sluggishness, a life of slackness and drift. Years of avoiding visits to the dentist will leave your teeth in a mess, and a constant evading of God's checkups will have the same decaying effect on your soul. Omitting medical checkups may mean that much goes wrong inside you unnoticed, and omitting God's checkups may let the equivalent of tumors, cysts and polyps grow unnoticed all over your inner self. Our praying is the index of our spiritual life quality; the dictum credited to Murray McCheyne is right: "What a man is alone on his knees before God, that he is, and no more." Our lack of love for praying may be an indication of all-round spiritual debility.

---

[10]P. T. Forsyth, *The Soul of Prayer* (1916; reprint, Vancouver, B.C.: Regent College Publishing, 1995), pp. 53-54.

Maybe we need to go to God for a major checkup straightaway in order to find out.

We can't say any more than that because from this point on each of our own stories and each of our reader's stories will be different. We are all different people; we are all in different places, with different problems. And the effect of divine searching and the changes that God will require us to make are distinctive to each of us. Whenever we read Scripture, meditate on it and seek to pray on the basis of what we read, "Lord, lead me in the way everlasting," we may properly say to God, "Lord, you are searching me even now; what are you seeing? Show me if there be any wicked way in me." That request ought to be a normal part of our praying, a regular invitation to God to examine our inner being, the part that no one else sees. What happens after that is between the Lord and each of us individually.

Here, then, is God's way of leading us all into the spiritual health of a lively faith, lively obedience and lively prayer. May we not hesitate to go along with him in this.

❧6❧

ASKING

This is the confidence that we have toward him, that if we ask anything according to his will he hears us. And if we know that he hears us in whatever we ask, we know that we have the requests that we have asked of him.

1 JOHN 5:14-15

Let thy merciful ears, O Lord, be open to the prayers of thy humble servants; and that they may obtain their petitions make them to ask such things as shall please thee; through Jesus Christ our Lord.

ANGLICAN BOOK OF COMMON PRAYER

Martin Luther's last written words were "We are all beggars. That is true."[1] Two days later he died. He was right, of course, in that final written testimony. If we think of ourselves or others as achievers, creators, reformers, innovators, movers and shakers, healers, educators, benefactors of society in any way at all, we are at the deepest level kidding ourselves. We have nothing and have never had anything that we have not received, nor have we done anything good apart from God who did it through us. In ourselves we are destitute, bankrupt and impotent, totally dependent on God at every point and in every respect. This is true, as Luther constantly insisted, with regard to the pardon of our sins and the

---

[1]Martin Luther, quoted in Stephen J. Nichols, *Martin Luther* (Phillipsburg N.J.: Presbyterian & Reformed, 2002), p. 63.

justification of our persons (that is, God's acceptance of us as righteous and acceptable, despite our ongoing sinfulness, by virtue of Christ's cross). And it is equally true of life, health, food, clothing, a job, a home, a family, a car, a bank balance in the black and every other good thing that comes our way. So before God's throne we *are* all beggars, and begging good gifts from God is what petitionary prayer is all about.

We ask God, as beggars, for what we need because he invites us to do so. Christians know this clearly, for God in Scripture is explicit about it, and the rest of mankind knows it also, after a fashion, through God's natural, or general, revelation of himself as the universal Creator and Supplier. The very nature of prayers of petition emphasizes our true relationship with God. He is the provider; we the receivers. He is the master of the universe; we are small and though, from our own standpoint, we are important and are truly valued by God as his image-bearers, yet from another standpoint we have to acknowledge that we are quite unimportant subjects within that universe. God is the maker of all things; we are completely dependent on what he gives. Could he get on without us? Yes. Does this fact make his actual generosity to us more and more marvelous to contemplate? Yes again.

In February 2004, Britain's BBC reported on a worldwide survey finding (among many other interesting bits of information) that almost 30 percent of the world's atheists admit that they "sometimes pray."[2] While Christian believers might smugly ask "to whom, or what?" we can reasonably assume that petitions make up most of those prayers. The sense of dependence runs inherent in the human soul. Even those who doubt God's reality come to him as "beggars," by inner instinct, "just in case," particularly when they are in trouble. And God in his kindness and grace is most forthcoming in inviting his own people to ask. But how are we to ask well when we pray? That is the subject of this rather lengthy chapter.

[2]"Nigeria Leads in Religious Belief," *BBC News,* February 26, 2004 <http://news.bbc.co.uk/2/hi/programmes/wtwtgod/3490490.stm>.

This book has so far been devoted to thinking through the believer's relationship with God (our union and communion with him), in order to see how an appropriate relationship with him and an appropriate understanding of the Christian life can generate good praying. The problem we are addressing is what we feel to be the poor quality of our praying, and this was the place we had to begin in order to speak effectively to our need. Commitment to the real God in real faith for the living of the real Christian life, and within that frame to the disciplines of brooding and praising and being searched, is the launching place of real prayer, and will continue to be so every day of our lives. But at the core, where all people of prayer bend their knees, prayer is asking, begging God to supply felt needs. In a broad sense, asking is the essence of praying. Whatever else we do in religion builds around the activity of asking as its center. All books on prayer affirm this, all who ever pray feel this, and all religions whatever their view of God or gods, agree on this. It is precisely because asking prayer comes so naturally to us, however rudimentary or wrong our idea of God may be, that we have delayed this chapter until midway through the book. Granted, a three-year-old can understand asking from a heavenly Father as from an earthly father, and God blesses children who pray. No doubt about that! But for adults to practice the petitionary mode of prayer in a way that honors God and leads to the joy of seeing answers, more is needed. So, building on the foundations we have laid, we will now offer what seems to us to be the key truths about human asking and divine answering.

WESTMINSTER DOCTRINE

In 1647, a company of theological experts put together a teaching document meant to be used by parents to bring up their children in the understanding of the Christian faith. As was common in those days, when books were relatively expensive and often unavailable, this curriculum was set up to be memorized in rote form, by questions and answers. The Westminster Shorter Catechism consists of a series of 107 questions and answers that cover major tenets of the Christian faith. Ninety percent of the scholars who shaped this catechism were Anglican, but historical Anglicanism has never shown much interest in it, while the document has always been embraced by Presbyterians as one of their official statements (or standards) of Christian theology—and it is still used in many Presbyterian homes and churches to teach both children and adults the basic outline of their faith. J. I. is Anglican and Carolyn is Presbyterian, and both agree that the Westminster Shorter Catechism is a handy tool from which to learn fundamental truths about prayer. Any readers who are nervous about human documents taking the place of the divinely inspired Word of God may rest assured that the scholars who shaped the Westminster Shorter Catechism believed Scripture, drew from Scripture and created this document as a distilled understanding of what Scripture teaches on the various subjects addressed, adding reference texts so that readers could check the validity of what they had done. So, as we try to learn better praying, let us begin with words from this catechism as cited below.

> *What is prayer?* Prayer is an offering up of our desires unto God, for things agreeable to his will, in the name of Christ, with confession of our sins, and thankful acknowledgment of his mercies. (Ps 62:8; 1 Jn 5:14; Jn 16:23; Ps 32:5-6; Phil 4:6)

> *What rule hath God given for our direction in prayer?* The whole Word of God is of use to direct us in prayer; but the special rule of direction is that form of prayer which Christ taught his disciples, commonly called the Lord's Prayer. (1 Jn 5:14; Mt 6:9-13; Lk 11:2-4)

Note the flow of thought in these two questions. Prayer asks God to fulfill desires. But the sinfulness of our twisted hearts leads to desires that are out of line with God's will. So we need guidance as to what desires we should bring to God. Also, since God is great, reverent and respectful, courtesy is called for when we address him, so we need to know the proper way to present our desires to him. The Bible overall, and the Lord's Prayer in particular, give us the guidance we need.

Think of young children in a family. They want something that the parent is happy to give them. A toddler will reach out and whine, "augh, augh." The mother says cheerfully as she reaches for the carton, "Can you say, 'Juice'? Can you say, 'I want juice'?" And so she teaches the child two things. The first is, that juice is something she is very willing to give, the second is to present wants in ways not as socially unpleasing as a whined monosyllable, which, while fine for a toddler, no doubt would be more than a little obnoxious by age ten. We are children of God; we too need to learn to ask properly for things that God is ready to give. These two things together—what to ask for and how to do it—are what learning to pray prayers of petition is all about.

The next four questions and answers about prayer from the Westminster Shorter Catechism help to clarify these matters. They show us how we should shape our own praying, guided by the prayer that Christ taught his disciples.

What doth the preface of the Lord's Prayer teach us? The preface of the Lord's Prayer (which is, *Our Father which art in heaven*) teacheth us to draw near to God with all holy reverence and confidence, as children to a father, able and ready to help us; and that we should pray with and for others. (Rom 8:15; Lk 11:13; Acts 13:5; 1 Tim 2:1-2)

What do we pray for in the first petition? In the first petition (which is, *Hallowed be thy name*) we pray that God would enable us, and others, to glorify him in all that whereby he maketh himself known; and that he would dispose all things to his own glory. (Ps 67:2-3; 83:18)

What do we pray for in the second petition? In the second petition (which is *Thy kingdom come*) we pray that Satan's kingdom may be destroyed; and that the kingdom of grace may be advanced, ourselves and others brought into it, and kept in it; and that the kingdom of glory may be hastened. (Ps 68:1; Rev 12:10-11; 2 Thess 3:1; Rom 10:1; Jn 17:9, 20; Rev 22:20)

What do we pray for in the third petition? In the third petition (which is,

Thy will be done in earth, as it is in heaven) we pray that God, by his grace, would make us able and willing to know, obey and submit to his will in all things, as the angels do in heaven. (Ps 67; 119:36; Mt 26:39; Job 1:21; Ps 103:20-21)

Again, note the flow of thought, this time in the first half of the Lord's Prayer, as the Catechism's answers to these four questions bring it out. The prayer teaches us, first, how to invoke God (as our Father through Christ, a Father who in his transcendent awesomeness is not at all remote, and who truly loves his children); and, second, how to adjust to God (by seeing ourselves as here to glorify him and by learning as lovers of him to desire that we and every rational creature should fulfill that goal). This is the basic desire that must undergird and shape all the rest of the desires that we voice in our petitionary prayers.

Having got this far, we will not follow the Catechism further but offer our own answer to four questions that now naturally arise for praying people. First, what is it right to ask for? What is to be the scope and range of our petitions? Second, what should be the reason for our asking, that is, our motivation? Third, what is our warrant for expecting God to answer our prayers? On what basis do we make our petitions? Fourth, how does God answer prayers? What should we expect when we make our petitions? The rest of this chapter will be addressing these questions in order.

Before we move into them, however, a caveat is needed. If we envisage God as doing no more than passively listening to us as we ask him for things, we are wrong. Petitioning God is a two-way street. In the last chapter we noted how Psalm 139 views God's constant searching of us as part of the reality of our relationship with him, whether we are aware of it at any particular moment or not. He is the one who searches hearts, and he never stops doing it. And we need to realize that when we ask him for things, laying before him our desires, hopes, dreams and goals, the distresses that we want him to handle for us and the needs we are begging him to meet, he is asking us questions about our asking: *Why do you ask for this? How serious is the matter to you, and how deep does your concern go?*

Why do you think that what you are asking for is in line with my will? Would something other than the precise thing you now request satisfy you equally? Tell me. Human fathers, confronted with passionate but irresponsible requests, sometime find it necessary to quiz their children in this way, and it is the same with God. As we pray, awareness of these questions will arise, and if we really are serious—which, alas, not all people with prayer lists are—we know that they are questions not to be evaded as we talk to our heavenly Father. Petitioning God is thus a demanding business, as again and again God makes it part of his program for maturing us into thoughtful spiritual adults, and we must be ready for that.

WHAT SHOULD WE ASK FOR?

This question has to do with the substance of prayer. We have already had a formula answer from the Westminster Catechism: we ask for things that accord with God's will and that we desire. In saying that, the catechism is picking up familiar thoughts from the New Testament. In his farewell discourse to the apostles Jesus spoke more than once of making requests to the Father in his name—with astounding promises attached:

> Whatever you ask in my name, this I will do, that the Father may be glorified in the Son. If you ask me anything in my name, I will do it. (Jn 14:13-14)[3]

> You did not choose me, but I chose you and appointed you that you should go and bear fruit and that your fruit should abide, so that whatever you ask the Father in my name, he may give it to you. (Jn 15:16)

> In that day you will ask nothing of me. Truly, truly, I say to you, whatever you ask of the Father in my name, he will give it to you. (Jn 16:23)

---

[3]Some manuscripts omit "me" and some omit the whole verse. But the text as we cite it is almost certainly correct. See D. A. Carson, *The Gospel According to John* (Grand Rapids: Eerdmans, 1991), pp. 497-98 (additional note).

These were words of great challenge and comfort to the disciples as they began to contemplate life without the bodily presence of their beloved Jesus. They are words of challenge and comfort for us all. But they raise questions.

What is the message here? Is Jesus giving his first disciples (and us with them) a blank check? An invitation to write in whatever amount, so to speak, for whatever we want or think we want—and God will make it happen? Only yielding to a reckless moment of greed (a possibility to which we are all, alas, more exposed than we like to think) would take us to such an interpretation, and clearly that is not what is meant. The thought from the text is that we should ask God for things that the Lord Jesus will also ask for on our behalf. We are to make requests to the Father that the Lord Jesus will back. Jesus will associate himself with us in our requests when our requests match what he wants for us. That is the meaning of asking in his name. Jesus looks forward to his disciples asking for things that can only become reality with his help and by his power, and that will make for his glory when they do. That is what it means to ask according to God's will, the will of the Father which the Son knows and does. We, God's adopted children, come to know his will through studying Scripture and brooding on its implications, and through directly seeking the Savior's face in prayer.

The apostle John, who recorded the words of Jesus that we have just quoted, echoes their thought when he writes in his first letter (maybe after coming up against frustrated prayers engendered by selfish greed among those he served): "This is the confidence that we have toward him, that if we ask anything according to his will he hears us. And if we know that he hears us in whatever we ask, we know that we have the requests that we have asked of him" (1 Jn 5:14-15). *Him* and *he* in this passage is the Son of God, our Lord Jesus Christ. Our confidence is to be directed toward him and centered in him. We are to aim at asking in accordance with his will (which, of course, is identical with the Father's will), and when we do so ask we receive what we ask for. This matches

Christ's promise: "If you ask me anything in my name, I will do it," It is plain, therefore, that our petitions may be addressed to both the Father and the Son, and if they match the one will of the two persons, the granting of each petition is guaranteed.

The idea of asking according to God's will sounds simple and clear when first stated, but in practice discerning the parameters of the divine will in the wide range of situations about which we make requests to God is not easy. Bible readers soon realize that the personal will of our personal God, like yours and ours, is a complex reality, and merely drawing the classical and sound distinction between God's will of command and his will of events does not get us very far in understanding it. The triune Lord, we see, has a moral character and what we call a value system, which his goals, plans and commands all reflect. His range of revealed purpose as he deals with this fallen world includes the producing of what is morally, spiritually, aesthetically and culturally good; making unbelievers godly through redemption, regeneration, sanctification, and glorification; advancing the kingdom of Christ worldwide; gathering and building up the one church of Christ in every place; maturing, enriching, and perfecting his adopted children in their relationship with himself; exposing and punishing evil; displaying the glory of his holy love, wisdom, truth, and justice, and of his unlimited cosmic and transcosmic powers, and eliciting praise for it all from angels and humans alike. All the specific acts of God in his sovereign ordering of world events and individual lives are means, one way or another, to the furthering of this array of ends, and into this frame of purposive divine action our petitionary prayers should fit, for then they too, in some way that is beyond our full understanding, will also be means toward these ends. How then are we to formulate petitions according to God's will? The answer is twofold: by following the guidelines of, first, observed need and, second, inner inclination.

In asking God to meet observed needs, the second half of the Lord's Prayer stands as a model. Here we pray for daily provision ("Give us each day our daily bread"—we need it), for daily pardon ("Forgive our sins"—we need that) and for daily protection ("Deliver us from evil"— we need that too, more than we know). And the plurals *us* and *our* are key words, which show that we are meant to make this prayer for other Christians besides ourselves. At this point further models appear, namely Paul's prayers for the spiritual advance of Christians in the churches that, with two exceptions, he himself had planted and, without exception, now served. Prayer for spiritual advance, both our own and that of others, is always in order, for all of us always need to go further in life with God than we have yet gone. The positive that corresponds to the negative "deliver us from evil," namely, (in substance) "make us more Christlike," is spelled out here in language of breathtaking range and force.

For the church at Ephesus, Paul prays that

> according to the riches of [the Father's] glory he may grant you to be strengthened with power through his Spirit in your inner being, so that Christ may dwell in your hearts through faith—that you, being rooted and grounded in love, may have strength to comprehend with all the saints what is the breadth and length and height and depth, and to know the love of Christ that surpasses knowledge, that you may be filled with all the fullness of God. (Eph 3:16-19)

For the church at Colossae (not of his planting, though he had strong links with it), Paul prays that

> you may be filled with the knowledge of [God's] will in all spiritual wisdom and understanding, so as to walk in a manner worthy of the Lord, fully pleasing to him, bearing fruit in every good work and increasing in the knowledge of God. May you be strengthened with all power, according to his glorious might, for all endurance and patience with joy, giving thanks to the Father, who has qualified you to share in the inheritance of the saints in light. (Col 1:9-12)

For the church at Philippi, Paul prays that "your love may abound more and more, with knowledge and all discernment, so that you may approve what is excellent, and so be pure and blameless for the day of Christ, filled with the fruit of righteousness that comes through Jesus Christ, to the glory and praise of God" (Phil 1:9-11).

For the church at Thessalonica, Paul prays: "May the God of peace sanctify you completely, and may your whole spirit and soul and body be kept blameless at the coming of our Lord Jesus Christ" (1 Thess 5:23).

What congregation, what Christian group—home meeting, para-church organization, whatever—would not be supremely blessed to have God fulfill toward them the fullness of this multiaspect work of illuminating, transforming and preserving grace, as these prayers spell it out? Can we doubt that making any or all of these petitions to God for any Christians or Christian communities—our own congregations, for instance—is to ask for enrichment that God will be delighted to bestow? Enrichment, therefore, that is in accord with his will every time it is sought? Enrichment that meets the real, observable needs of all Christian individuals and communities all the time? When Christians echo and elaborate these thoughts in their prayers for each other, they are therefore entitled to expect their prayers to be answered.

Beyond this, however, questions still arise. When we pray for individuals who in one way or another are close to us—family, friends, mentors, leaders, Christian workers at home and abroad whom we support, and so on—we become specific in asking God to do certain particular things to meet their particular needs. Often that is exactly what the people concerned have asked us to do. But since many of the details of God's plan are unknown to us, when we have told God what we would most like to see happen, some degree of uncertainty must remain as to whether or not we prayed according to his will. What to do then? Two things. First, we should lay before God, as part of our prayer, the reasons why we think that what we ask for is the best thing. Second, we should tell God that if he wills something different we know it will be better, and it is that (rather than the best we could think of) that we really want him to do.

A word now about these two moves.

First, about giving God reasons. The Puritans used to speak rather grandly about using argument in prayer.[4] By this they did not mean pressing God to fall in line with our own desires ("My will be done"); what they meant was telling God why what we have asked for seems to us to be for the best, in light of what we know God's own goals to be (generating good, saving sinners, extending the kingdom and enriching the church of the Lord Jesus Christ, and glorifying himself by so revealing his transcendent triune glory that his rational creatures give him glory by their thanks and praise). Here, now, is a sample Puritan, Stephen Charnock, making the point in his own way:

> Our praying . . . should consist of arguments for God's glory and our happiness: not that arguments move God to do that which he is not willing of himself to do for us . . . as though the infinitely wise God needed information, or the infinitely loving God needed persuasion, but it is for strengthening our faith in him. All the prayers in the Scripture you will find to be reasoning with God, not a multitude of words heaped together; and the design of the promises is to furnish us with a strength of reason in this case: Dan 9:16, "Now according to all thy righteousness, I beseech thee, let thy anger and thy fury be turned away from thy city Jerusalem." He [Daniel] pleads God's righteousness in his promise of the set time of deliverance; after he had settled his heart in a full belief of the promise of deliverance, he shows God's own words to him. The arguments [in this and all biblical prayers] you will find drawn from the covenant in general, or some promise in particular, or some attribute of God, or the glory of God.[5]

---

[4]Thus the answer to question 196 of the Westminster Larger Catechism reads as follows: "The conclusion of the Lord's Prayer (which is, *For thine is the kingdom, and the power, and the glory, forever, Amen.*) teacheth us to enforce our petitions with arguments, which are to be taken, not from any worthiness in ourselves, or in any other creature, but from God."

[5]Stephen Charnock, *Works* (Edinburgh: James Nichol, 1865), 4.8. Dan 9:4, 7-9, 16-19 is the passage that answer 196 in the Larger Catechism quotes to illustrate argument in prayer (see note 4).

Second, about embracing God's will. Giving God reasons shows the boldness of humility; embracing God's will shows the submissiveness of humility. In the former, faith engages with God's wisdom; in the latter, it bows to his authority. What that means is most tellingly shown us by the account of Jesus praying in Gethsemane. Matthew records his words thus: "My Father, if it be possible, let this cup pass from me; nevertheless, not as I will, but as you will. . . . My Father, if this cannot pass unless I drink it, your will be done" (Mt 26:39, 42). Mark has: "Abba, Father, all things are possible for you. Remove this cup from me. Yet not what I will, but what you will" (Mk 14:36). Luke gives us: "Father, if you are willing, remove this cup from me. Nevertheless, not my will, but yours, be done" (Lk 22:42). These are interpretive renderings in Greek of what the eleven undoubtedly heard Jesus say in his home language, Aramaic. The "cup" was the atoning death for us that the Son was sent from heaven to endure. The prayer, even when it becomes two or three sentences in English, is a single unit of heartfelt, agonized expression, with the "amen" (so to speak) not coming until the Lord has affirmed the priority of his Father's known will over the involuntary longing for release from the coming ordeal that he finds within himself. We walk in the footsteps of our Savior when we tell him and the Father that however much we find ourselves longing for something else, the Father's will has priority for us; we do not want to receive what is not part of that will; we want our Father's will and only his will, whether or not at the moment we know how much it involves

It is sometimes said that we should get our petitionary prayers from God himself, and that is true, in the same sense to which the foregoing paragraphs point. In each case we should ask ourselves what we see as truly and centrally needing to happen in the life and need situation we are praying about, and what is the immediate event which, if it took place, would be the most direct step toward making the desired change result. We should check that, so far as we can tell, both the end and the means that we envisage as best will not be out of line with God's goals, character and scale of values, but will rather make for his glory; then we should take our request submissively but confidently to God, stating our arguments and knowing that in making this request we have done all we could to discern and fit into this will. Following this procedure in a spirit of pure-hearted praise, we can know for sure that he will certainly "hear" (take note) and answer us, even if not entirely in the way we had hoped.

In answering the question, What should we ask for? we also see the answer to its negative counterpart, What should we *not* ask God for? The short statement of that answer is: things we want and now request just because we want them and for no higher reason than that. It is sadly possible to say, in effect, "Lord Jesus, heavenly Father, *my* will be done if you please; this is what I want. And the mere fact that I want it is my warrant for asking you to supply it." There are praying people who get no further in their petitions than listing items tagged, so to speak, with the formula "This is what I want." And they look to God as if he is simply there to do like Jeeves in the P. G. Wodehouse stories, whose role is to wonderfully supply the various felt needs of the young master and get him out of scrapes. When Martha asked Jesus to send Mary into the kitchen to help her, and a man asked him to tell his brother to divide a legacy fairly (Lk 10:40-42; 12:13-15), Jesus gave them sharply negative answers. Jesus would not be manipulated that way then, and the holy Three will not be manipulated that way now, even in face of repetitious prayer that seeks to wear down all divine resistance.

In the Sermon on the Mount Jesus says: "When you pray, do not heap up empty phrases as the Gentiles do, for they think that they will be heard for their many words" (Mt 6:7). He is not here talking about asking for wrong things but of asking for anything, whether right or wrong, in the wrong way. What Jesus is objecting to is the fact that some people think that if they say often and insistently enough to God, "This is what I want; please do it," they will twist God's arm and thereby secure what they ask for. But real prayer is not like that and right requests become wrong if presented in that fashion. That is superstitious, irreverent and pagan, even when those who think and act like this are regular church-goers. It is never the way to petition almighty God.

The lack of forthrightness in petitioning God is not right either. When we are clear that what we are asking him to do is to meet a real need and that he will glorify himself by doing so, we should make our request boldly and persistently, thus showing strong faith in his holy goodness. Two of Jesus' parables make this point, by "how-much-more" reasoning, though in the first case Jesus leaves the disciples (and us!) to work this out for ourselves.

The first story (Lk 11:5-8) is of the man who at midnight rouses his friend from bed in order to borrow three loaves so that he can fulfill East-ern society's sacred duty of hospitality and feed another of his friends who, unannounced, has just dropped in for the night. The roused sleeper feels this is an abuse of friendship but nonetheless gets up and meets the request because of the asker's "impudence"—shameless per-sistence, unabashed cheek, and refusal to take no for an answer. How much more, then, can we expect God to respond with actions when we ask him to meet our own real and urgent needs (vv. 9-13)!

The second story (Lk 18:1-8) is of the unprincipled judge who vindi-cated the widow, not because justice so required (though it did) but be-cause she had made herself a nuisance to him. This time Jesus made the how-much-more point explicit: "Hear what the unrighteous judge says. And will not God give justice to his elect, who cry to him day and night?" (vv. 6-7). Both stories were told to make us bold in petitionary prayer. Humble boldness and pertinacity as we engage with God in making any request is part of the biblical prayer pattern.

WHY SHOULD WE ASK?

This second question has to do with the motivation of all our asking. Once more we take our lead from the pattern of petition in the Lord's Prayer. The Westminster Shorter Catechism told us, at least in outline, the significance of "Hallowed be your name / Your kingdom come, your will be done," in terms of specific realities to request. Now we must dwell a little further on the significance of these phrases as model expressions of the desires that drive the regenerate heart.

The Bible perspective throughout is that with God—the Searcher of hearts—the inner realities of motivation, purpose and desire that prompt and energize our actions are just as important as the performance of the actions themselves, viewed from the outside. Petitionary praying (or any other sort of prayer, for that matter) that is performed mechanically, without any focused thought (as when we clean our teeth) and in a state of suppressed resentment, perhaps, at having to do it, or at something God has previously done or not done, is prayer from a heart that is not as it should be, and so the performance is in God's eyes hypocritical to a degree. God assesses all our actions from the inside as well as the outside, as Jesus tried (unsuccessfully) to teach the Pharisees.

Our positive point, now, can be stated thus: "Hallowed be your name"—which means, may you, God, be always and everywhere honored, exalted, magnified, glorified and praised for all that you are and do—is the basic petition of the entire Lord's Prayer, the global ideal and desire that all the other petitions are actually spelling out and specifying in one way or another. Just as this petition is the controlling thought of the Lord's Prayer as a whole so the longing to see it fulfilled should be the controlling desire of the heart whenever God's children pray. We have been given the Lord's Prayer so that we might learn from it not just the wording but the spirit, the animating attitude, of this authoritative model.

So we are to pray to God in order to further the praise of God first and foremost, not to gratify selfish concerns in which God has no place. Why then should we ask for what we do ask for? Our honest answer to that question should point toward God: his name, his glory, his nature, his kingdom. Often, however, our asking is more murkily motivated. James shows this in a specific way as he opens the fourth chapter of his letter. "What causes quarrels and what causes fights among you? Is it not this, that your passions are at war within you?" (We are fighting not only other people's passions but also the passions within own hearts.) "You desire and do not have, so you murder. You covet and cannot obtain, so you fight and quarrel." (That was what was going on in the churches that James addressed. It was a good thing that he took time out to write about it, because quarrelsome passion has infected churches again and again ever since James's day, though not often, thank God, to the point of physical murder. Murder in the heart, however—"I hate so-and-so"—has undoubtedly often been present.) Now comes the key truth James has been working up to: "You do not have, because you do not ask. You ask and you do not receive, *because you ask wrongly, to spend it on your passions*" (Jas 4:1-3, emphasis added). Here we see James highlighting self-focused motivation that produces self-focused desires and the "my will be done" type of asking. Compare with that, now, the two following examples of intercessory requests.

Abraham, a prophet (Gen 20:7) but temperamentally a quiet, unassuming and unheroic man, has just heard from God, who has appeared to him by a theophany in human form, that destruction faces the city of Sodom for its sins. Abraham is concerned for his nephew Lot and Lot's branch of the family, who have settled in Sodom, and so he asks God to spare the city if fifty—forty—thirty—twenty—ten godly people live in it, obviously with Lot and his household in mind throughout. But the "I want" of his praying is absorbed into a stated concern for God's glory as a just judge, and there is no reason to doubt that this genuinely expressed the God-centeredness of Abraham's heart. "Suppose there are fifty righteous within the city. Will you then sweep away the place and not spare it? . . . Far be it from you to do such a thing, to put the righteous to death with the wicked! . . . Shall not the Judge of all the earth do what is just?" (Gen 18:24-25). What comes first with Abraham is the hallowing of God's name. Beyond the typical Eastern step-by-step presentation of Abraham's request in his unique to-and-fro exchange with his theophanic Lord, Abraham shows that God's honor is the supreme target of his prayer, and over and above the love, boldness, humility and faith that Abraham's praying displays, his desire for God to be honored is the supreme quality for us to imitate as we labor to pray for people and situations that weigh heavily on our own hearts.

Set alongside this, now Daniel's prayer that God will deliver his people from their exilic captivity. Daniel, though a major figure in Babylon, is an Israelite patriot, and his prayer shows him longing for Israel's restoration. But central to his prayer is celebration of God's covenant and justice and mercy (Dan 9:4, 7, 9), and the conclusion to which he works up is this: *"For your own sake,* O Lord, make your face to shine upon your sanctuary, which is desolate. . . . Delay not, *for your own sake,* O my God, because your people and your city are called by your name" (Dan 9:17, 19, emphasis added). In other words, in and through action to restore us, display yourself, vindicate yourself, glorify yourself. In other words, hallowed be your name. The quality test of all our petitionary praying is the clarity test, whether we make it apparent that God's yes to our requests will in fact be or become a means to the hallowing of his name in praise for his demonstrated praiseworthiness. In this Daniel, like Abraham, is showing us the way.

ON WHAT BASIS DO WE ASK?

This third question about asking God for things raises the issue of expectations—and our basis for those expectations. What reasons have we to look for answers to our prayers? What reasons have we to expect that God will move, that divine action will be taken in response to the requests we make? The answer is that there is a solid foundation for these expectations in a trio of factors, which we may picture as the legs of a three-legged stool. As the stool will only stand if all three legs are in place, so we may expect answers to our prayers only when (1) our adoptive relationship with God, (2) the mighty promises of God, and (3) personal faith-full purity of heart are together. Scripture has much to say to us on these three themes.

The first leg of our stool is our knowledge that God is now our Father by adoption and grace. We weren't born God's children, nobody is, but we become God's children through faith in Jesus Christ. He, who is the eternal Son of the Father by nature, brings us into the family as adopted children, and henceforth he is our elder brother. Our relationship with the Father of Jesus as our own Father is basic to all that we ask in prayer. Fathers give good gifts to their children, and that should give us boldness in making our requests.

In the Sermon on the Mount Jesus gives an intimate family invitation to

> Ask, and it will be given to you; seek, and you will find; knock, and it will be opened to you. For everyone who asks receives, and the one who seeks finds, and to the one who knocks it will be opened. Or which one of you, if his son asks him for bread, will give him a stone? Or if he asks for a fish, will give him a serpent? If you then, who are evil, know how to give good gifts to your children, how much more will your Father who is in heaven give good things to those who ask him? (Mt 7:7-11)

This invitation is addressed to all disciples of Jesus, all who through faith are children of God—and therefore it is a word from our Master and Brother meant specifically for us.

Observe the context. Matthew 6, where Jesus teaches the Lord's Prayer, is the midsection of the Sermon on the Mount and consists entirely of teaching on three of the realities of life with our heavenly Father: practicing piety to please him alone (vv. 1-18), living single-mindedly as his heirs and servants (vv. 19-24), and trusting his fatherly care in daily life (vv. 25-34). It is within that family frame that in chapter 7, having warned us against sibling savagery in God's family (vv 1-5), Jesus invites us to offer petitions to our Father in heaven. Jesus addresses these words to all who know they are children of God through faith in himself, so with a humble boldness we can rightly say that our relationship with

God as children to a Father is a solid basis for *expecting* that our asking
will receive a positive answer.

A second leg of our stool is the promises of God as set forth in Scripture.
Our God has given us promises in writing, and since he is a faithful
God, we may confidently claim those promises, invoking them explicitly in our petitionary prayers. When we do this, we please and honor
our Father by our trust. In Romans 4, Paul celebrates the faith of the
aged Abraham and his equally aged wife, to whom God had promised
the gift of a child. Measured by all human reason and all the circumstances, that promise was an impossibility. But, says Paul, Abraham
didn't stagger (as the KJV puts it) at the promise of God, that is, he did
not vacillate in his certainty that God would keep his word; he trusted
that God was able to fulfill his promise and actively expected him to
do so. "No distrust made him waver concerning the promise of God,
but he grew strong in his faith as he gave glory to God, fully convinced
that God was able to do what he had promised" (Rom 4:20-21). Abraham was sure that God could and would do what he promised—and
of course it happened.

The promises of God are trustworthy. When we ask favors of God, we
can rely on those promises, and to the extent that we are asking for what
God has already promised to do, we should be free from all doubt that
answers will come. But let us take care to get our perspective right. Peter
generalizes about what is central in God's promises to us. If we are looking for, say, a new car, a new spouse, perfect health, vocational success
and public influence, as exponents of the once-popular "name it and
claim it" teaching would encourage us to do, Peter's view of God's promises will seem disappointing and unhelpful. But what Peter allows us to
glimpse of God's promises is something truly better than any of these
items.

> [God's] divine power has granted to us all things that pertain to life
> and godliness, through the knowledge of him who called us to his

own glory and excellence, by which he has granted to us his precious and very great promises, so that through them you may become partakers of the divine nature, having escaped from the corruption that is in the world because of sinful desire. (2 Pet 1:3-4)

What does God promise us? That we will be "partakers of the divine nature," that we will be rescued from "the corruption . . . of sinful desire." What kinds of petitions will lead God to keep those kinds of promises? Clearly, not prayers for personal convenience but for personal sanctity, not for increasing affluence but for growth in grace. "Lord, make me as holy as it is possible for a saved sinner to be," is a prayer ascribed to Murray McCheyne. That is how Peter would have us all pray. It should not surprise us that God's promises to and purposes for us have more to do with our spiritual development than our physical comfort. Certainly, God promises to provide for our material needs (note: needs, not dreams; look at Mt 6:19-21, 25-34) for as long as he plans that our earthly life should last. But what he primarily has in view for us is a destiny of Christlikeness, and where Christlikeness is not being sought he may well withhold some of the benefits to which his promises refer, just as long ago he withheld rain and good harvests from idolatrous and immoral Israel.

One of the difficulties with promises is waiting. A small child waits endlessly, or so it seems, for the afternoon snack that mother is already retrieving from the refrigerator. Our own petitionary prayers, based on God's promises, are likely to generate similar impatience in ourselves. "God has already promised to . . ." we say. "Why must I wait for it? Why must I even ask?" Godly people in the Old Testament often pleaded with God to finally grant them the land and prosperity he had promised them, or to release them from captivity, or from ongoing hostility and ill-treatment, when God's fulfillment of his word had been delayed. This must have felt particularly painful during Israel's wilderness wanderings as children watched their grandparents die—the promise of land of their own yet unfulfilled; and during the exile, as parents watched their children attain adulthood—still in captivity; and in the post-Solomon era as one evil ruler after another occupied the throne, their misdeeds apparently going unpunished, and the moral and spiritual revival that the faithful sought not taking place.

Similarly, in New Testament times some faithful believers thought God was delaying the fulfillment of the promise of Christ's return. Near the end of his second letter, Peter speaks directly to unrest and skepticism about Christ's reappearing, and does so in a way that throws light on the whole issue of God's apparent delays, whether in the past or as may arise in the future. Says Peter: "The Lord is not slow to fulfill his promise as some count slowness, but is patient toward you, not wishing that any should perish, but that all should reach repentance. . . . [C]ount the patience of our Lord as salvation, just as our beloved brother Paul also wrote to you according to the wisdom given him" (2 Pet 3:9, 15). Our desire for instant action in response to our prayers reflects the limitation and smallness of our view of things compared with God's. God fixes his time for doing what he has promised (and what his people look to him to do) in light of long-term purposes of goodness and wisdom involving far more than we can ever be aware of. "That *all* should reach repentance" is a case in point: who were Peter's first readers, and who are you and we today, to compute God's "all"? The principle that Bible-believers must grasp is that it is God's prerogative to do what he promises in what he knows to be the best and wisest way, at what he knows to be the best and wisest time. Seeing this will help us to develop the patience and settled trust that God desires to shape in us, and will stabilize our hope when our hearts move us to pray "Lord, how long?"

Sometimes God moves his people to engage in promise-based praying at trigger points in linear time so that the link between the asking and the answering is prompt, direct and obvious. This was true of Nehemiah near the end of Israel's captivity under Persian rule. In chapter 1 of Nehemiah's memoirs, we see him, having heard the bad news of Jerusalem's

sorry state, reminding God of his former promises, arguing that certainly
the time was ripe for God to fulfill those promises and begging God for
some part in the action—which, as the rest of the book bears out, God
granted him. The large events of the book begin with this prayer of asking. We hear Nehemiah say:

> Remember the word that you commanded your servant Moses, say-
> ing, "If you are unfaithful, I will scatter you among the peoples, but if
> you return to me and keep my commandments and do them, though
> your dispersed be under the farthest skies, I will gather them from
> there and bring them to the place that I have chosen, to make my
> name dwell there." They are your servants and your people, whom
> you have redeemed by your great power and by your strong hand. O
> Lord, let your ear be attentive to the prayer of your servant, and to the
> prayer of your servants who delight to fear your name, and give suc-
> cess to your servant today, and grant him mercy in the sight of this
> man [the king, whom Nehemiah served as cupbearer]. (Neh 1:8-11)

The rest of the book tells how the king of Persia granted Nehemiah a
leave of absence and governor status to head up a construction project
that eventually rebuilt the walls of Jerusalem, despite opposition, in no
more than fifty-two days, how then he reorganized the city and renewed
its commitment to God, and finally how, in a second term as governor,
he brought that reformation, which was crumbling, to renewal.

Self-quotation is commonly viewed as a vice, but J. I. is prepared to
take a risk on that by citing what he wrote elsewhere about Nehemiah as
a praying person.

> Nehemiah's walk with God was *saturated with his praying,* and praying
> of the truest and purest kind—namely, the sort of praying that is al-
> ways seeking to clarify its own vision of who and what God is, and to
> celebrate his reality in constant adoration, and to rethink in his pres-
> ence such needs and requests as one is bringing to him, so that the
> stating of them becomes a specifying of "hallowed be thy name . . . thy

will be done . . . for thine is the kingdom, the power, and the glory."
. . . Nehemiah punctuates his story with prayers to "my God," who is
"our God." He starts his book with a full transcript of his plea for the
covenant people (1:5-11), he ends it with four "remember me" petitions, the last of which is actually his sign-off line (13:14, 22, 29, 30-
31), and he goes out of his way to record several other prayers in the
course of his narrative [see 2:4; 4:4-5, 9; 5:19; 6:14]. . . . It is clear that
as a writer he understands, and now wants his readers to understand,
that only ventures that are begun in prayer and bathed in prayer
throughout are likely to be blessed as the venture of rebuilding Jerusalem's walls was blessed, and he so selects and arranges his material
as to project this truth without having to put it into words.[6]

Nehemiah's leadership in the restoration of Jerusalem was outstand-
ing for his openness to God's leading (see esp. chap. 2), his wisdom in
planning for God's glory (see esp. chaps. 2, 7-12), his refusal to cave in
to hostile pressures and ridicule (see esp. chaps. 4, 6), his zeal to work
hard for God and motivate others to do the same (see esp. chaps. 3-4),
his particular care for the needy and distressed (see chap. 5), his self-
effacing humility in times of success, and his tenacity in correcting dis-
orders that made his previous efforts look like failure (see esp. chap. 13).
But his leadership would not have been what it was without his praying,
and his praying would not have been what it was without his confidence
that he served a covenanting God who keeps his promises (Neh 9:8, 32;
cf. Neh 1:8-9): a God of utter faithfulness, who can be utterly trusted.

*The third leg of our stool, that entitles us to expect God to answer our peti-
tionary prayers, is purity of heart,* our own purity of heart before the holy
God to whom we pray. By this we mean, in general, all that Kierkegaard
meant when he titled one of his books *Purity of Heart Is to Will One Thing,*
namely, thoroughgoing God-centeredness. The Bible uses *heart* to desig-
nate the core of the person, from which come all our thoughts and de-

---

[6]J. I. Packer, *A Passion for Faithfulness* (Wheaton, Ill.: Crossway, 1995), pp. 44-45.

sires, all the dispositions, inclinations, and strategies that shape our lives. The pure heart is the heart that seeks and serves God in everything without wavering, and rejects all alternatives to this agenda all the time. When Jesus said: "Blessed are the pure in heart, for they shall see God" (Mt 5:8), he spoke out of his knowledge that seeing God will be the fulfillment of the pure-hearted person's deepest longing. The principle we affirm here is that potent praying presupposes purity of heart as described. Before we say anything to God, therefore, we need to check up on ourselves to make sure, so far as we can, that nothing in us—no "grievous way," as Psalm 139:24 puts it, no ongoing willful sin—is going to impede God's positive answer to our prayers.

If we approach God with impure hearts, we are like children who are trying to fool their parents and whose parents can see quite clearly what the kids are up to. If a child asks the parent for twenty dollars in order to buy a video game, a wise parent will not respond positively if the proposed game is X-rated for graphic violence. If the child objects to this refusal by stomping and yelling and pretending to shoot every object in sight, those actions reveal a "heart condition" that puts an obstacle in the way of the parent granting that specific request at any time in the near future. We now follow the Bible in pointing to the behavior that puts an obstacle in the way of God granting our prayers. In Psalm 66:18-19 we read:

> If I had cherished iniquity in my heart,
>   the Lord would not have listened.
> But truly God has listened;
>   he has attended to the voice of my prayer.
> Blessed be God,
>   because he has not rejected my prayer
>   or removed his steadfast love from me!

God has granted the request of the psalmist, but would not have done so had he "cherished iniquity in his heart"—that is, held on to anything

in his life or his life plan that he knew was wrong. Under those circumstances the Lord would not have "listened to" his prayer: that is, given it
a positive answer. God knows all things, including the thoughts behind
our askings. But does God always "listen" to us when we ask? That, it
seems, depends in part on the condition of our hearts. Willful children,
storming at their parents as they try to force them to do something, may
call forth the response, "I can hear what you say, but I'm not listening,"
or simply "I'm not listening." Petitions from an impure heart evoke just
that response from God.

The prophet Isaiah helps us to comprehend God's "nonlistening"
more clearly—and not confuse it with any limitation of power.

> Behold, the LORD's hand is not shortened, that it cannot save,
>   or his ear dull, that it cannot hear;
> but your iniquities have made a separation
>   between you and your God,
> and your sins have hidden his face from you
>   so that he does not hear. (Is 59:1-2)

Isaiah tells these people, God hears you all right, in the sense that he
knows what you are asking, but he doesn't hear in the sense of responding to your request. Why not? Because of the sins, the perversities, the
things you know are wrong which nonetheless you are cherishing. Be
honest, admit your error, give it up, repent of it, and so purify your
hearts (James's phrase, Jas 4:8) before you bring requests to God. To be
sure, purity is not a bribery tool, as if when we give up enough of ourselves, we prevail on God finally to act. The emphasis of Isaiah 59 is on
God's prerogative, not ours. But we should approach a holy God of unlimited power with inner purity; otherwise, we are asking God, in effect,
to turn a blind eye to any sins and vices, which of course he cannot and
will not do. This is part of learning to pray not only with our words but
with our whole being.

In summary, then, when God's fatherly relationship with us and his faithfulness to us as promise keeper are linked with our own cultivated and disciplined purity of heart, we have a warrant for expecting answers to our requests, and that is both startling and thrilling to know. What, from God's standpoint, appear as serious, faithful, sustained prayers from his own children are all going to be answered in what, from his standpoint, are thoroughly positive terms.

How Does God Answer Our Prayers?

All this leads to our fourth and last question. How does our God answer our prayers? It is often said that he gives us one of three answers: yes, no and wait. This is not wholly wrong, but the matter can, we think, be made much clearer as follows.

Every petitionary prayer brings before God a situation of need that we are asking him to meet. Regularly we tell him just how, as we see it, he can best take action to meet that need. It is clear from the number of specific prayers recorded in the Bible that that is how our God wants us to pray; indeed the truth is that as both the Father and the Son invite us to present our petitions, so the Holy Spirit within us stirs us up to do just that. The overall thrust of all the Spirit's many ministries to each believer is ever to deepen, enrich and make closer our fellowship with the Father and the Son, and prompting us to intercessory involvement with both is one means by which he achieves this end. We are, then, constantly to be using our limited wisdom to work out what might most fully advance the good of those for whom we pray, the relief of each need about which we pray and the glory and praise of our prayer-hearing, promise-keeping heavenly Father, the universal provider from whom all good things come. If our reasoning was right, what he does is what we asked; if our wisdom failed, what he does is what we *should have* asked. He knows *and* does what is better in every situation—situations, remember, of which the prayers we have made are now part. A moment ago we said that God always answers his children's prayers positively, and that is the clue we need to understand the actual outcomes of our praying. God's yes is regularly a case of "your thinking about how I could best meet this need was right"; his no is a case of "not that, for this is better"—and so is really a yes in disguise!—and his wait (which we infer from the fact that though we have asked for action, nothing yet has changed) is a case of "wait *and see;* I will deal with this need at the best time in the best way. Whether or not you will be able to discern my wisdom when I do act, that is what in fact I am going to do. Keep watching, and see what you can see."

Examples may help to clarify this. Here, first, is a biblical example of God's no being a yes in disguise. When Paul asked the Lord Jesus for miraculous healing for his thorn in the flesh, the Lord's response was to say, in effect, Paul, I've got something better in store for you than healing. My grace is sufficient to keep you going, though you remain unhealed (2 Cor 12:7-10). No doubt Paul had thought that his ministry would be curtailed by his continuing disability, and he knew that miraculous healings brought glory to Christ; so here were two strong arguments to back his petition as in three solemn sessions of prayer he pleaded for the miracle to happen. But now he understood that Christ's answer (though painful) was better than his request, and so he tells the Corinthians, "I will boast all the more gladly of my weaknesses, so that the power of Christ may rest upon me" (v. 9). That was the Lord changing for the better a request that had been made honestly and with a purpose of glory for God and out of a truly pure heart. Paul's need was actually met, though not in the way he had asked for; his ministry (miraculously) went on undiminished; and Christ was glorified; thus prayer was answered.

Carolyn, when teaching young children to pray or adults newly arrived at prayer as a discipline, is fond of saying, "God fixes our prayers on the way up!" Some people get so entangled in the various dos and don'ts of prayer, so transfixed by the problem of sorting out what is our part and what is God's part, so bogged down fretting over whether they, as mere flawed humans, should ask anything of a holy, almighty God or conversely whether there is any point in asking since God will do what he wants anyway that they become paralyzed about praying. "Why ask

God for anything? There is no way to get it right." Romans 8:26, however, provides wonderful release from this paralysis. "For we do not know what to pray for as we ought, but the Spirit himself intercedes for us with groanings too deep for words." We as praying persons are being prayed for by the Holy Spirit himself! So Carolyn knows she is entitled to say, "Don't fret; just pray. God fixes our prayers on the way up." If he does not answer the prayer we made, he will answer the prayer we should have made. That is all anyone needs to know.

But what about timing? *When* will God answer our prayers of asking? When we ask God for things, we always hope that they will be given straightaway. We humans are always in a hurry, but God sometimes keeps us waiting because he is not. Luke 18:3-5 points to this: the unjust judge kept the widow waiting before he gave her justice. God has his own time frame and his own plan, which reflects his exhaustive knowledge. He knows the best time at which to answer our prayers as well as the best way to do it. "The Lord is not slow to fulfill his promise," says Peter: with God a thousand years is as a single day. God's time frame, different as it is from our own, provides no grounds for complaint that God is keeping us waiting. He knows what he is doing: he is working according to plan; it is for us to adjust to him, not the other way around.

Sometimes the things that we ask for involve more than we realize, and God, who loves us, gives us more than we knew we were asking for as he responds to our requests. This is especially so when we pray about our own spiritual lives, where knowledge of what we really need is regularly lacking. The great hymn writer John Newton—who was a boy sailor, a navy deserter, then a slave trader, then a Christian convert, a friend of William Cowper, John Wesley and George Whitefield, who went on to become pastor first of Olney Church and then of St. Mary Woolnoth in London, and ultimately was a major evangelical leader for a generation and more—speaks poignantly of this in a hymn he wrote looking back on God's work in his life. His words should make us think deeply about our own prayers—both for ourselves and for others.

I asked the Lord that I might grow
In faith and love and every grace;
Might more of his salvation know,
And seek more earnestly his face.

'Twas he who taught me thus to pray,
And he, I trust, has answered prayer;
But it has been in such a way
As almost drove me to despair.

I hoped that in some favored hour
At once he'd answer my request;
And by his love's constraining power,
Subdue my sins and give me rest.

Instead of this he made me feel
The hidden evils of my heart,
And let the angry powers of hell
Assault my soul in every part.

Yea more, with his own hand he seemed
Intent to aggravate my woe;
Crossed all the fair designs I'd schemed,
Blasted my gourds and laid me low.

"Lord, why is this," I trembling cried;
"Wilt Thou pursue thy worm to death?"
"'Tis in this way," the Lord replied,
I answer prayer for grace and faith.

These inward trials I employ
From self and pride to set thee free
And break thy schemes of earthly joy,
That thou mayest seek thy all in me.[7]

---

[7]John Newton and William Cowper, *Olney Hymns in Three Books,* 1879. The "gourds" and the "worm" are images taken from Jn 4:6-7 (KJV) and Ps 22:6; Is 41:14.

That is how the Lord sometimes answers prayer for spiritual advance.

We have it on firm scriptural authority that the Father's response to requests faithfully, humbly, hopefully, expectantly made by his own children, out of a pure heart and an honest desire for God's glory, is never going to be a flat no. One way or another God's response will be a positive response, though it may be "I am adjusting the terms of your prayer to give you something better than you asked for." Or it may be, "I know that this isn't the moment in which answering your prayer would bring you and others most blessing, so I'm asking you to wait." Or it may be, "I am answering your prayer, but you don't know the strategy I'm working on, and it doesn't at the moment feel or look like an answer at all. Nonetheless, it is. Keep praying, keep trusting, and keep looking for what, down the road, I may be able in wisdom to let you see."

We are not implying, however, that the pain of seemingly unanswered prayer—honest, earnest, pure-hearted, long-term petition—will ever be eliminated entirely from our lives as long as we are here on earth. Scripture seems clearly to indicate the contrary, particularly in connection with persons close to us whom we very much love: family, colleagues, friends. We find it unimaginable, for instance, that David did not regularly pray for his scapegrace son Absalom, whom he loved so much, whatever mistakes he may have made in parenting him; yet Absalom, rebelling against his father, came to a thoroughly bad end (2 Sam 18). And Paul tells us that he prayed with agonized love throughout his ministry, presumably for the Jews whose rejection of Christ and Christians had put them squarely under God's wrath (Rom 9:1-3; 10:1; 1 Thess 2:14-16). Members of Paul's immediate and extended family, former friends and fellow Pharisees must have been in Paul's mind here, along with the Jewish community in general. Can we doubt that pioneer Puritan pastor Richard Greenham and pioneer missionaries Carey in India, Judson in Burma and Morrison in China, all of whom saw virtually no converts among those whom over the years they sought to lead to Christ, prayed for the communities in which they worked, and for individuals within those communities, the way Paul prayed for the Jews? That petitionary prayer makes a difference, and that in heaven we will find what difference our prayers made, and that here on earth we are to go on praying for the physical and spiritual needs of others as love and compassion prompt us is not to be doubted, but here on earth the pain of not seeing all the changes in all the people that we longed to see is something we have to live with. The Lord Jesus himself, our prime model in praying, knew this particular heartache, as his tears over Jerusalem showed: "Would that you, even you, had known on this day the things that make for peace! But now they are hidden from your eyes" (Lk 19:42; cf. Mt 23:37-38). We will find that Jesus our Master upholds us when our experience of disappointment after praying comes close to his.

And it is as if the Lord adds, "By the way, always check when you ask me for something whether you yourself should be the beginning of the answer to your own prayer by doing something that you have not yet ventured to do." Here we should recall that Jesus' prayer for Jerusalem, implicit in the lament just cited, was truly answered when—after he had endured death, then risen and returned to glory—thousands in the city came to faith. Sometimes praying without action is as defective as is action without prayer, and our own inaction may be the factor that blocks the blessing we pray for. Let us not forget this as we move on.

If what this chapter has said is right, our practice of intercession may benefit from overhaul. Many pray for people and causes from lists that they compile to jog their memories. That is undoubtedly wise and good, but as life goes on, their lists lengthen so that increasingly they run through names and proposed needs at high speed each time, and the conversational discipline of backing our requests with reasons why God should do this or that is squeezed out. So, too, does the task of asking God what we ourselves might need to do to implement answers to our prayers. That is not good at all. Laying before God specific requests that one has been asked to make or that goodwill has suggested, adding "if it is your will" and then hurrying on, falls short of the intercessory pattern that we meet, for instance, in Abraham's prayer for Sodom (Gen 18:23-33), and Ezra's and Nehemiah's and Daniel's and the psalmist's prayers for Jerusalem (Ezra 9; Neh 1; Dan 9; Ps 74; 79).

Now if we are going to take time to think our way into the situations and personal lives on which our intercessions focus, we may have to limit the number of things we undertake to pray for. But our amplifyings and argumentation will lift our intercessions from the shopping list, prayer-wheel level to the apostolic category of what Paul called "struggle" (Col 2:1-3), and may well enrich our experience of the truth declared by James: "The prayer of a righteous person has great power as it is working" (Jas 5:16). It would seem, therefore, that all of us are likely to benefit from talking over with our heavenly Father from time to time how we should order our personal intercessory prayers.

Here, now, is a true story (name and location not given for obvious reasons) offered by J. I. that illustrates some of what we have been saying: She lived in Eastern Europe and had come to a living faith in Christ. She wanted to go to the United States for Christian theological education. So twice, after prayer and praying each moment, she went to the U.S. embassy to apply for a one-year visa, but each time her request was denied. She went a third time, and now her passport was stamped with a prohibition against applying again. As she turned away from the desk she told the Lord that she accepted this as his will. Suddenly she was recalled, her passport was requested, and without explanation the prohibition was struck out and a one-year student visa stamped in. To this day she does not know why that was done. Her prayer had been answered positively, but in a way that tested both her persistence and her submission to God's will. She serves God joyfully in the United States today.

Yes, God answers prayer, at the best time and in the best way. Never doubt that as you bring your requests to him today.

7

COMPLAINING

I call to God,
and the LORD will save me.
Evening and morning and at noon
I utter my complaint and moan,
and he hears my voice.

PSALM 55:16-17

Complaining is not an activity that we admire or enjoy (unless we are of an unusually cantankerous bent), nor do we think highly of people who are always complaining. To characterize someone as "a complainer" is *not* a compliment; on the contrary, it tags that person as a really pathetic specimen of humanity. What place then is there for complaint in an activity as holy as prayer?

Sometimes, of course, complaints are a form of public service. We rightly complain of something that has gone wrong for the sake of other people who come after us. If a highway intersection is so designed as to invite an accident, which perhaps we ourselves have only narrowly escaped, it is quite right to complain to the highway authority in hope that they will redesign this stretch of road in order to keep more fenders and lives intact.

But what of complaint focused only on self? In general we admire people like Disraeli, that nineteenth-century English prime minister whose constant maxim was "Never complain." We tell ourselves with a small pat on the back, "Well, *I'm* not going to complain." There is, however, a good deal of pride as well as a certain amount of self-pity involved in our contemplating these complaints that we decide not to make. Ancient Stoic philosophers, along with their modern counterparts sometimes found in the military or the Boy Scouts or a suburban kitchen, have taught that keeping a stiff upper lip and declining to complain when things go maddeningly and hurtfully wrong is a sort of virtue and a sign of strength. Maybe so, but it is commonly a mark of conceit and contempt as well. ("I'm not the complaining type—I'm made of stronger stuff than old so-and-so.") Self-focused complaining is a vice, and self-focused noncomplaining is ordinarily a vice as well.

Yet we constantly find in the Bible that when bad things happen to good people, so that they feel totally at the end of their tether, they complain with great freedom and at considerable length to their God. And Scripture does not seem to regard these complaining prayers as anything other than wisdom. Particularly in the psalms we meet the sentiment: Things are out of hand, I'm isolated, I'm helpless, I feel hopeless, I'm hurting. Lord, *do something!* The phrase "How long?" appears in the psalms nearly twenty times. It is almost a technical phrase expressing this kind of complaint. The psalmist is saying in so many words, "Lord, I'm looking to you to do something about a situation that is beyond my control. Lord, how long?" He is asking: How long will I have to wait? How soon will you act?

BIBLICAL COMPLAINING

Biblical prayers of complaint come from a variety of situations. Following betrayal by a close friend, David prayed like this:

> Give ear to my prayer, O God,
>   and hide not yourself from my plea for mercy!
> Attend to me, and answer me;
>   I am restless in my complaint and I moan
> because of the noise of the enemy,

because of the oppression of the wicked. . . .

But it is you, a man, my equal,
   my companion, my familiar friend.
We used to take sweet counsel together;
   within God's house we walked in the throng. . . .

Evening and morning and at noon
   I utter my complaint and moan,
   and [God] hears my voice. (Ps 55:1-3, 13-14, 17)

Now look at Job. He was handed over to Satan for Satan to do to him whatever he liked—up to the point of taking his life, which God told Satan he must not do (Job 1). But God did give Satan permission to take everything else that belonged to Job, and this in effect Satan did. Job, a rich, prosperous, capable man, husband of one wife, father of many children, loses in rapid succession his wealth, his health and his children too. (Perhaps Satan leaves his wife intact because she was more likely to hinder Job than to help him. She, after all, was the one who told him to, "Curse God and die" [Job 2:9].) Job is left feeling that he has lost everything that mattered to him. And so he complains—to God.

If Job could have looked behind the scenes, as we can, and known of the private exchanges between God and Satan, he might have been even more horrified than he was. But that was something he did not know at any stage. All he knew was that, for no reason that he could imagine, the God he served was exposing him to hell on earth. Through the eyes of his book, we watch Job's friends come and sit with him in silence—for a whole week. Finally, Job breaks the silence, and the friends begin to talk. They are full of sympathy for Job, but they can only ring changes on the thought that he is a sinner now provoking God by refusing to admit it: a gratuitous guilt trip for Job that only makes him feel worse. Eventually, Job, spiritually exhausted by the horrific events and goaded by the platitudes his friends offer, begins to pour out torrents of complaint.

I loathe my life; I will give free utterance to my complaint.
  I will speak in the bitterness of my soul.
 I will say to God, Do not condemn me;
   let me know why you contend against me.
Does it seem good to you to oppress,
    to despise the work of your hands
    and favor the designs of the wicked? . . .
Your hands fashioned and made me;
    and now you have destroyed me altogether.
Remember that you have made me like clay;
    and will you return me to the dust? . . .
You clothed me with skin and flesh,
    and knit me together with bones and sinews.
You have granted me life and steadfast love,
    and your care has preserved my spirit. . . .

Why did you bring me out from the womb?
    Would that I had died before any eye had seen me
and were as though I had not been,
    carried from the womb to the grave.
Are not my days few?
    Then cease, and leave me alone, that I may find a little cheer
before I go—and I shall not return—
    to the land of darkness and deep shadow.
        (Job 10:1-3, 8-9, 11-12, 18-19)

Is this the same Job that God described to Satan as "my servant, . . . a blameless and upright man, who fears God and turns away from evil" (Job 1:8). Yes, but this is Job distraught by grief and human pain, goaded to despair by his well-meaning friends, speaking his words of complaint to the safest possible source: God.

Thirteen chapters later, the scene is not much better. Again we hear Job's complaint to God, but this time with a sense of longing and even hope:

Today also my complaint is bitter;
  my hand is heavy on account of my groaning.
Oh, that I knew where I might find him,
  that I might come even to his seat! . . .
Behold, I go forward, but he is not there,
  and backward, but I do not perceive him;
on the left hand when he is working, I do not behold him;
  he turns to the right hand, but I do not see him.
But he knows the way that I take;
  when he has tried me, I shall come out as gold. . . .
But he is unchangeable, and who can turn him back? . . .
For he will complete what he appoints for me.
      (Job 23:2-3, 8-10, 13-14)

Job wonders aloud in prayer, *Why is God doing this to me? God doesn't tell me, but I want to know.* Those who have read the end of Job's book will know that God did indeed meet with Job as Job had invited him to do. But explanations are lacking even then; God does not need to explain. Still, he responded to Job's complaint—and Job was content.

Jeremiah was also a complainer, so much so that readers have long dubbed him "the Weeping Prophet." Jeremiah's long life spanned the optimistic days of godly king Josiah (640-609 B.C.), when boundaries became secure against a declining Assyria and the Hebrew people returned to worshiping the true God in his temple; the foreboding days of Jehoiakim (609-598), when Babylon threatened at Judah's boundaries; the beginning of the Babylonian exile (597 and following); and the decisive deportation in 587 when Zedekiah, the last Jewish king, was carted off to Babylon, blinded and led like an animal in chains (2 Kings 25:6-7). Jeremiah was among the few people left amid the pitiful ruins of Judah after the rest of his nation had been forcefully removed some six hundred miles to the northeast. Eventually Jeremiah himself was forced into Egyptian exile, which is probably where he died.

God had given Jeremiah a tough assignment. While all was well in

Judah under the reign of Josiah, God said to Jeremiah:

> See, I have set you this day over nations and over kingdoms,
> to pluck up and break down,
> to destroy and to overthrow,
> to build and to plant. . . .

> Behold I make you this day a fortified city, an iron pillar, and bronze
> walls, against the whole land, against the kings of Judah, its officials,
> its priests, and the people of the land. They will fight against you. (Jer
> 1:9-10, 18-19)

As God's prophet Jeremiah knew long ahead of time the destruction
that was to come—and that his own people would reject the warnings
that he was assigned to give them. As would most of us in any similar
setting, Jeremiah complained over and over to God. Because of the intimate tone of the various conversations between Jeremiah and God recorded in this long book, we sense that perhaps God expected or even
invited these complaints. For example, in Jeremiah 12, we read:

> Righteous are you, O LORD,
>   when I complain to you;
>   yet I plead my case before you.
> Why does the way of the wicked prosper?
>   Why do all who are treacherous thrive? . . .
> You, O LORD, know me; you see me,
>   and test my heart toward you. (Jer 12:1, 3)

Jeremiah asks the age-old question: Why does a righteous God allow
the bad guys to prosper and the good guys (like himself or ourselves) to
suffer? And God is silent toward Jeremiah—at least on that subject. In
chapter 20, Jeremiah picks up another line of complaint, this time making a verbal assault on God's own relationship with him.

> O LORD, you have deceived me,
>   and I was deceived;

you are stronger than I,
    and you have prevailed.
I have become a laughingstock all the day;
    everyone mocks me.
For whenever I speak, I cry out,
    I shout, "Violence and destruction!"
For the word of the LORD has become for me
    a reproach and derision all day long. (Jer 20:7-8)

Jeremiah complains of his assigned mission as if to say to God, "You've led me into something that you never enabled me to foresee. You've put me in a situation where I wouldn't have gone if I'd been able to resist your pressure, but I couldn't resist it. You forced me into this. And now I've become a joke, every word I speak brings derision. People laugh at me for saying these things." Jeremiah was a godly man, practicing piety in the Old Testament way, doing his God-assigned job as prophet, yet from time to time making explicit complaints to God. And we see no specific rebuke to Job or Jeremiah or the psalmists for complaining. God did tell Job to stand up like a man (meaning not very high) and put his hand over his mouth while God talked to him for four chapters (38—41), but that was to tell him, not that he should not have complained, only that his complaint had reflected his ignorance about God's wisdom. The complaints as such, it seems, were acceptable and were accepted. What are we to make of this?

THE DOWNSIDE OF HIKING

In chapter two of this book, we pictured the Christian life as hiking with the Lord, and this image will help us here. Hiking with the Lord sounds very upbeat, very adventurous, very romantic. From one standpoint the Christian life is like that: it is a richer, more joyful life than any other. But when you go hiking with someone who undertakes to lead you through country where you have never been before, again and again there are downs as well as ups. And you find yourself in places where you feel,

Now if I'd been planning this, I wouldn't have involved myself in what we've got here. For what is it that we have here? Mud, perhaps, or rock or shale or nettle beds or thorns or cactus. Or laurel branches. Let Carolyn speak to this.

Three summers back, while doing youth ministry, I (Carolyn) had an adventure with a highly capable young woman who had lived her entire seventeen years in rural Appalachia. Hannah invited me to hike with her to the bottom of a ravine in the back of their property. I should have noticed the twinkle of challenge in her eye, but I can't think when I have ever refused a hike. So I laced up my hiking books and we struck out. What Hannah had neglected to tell me was that this "hike" had no marked trail, that we would slide on our backs under creeping laurel bushes, where we couldn't see inches ahead, down the steep side of a canyon, that we would traverse a shale wall high above the stream below with only slippery inches of stone as finger grips, and that (as for finger grips) we'd hardly ever see where we were putting our hands. Did she mention that copperhead snakes lived there too? I was finally reduced to saying amid chuckles, "Hannah, if one of us gets snake-bit, I hope it is me and not you. There is no way I can get myself out of here without you!" We did get to the bottom and rested on mossy rocks along a sparkling stream; and we also climbed back out (equally challenging). Once back on top Hannah admitted that I'd done at least as well as the college football player she had once "guided" down there. And at least we had not gotten stuck in the ravine all night as did, on one occasion, her pastor-father, who barely climbed out in time to give his Sunday sermon!

Hiking through life with the Lord at our side is sometimes that kind of challenge. In the New Testament we hear a kind of drumbeat insistence that those who follow the Lord Jesus Christ will certainly be involved in troubles: they will experience downs as well as ups. In preaching, teaching and fellowship discussions, we fellow pilgrims are inclined to stress the joy and the glory of the Christian life, and it is a real delight to share with each other and with unbelievers our testimony to the constant provision we receive from the Lord who loves us. But in the New Testament the emphasis on joy is balanced by a whole series of passages about tribulation, affliction, suffering, even chastisement coming from the same Lord. Thus, as it were, a hike with Jesus means at times scrambling blind-eyed under creeping laurel and clinging to inch-wide rock, not daring to look below.

Here are three examples. First, in Mark 4:35-41 we read that after a long day of teaching near the shore of the Sea of Galilee, Jesus said to his disciples, "Let us go across to the other side." So the disciples got into the boat and pushed out and started rowing, while Jesus, who was exhausted, went to sleep. A storm came up and they woke him and said (screamed probably), "Teacher, do you not care that we are perishing?" Their situation was out of hand; they could no longer control the boat, and it was filling with water. Jesus, we know, stilled the storm, but the point is that they would not have been in that desperate situation if Jesus himself hadn't said, "Let us go across the lake right now." Being a disciple to Jesus will again and again get us into situations of trouble that otherwise we could and would have avoided. We must expect it.

Second, look at the narrative in the book of Acts as it tells Paul's story of how the gospel came to Europe. In Acts 16, we learn that the Holy Spirit has restrained Paul and Silas from missioning in Asia Minor as planned, and so they had stayed on the high road west, which took them to Troas. That night Paul dreamed of a man of Macedonia saying, "Come over and help us"; they interpreted this as a call from God and crossed the Aegean Sea to Philippi, where they started preaching the gospel, and very soon Paul and Silas were in prison with their feet in the stocks. If they had not been following their Lord's leading, they would not have been in Philippi to experience its prison; they wouldn't even have been in Europe. They would have been missioning in Asia Minor, as they originally had intended. We know that they sang hymns and that there was an earthquake, which released them from their chains, and the jailer was converted. So this part of their hike with God ended in jubilation. But up to that point their experience in Europe had been rough. What about those hours when Paul and Silas were sitting in prison? What would have gone through their minds? They must have wondered whether it really was worth it to be the Lord's agents spreading the Word and thereby getting themselves into this kind of trouble. They must have felt like complaining, even though they settled for singing hymns. For us, too, God's service may mean trouble, trouble, trouble all the way. It seems we must expect that.

Finally, in Luke 21, a (deliberately?) enigmatic discourse about the future, Jesus tells his disciples, in a series of traumatic images, what their own future holds.

> They will lay their hands on you and persecute you, delivering you up to the synagogues and prisons, and you will be brought before kings and governors for my name's sake. This will be your opportunity to bear witness. Settle it therefore in your minds not to meditate before-hand how to answer, for I will give you a mouth and wisdom, which none of your adversaries will be able to withstand or contradict. You will be delivered up, even by parents and brothers and relatives and friends, and some of you they will put to death. You will be hated by all for my name's sake. (Lk 21:12-17)

Be realistic, says the Lord Jesus. Trouble is coming for the whole world (vv. 6-11), but especially for you *because* you are my disciples. So Christians too, like Job and Jeremiah, will have something to complain about. We must expect that—and expect to have to pray accordingly.

A century ago E. M. Bounds penned, or quoted, two simple verses, which made coping with all such things sound easy and happy:

> Trials must and will befall;
> But with humble faith to see
> love inscribed upon them all—
> this is happiness to me.

> Trials make the promise sweet,

Trials give new life to prayer;
  Bring me to my Savior's feet,
  Lay me low, and keep me there.[1]

We might dismiss these lines as shallow and superficial, infused with too much nineteenth-century prettiness, but look at the author. E. M. Bounds (1835-1913), best known for his writings on prayer. He gave up a law career to serve as a minister of the gospel. He was an army chaplain in the American Civil War—on the losing side. He was imprisoned in Nashville, then returned to the South to endure the hardships of rebuilding in what had become both a material and a spiritual desolation. Getting to the point of singing his hymn honestly and joyfully, for us as evidently for him, is not at all easy. Lived out, these poetic lines are not necessarily shallow and complacent. Given the harsh turns in most of our lives, it is far from easy to get to the place where we can say these calm words from the heart and then live by them. We New Testament Christians, even without enduring anything like the Civil War, have much to complain about, as did Job and Jeremiah and the psalmists, and with them E. M. Bounds. Realism compels us to face this. It is the grueling part of the hike.

THE CATEGORY OF COMPLAINT

Let us now pull some threads together and summarize and contextualize what we have seen so far. Complaint is a kind of speech that blends lamentation (raging, glooming and despairing over what is bad, frustrating and hurtful) with supplication (begging and pleading that someone will do something about it). Wisely or foolishly, the Northern European-influenced culture that shaped us, and many of our readers with us, has historically embraced the stiff-upper-lip ideal of human behavior, and habitually looks down on people who voice personal complaints in public as morally inferior weaklings. Western Christianity has followed suit,

---

[1]E. M. Bounds, *The Essentials of Prayer* (Grand Rapids: Baker, n.d.), p. 54.

stressing how faith gives strength to quietly endure pain and grief and the frustrations of isolation and desolation, and the many malfunctions of body and mind that come our way.

So it does. But the idea that full humanness involves the habitual stifling of strong emotion so that reason may rule in unbroken calm belongs to the legacy of Platonism in post-Renaissance Western culture rather than to any form of biblical Christianity. Plato thought we must corral and damp down our emotions so that they will not disrupt the smooth working of our minds, and as advice to fallen and disintegrated human beings like ourselves there is much wisdom in that. But Plato regarded the disjunction between the soul's energy of thought and the distracting urges of emotional surges, in other words, between the workings of the mind and of the body, as ultimate. This is not the Christian view, though many, having been reared on it at home, in school and in church, think it is. The Bible indeed teaches self-control, but the Platonic ideal of calm stoical strength should not be thought definitive for the people of God.

Scripture, in which the mind of God, the world's Creator, is made plain, conceives the life of the human individual not as a body-and-soul duality, nor as a mind-and-emotions tug-of-war, but as a unity. Central to that unity is the heart, as we have said, understanding the word to mean the central core of the personal self as the physical heart is the central organ of the physical body. Out of the heart flow the thoughts, desires, motivations, emotions, dreams, attitudes, plans, hopes, reactions, relational outgoings, and everything else that enters into both the conscious and the unconscious or unrecognized aspects of every person's living. The personal self (soul, spirit) is unitary in itself and uses the physical body, via which it lives, to express itself. The human individual could be described as either an embodied soul or an ensouled body. Such is each man and woman in God's world.

Now, the creational ideal was that each individual should be irradiated by the light of God's revelation (his *general* revelation, as most scholars today call it), that this revelation should be recognized for what it is, and that it should evoke a wholehearted commitment—that is, a harnessing and deploying of all a person's powers—to communion—that is, fellowship, interactive togetherness—expressed in responsive worship and thanksgiving and in obedient service of the Creator. So if we say that mankind was made to praise and pray, we will not be wrong. This was the formula for life in the image of God, the pure quality of life that Adam and Eve forfeited and that only ever reappeared in the earthly life of God's incarnate Son. Part of our legacy from Adam is that within the unitary human being, now subject to death and all that that means, the personal self has disintegrated to a degree, so that throughout history intellect and emotion have appeared as Plato saw them, that is, as two distinct energies constantly pulling against each other. But from the moment of our regeneration in Christ, through the implanting of a new, unifying, Godward energy (the new creation of 2 Cor 5:17 and Gal 6:15, the new heart of Ezek 36:26), and through the indwelling of the Holy Spirit to sustain and channel this dual energy, God is at work reintegrating us: putting us back together, that is, as the thinking-and-feeling creatures, praising and praying, that we were always meant to be. Regenerate people feel through their minds and think through their feelings. They are self-aware in a God-conscious and God-centered way that is beyond the understanding of those who do not actually share this life quality.

All this has been said in order now to make the point that complaints such as we have been examining are integral to this new, regenerate life of communion and prayer and fellowship and worship and seeking God's honor and praise. The almost lurid intensity with which psalmists and others describe the sad situations out of which they pray is not just ancient Eastern imaginations going strong, though it is that, but essentially it is the God-centered feeling intellect and the God-centered thoughtful emotion of regenerate hearts contemplating the distance between God's best and the way things have now turned out. We see this on a grand scale in the book of Lamentations, which mourns the fall of

Jerusalem. The complainers in each situation are regenerate children of God (regeneration was an Old Testament fact, though the theology of it was not made known until Christ came) and their complaints are fundamentally prayers for deliverance from evil and for the fulfillment of promises of protection, provision and relational enrichment that God himself gave. The plea embedded in their complaints is that joyful fellowship with God may be restored and present pain become a thing of the past. Feeling with their minds and thinking with their feelings, their emotions of distress are as vivid and intense as are their perceptions of current disaster due to God's nonintervention. In terms of direction and intention, their lament and complaints to God are acts of petition and promise-claiming, in a very strong form.

So complaint will be, or at least should be, a recurring element in the praying of the born again. The presence of complaint prayers in God's prayer book (for that is what the Psalter really is) shows that, so far from being irreverent, prayers of this kind, describing the distress of oneself and others in the freest and most forthright, forceful language imaginable, are entirely in order. Ignoring in our prayers situations that are not "just fine" would by contrast be barren unrealism. For this world is a battleground on which Satan and his hosts strive desperately to obstruct and spoil God's work in every way they can; the book of Revelation reveals that in this war all sorts of bad and destructive things will happen to Christians, churches and the larger human community; thus there will always be things to pray about in complaint terms as part of one's regular petitions. Using cursing psalms as complaint prayers against Satan and his forces might be a good way to begin. Non-Christians may find the idea of Christians taking complaints to their God pathetic, but complaint prayers are among those that we were made and are now redeemed to offer. Telling it like it is and piling on the agony of our feelings about it is not merely *safe,* because of who God is (the hurting of the child engages the Father's helpfulness, not his hostility), nor is it merely a *solace,* because of who we are (for humans always find it a relief, a re-

freshment even, to tell their deepest troubles to someone who sympa-
thizes), it honors God by *submitting* to his ordering of events thus far,
however painful, and it is *sanctifying* in its Christlike honesty and adher-
ence to God's ongoing purpose. What Christ uttered in Gethsemane, after all, was essentially a prayer of complaint.

The remainder of this chapter will look at three areas: the *range* of the
believer's complaining, the *rationale* of the believer's complaining, and
the *response* of God to the believer's complaining.

THE RANGE OF OUR COMPLAINT

What circumstances may rightly prompt a complaint to God? Most of us
are quick to gripe (mentally if not aloud). What constitutes just cause for
complaining prayer? As always, Scripture provides a sure and solid
guide. There we find at least four major circumstances that over and over
elicit prayers of complaint: *opposition, deprivation, isolation* and *depression*. If we page through the Psalter, we find frequent reference to all of
these.

Let us begin with *opposition*. Psalm after psalm speaks about "my enemies," "the people who set themselves against me," by reason of the
writer's life and loyalty in God's service. This kind of opposition to God's
people *because* they were the people of God has been reproduced over
and over in Marxist countries in our era. It remains a reality in Muslim
countries today with particular violence appearing along the boundaries
where Islam and Christianity meet. It would be naive, self-congratulating
and untrue to say that all of Christian-Muslim violence proceeds in only
one direction. Sadly, people from Christian nations also perpetuate religious violence. But "enemies" do sometimes go after a follower of Jesus
just because that person is a Christian believer.

Moreover, Christians in comfortable settings, far from bullets and
bombs, may encounter personal betrayal by someone they trusted. You
thought they would stand by you and thereby sustain you, but no, they
have quietly melted away; they have let you down, and so you are left in

much more painful isolation than ever you anticipated—and it is bitter. This kind of betrayal happens in the workplace, in friendships, in families and even in the church. Psalm 13 illustrates:

> How long, O LORD? Will you forget me forever?
>   How long will you hide your face from me?
> How long must I take counsel in my soul
>   and have sorrow in my heart all the day?
> How long shall my enemy be exalted over me? (Ps 13:1-2)

Psalm 55 pictures this kind of hurt, as if someone were standing high above you on a wall dropping stones on your unprotected head.

> Give ear to my prayer, O God,
>   and hide not yourself from my plea for mercy!
> Attend to me, and answer me;
>   I am restless in my complaint and I moan
> because of the noise of the enemy,
>   because of the oppression of the wicked.
> For they drop trouble upon me,
>   and in anger they bear a grudge against me. (Ps 55:1-3)

Psalm 55 goes on with words quoted earlier in the chapter where David grieves that the person who now taunts him is his former friend. David's "enemy" in this prayer is not a Muslim or a communist, a Canaanite pagan or an Assyrian warrior. This "enemy" is a God follower, a friend, who has gone over to the other side. So David pours out his deep hurt in complaint prayer. Are we faced with betrayal in marriage, alienation from a brother or sister in our church, unfair competition from a work colleague or outright persecution in a Christ-hating environment? If so, David gives us words for our complaining prayer, plus a word of comfort for our aching hearts:

> Cast your burden on the LORD,
>   and he will sustain you;

He will never permit
>   the righteous to be moved. (Ps 55:22)

Deprivation is also a matter for complaint. Job had lost his health, his wealth and his family. Several of the psalmists found themselves physically ill, and they too cried to God about that. Take Psalm 6, for instance.

> O LORD, rebuke me, not in your anger,
>   nor discipline me in your wrath.
> Be gracious to me, O LORD, for I am languishing;
>   heal me, O LORD, for my bones are troubled.
> My soul also is greatly troubled.
>   But you, O LORD—how long?
> Turn, O LORD, deliver my life;
>   save me for the sake of your steadfast love. . . .
>
> I am weary with my moaning;
>   every night I flood my bed with tears;
>   I drench my couch with my weeping.
> My eye wastes away because of grief. (Ps 6:1-4, 6-7)

Psalm 38 is another complaint prayer written by a man who is sick and sad. This time it seems that God himself has deprived David of physical health and spiritual well-being. Here we see the possibility of God using deprivation as a form of discipline and eventually correction, for sin—a divine routine to which we must all be open.

> O LORD, rebuke me not in your anger,
>   nor discipline me in your wrath!
> For your arrows have sunk into me,
>   and your hand has come down on me.
>
> There is no soundness in my flesh
>   because of your indignation;
> there is no health in my bones
>   because of my sin. . . .

My wounds stink and fester
    because of my foolishness,
I am utterly bowed down and prostrate; . . .

For my sides are filled with burning,
    and there is no soundness in my flesh.
I am feeble and crushed. (Ps 38:1-3, 5-8)

The three psalms below are among the many prayers of complaint in the face of *isolation*. In David's Psalm 39, we see that David has chosen to isolate himself from God's enemies, but he also senses that he is isolated from God, as if God is physically beating him one stroke after another. So David complains; he pleads for relief, and in so doing he acknowledges God as the source of all true hope.

I said, "I will guard my ways,
    that I may not sin with my tongue;
I will guard my mouth with a muzzle,
    so long as the wicked are in my presence." . . .

O LORD, make me know my end
    and what is the measure of my days;
    let me know how fleeting I am! . . .

And now, O LORD, for what do I wait?
    My hope is in you. . . .

Remove your stroke from me;
    I am spent by the hostility of your hand.
When you discipline a man
    with rebukes for sin,
you consume like a moth what is dear to him;
    surely all mankind is a mere breath! (Ps 39:1, 4, 7, 10-11)

Other psalms wail about isolation: loss of health, of goods and also of companionship. We see this particularly in two psalms of lament surrounding the ruin of Jerusalem. Here the psalmist Asaph expresses his pain and isolation as he contemplates Jerusalem laid waste. He also acknowledges the part that sin had in triggering these circumstances, and so he prays for (and believes in) God's salvation.

> We do not see our signs;
>   there is no longer any prophet,
>   and there is none among us who knows how long.
> How long, O God, is the foe to scoff? (Ps 74:9-10)

> O God, the nations have come into your inheritance;
>   they have defiled your holy temple;
>   they have laid Jerusalem in ruins.
> They have given the bodies of your servants
>   to the birds of the heavens for food,
>   the flesh of your faithful to the beasts of the earth.
> They have poured out their blood like water
>   all around Jerusalem,
>   and there was no one to bury them. . . .

> Do not remember against us our former iniquities;
>   let your compassion come speedily to meet us,
>   for we are brought very low.
> Help us, O God of our salvation,
>   for the glory of your name;
> deliver us, and atone for our sins,
>   for your name's sake! (Ps 79:1-3, 8-9)

Depression is part of the range of complaint illustrated in Scripture. Depression is our state of self when we feel that the pressure is intolerable and its accompanying physical and mental symptoms shade all of reality. We cannot see any way out, so that any hope we once had is swallowed in despair. Psalm 88 delineates in vivid and poignant language what depression does to the human soul.

> O LORD God of my salvation;
>   I cry out day and night before you. . . .

You have put me in the depths of the pit,
>   in the regions dark and deep.
Your wrath lies heavy upon me,
>   and you overwhelm me with all your waves.

>   *Selah*

You have caused my companions to shun me;
>   you have made me a horror to them. . . .
Every day I call upon you, O LORD.
>   I spread out my hands to you. . . .

I, O LORD, cry to you;
>   in the morning my prayer comes before you. . . .
You have caused my beloved and my friend to shun me;
>   my companions have become darkness. (Ps 88:1, 6-9, 13, 18)

The psalm ends as it begins—in darkness. One translation of its final phrase is "darkness has become my only companion."[2] For those who have battled depression, this prayer has a stark reality that we would rather not remember. But it is *prayer,* an honest prayer of complaint that makes no pretense of prettiness. This is a voicing of the psalmist's present reality, and we would be foolish to turn our back on it and suppose that it will never become ours. The good news is that God invites us to pour out our hearts to him—even from our darkness—and he never lets go of us once we are in his grip.

THE RATIONALE OF OUR COMPLAINTS

Are believers entitled to look to their God to restore the situation that called forth their complaints? Have they any warrant for expecting him to do that? Yes, and yes. The warrant for hope here lies in the filial relationship between us and the Father of our Lord Jesus Christ, who in love has adopted us into his family and become our heavenly Father for time and eternity.

---

[2]See the ESV note on v. 18.

An adoptive parent, such as are both the present writers, is truly a parent and can make a point of telling the child: "You are special to me; I chose you." That in effect is what our God says to each believer, corresponding to what he said to Israel corporately long ago (see Deut 7:6-16). Now, it is the way of parents to care when their children come to them in distress. It is natural for children in a healthy family to run to a parent when they feel swamped and panicky (J. I. remembers his young son running to him because a playmate had produced a knife), and it is natural then for the parent to do something about it. As we learned in the last chapter from the parable of the unjust judge, God's providential plan may involve waiting time for us that we had not envisioned, and Paul's account of his thorn in the flesh showed us that sometimes God's answer to our complaint is to strengthen us to carry on rather than change the situation. But it is guaranteed that the moment will come—whether in this world or, as with the martyrs, in the next—when we are found testifying that we went to our God in our distress, and he delivered us. Because he is a faithful Father, we knew he would, and he did.

GOD'S RESPONSE TO OUR COMPLAINTS

How does God respond to the believer's complaint? Our answer begins by flagging the fact that our heavenly Father shapes everything that happens to us for our nurture. We must never lose sight of this basic New Testament truth. The writer to the Hebrews hammers away at it in chapter 12 of that letter. This unknown author is writing, so it seems, to Jews who have become Christians, whose former friends resent this and are persecuting them in one way and another (see Heb 10:32-34) in the hope of breaking their spirit and bringing them back to the synagogue. Now in chapter 12 the writer says, "Have you forgotten the exhortation that addresses you as sons?" Then comes a saying from their Jewish wisdom literature as phrased in Proverbs 3:11-12: "My son, do not regard lightly the discipline of the LORD, / nor be weary when reproved by him. / For the LORD disciplines the one he loves, / and he chastises every son whom he receives." "My son?" This term includes, of course, men and women, sons and daughters together; it is the inclusive masculine, as grammarians say. "It is for discipline that you have to endure," explains the writer. "God is treating you as sons. For what son is there whom his father does not discipline?" (Heb 12:7-8). The purpose of this discipline is our holiness (v. 10), that is God's work of remaking us in character and attitude so that we bear the moral and spiritual image of Jesus our Savior. Suffering—meaning strain and pain, physical, mental and spiritual—is part of God's universal nurturing discipline, and his usual answer to complaint prayers about it is not to remove it but to teach us how to handle it. So now, within that frame of reference, let us look at two basic ways in which God responds to our prayers of complaint—and be encouraged.

First, observe how God *sustains* us in our weakness and keeps us going despite our pain. The classic New Testament passage on this is Paul's account in 2 Corinthians 12 of how the Lord Jesus responded to his complaint about his thorn.

We have referred to this before, but now is the time to look at it more fully. "To keep me from being too elated by the surpassing greatness of the revelations, a thorn was given me in the flesh" (2 Cor 12:7). Paul would not have said "in the flesh" if it had not been physical, and he would not have said "a thorn" if it had not been painful. It was then a painful physical condition of some kind. Paul describes it as "a messenger of Satan to harass me" (v. 7). What does that mean? It means that God has allowed Satan to inflict it, just as he once allowed Satan to inflict distress on Job. And now Satan encourages brooding on the pain in order to arouse in Paul's heart negative and self-pitying notions about the apparent lack of goodness and wisdom in his heavenly Father and the likely diminution of his ministry if the thorn remained. Satan's message at this point was a huge depressant, for, as Paul showed very fully in the second part of chapter 11, his ministry was very much his life. What to do? Well, Paul knew that Jesus was the great healer, and he had been used himself as Jesus' agent in healing, as the book of Acts records (see Acts 14:3, 8-10; 19:11-12). So now Paul asks the Lord Jesus to heal *him:* a perfectly appropriate thing for him to do. Paul says:

> Three times I pleaded with the Lord about this, that it should leave me. But he said to me, "My grace is sufficient for you, for my power is made perfect in weakness." Therefore, I will boast all the more gladly of my weaknesses, so that the power of Christ may rest upon me. For the sake of Christ, then, I am content with weaknesses, insults, hardships, persecutions and calamities, for when I am weak then I am strong. (2 Cor 12:8-10)

In other words, Jesus Christ, speaking from the throne, said to him, "No, Paul, I'm not going to heal your thorn in the flesh. But my grace is going to keep your ministry going, even though your thorn remains. For your life will become a large-scale demonstration that my power, which sustains your ministry, is made perfect in your human weakness." Thus the Lord Jesus dealt with Paul's complaint.

Paul could then truthfully say, "When I am weak, then I am strong." This is his testimony! The Lord was keeping him going, despite disability. And so it was to the end of Paul's ministry; you never hear about the thorn in the flesh again. Paul lived with it, lived with the ongoing pain, but he did not complain further about it. The story of his thorn (whatever it was) is a wonderful demonstration that the Lord does sustain us and keep us going in our weakness, even when we feel that we are under pressure that must make us crumple.

Second, observe what God shows us in his wisdom, to keep us *trusting* despite the circumstances. Look for this in the last chapter of the book of Job. Job, goaded by his friends, has said all kinds of wild things in his distress, coming back again and again to the thought that he wishes he could talk face to face with God and make sure that God at least understood his complaint. Job has never been told that it was God demonstrating to Satan that Job would honor him by faithfulness, in spite of what Satan might do. We know that; Job doesn't.

Now, however, comes Job 38:1 where we read, "Then the LORD answered Job"—yes, *answered* him in the sense of responding to him regarding the things Job had been speaking (praying, complaining) about. But "the LORD answered Job out of the whirlwind"—an emblem of his immeasurable and inscrutable power—and his answer was not the explanation Job had cried out for. The Lord said: "Who is this that darkens counsel by words without knowledge? Dress for action like a man; / I will question you, and you make it known to me. / Where were you when I laid the foundation of the earth?" God then batters Job with a series of questions making the point that God knows what he is doing throughout his world in relation to all that happens. All events, circumstances and realities are under God's control and always have been. God asks Job over and over: What do you know about all of this? Are you able to measure my wisdom in managing creation? And, within the created order, the animal kingdom in particular? Do you know when the mountain goats give birth? Do you control the wild donkey? The ostrich? The horse? The hawk? Behemoth (probably the hippopotamus)? Leviathan (probably the crocodile)? And so it goes on for four chapters (38—41) with a total of some four dozen questions, all rubbing in God's point.

What God is saying to Job essentially is, "Look, you see how much wisdom I have at my command when it comes to creating and managing my world. You see some of the wonderful creatures that I have made. You couldn't handle them, but I can and I do. Every action of theirs is under my control. Now, if I govern the natural order in my providence in this way, can't you believe that the same wisdom is operating in your case? Can't you believe that I know what I'm doing when I expose you to what you have been through?" That is God's counter-question to Job about the questions Job has been raising. And Job has an answer to it, which is a great answer, all the greater for its brevity. "Behold, I am of small account; what shall I answer you? / I lay my hand on my mouth" (Job 40:4). Job's hand on his mouth is a wordless gesture of humility. Job will not say any more; rightly, he feels small, for compared with God, so he is.

Let us be clear: it can be spiritually healthy to feel small, as the bigness and complexity of things that God has created sometimes makes us do, and deliberately to fill our mind with thoughts of the greatness of God's wisdom, power, and love. Have you ever stood on the edge of the Grand Canyon? It is impossible to do so without a powerful rearrangement of your sense of size. In that awesome setting, you simply feel tiny. That feeling is a this-world counterpart of what God is teaching Job as he takes him to the zoo (so to speak) and talks to him about the wonders of the world's animals and birds, all of which he himself invented and controls. Small—the sense of being in every way limited—is healthy in the presence of God. It seems clear that when Job realized that and turned back from agonizing self-dramatizing to simple, humble, patient trust in his God through thick and thin, he found peace.

And so we live, passing through life's ups and downs. Nobody's Christian existence is wine and roses all the way. Some of us experience horrible losses, even bordering on the losses of Job: belongings lost, health lost, human respectability lost, friends lost and (perhaps most painful) spouse and/or children lost. These losses are not beyond the bounds of possibility for any of us and are actuality for some of us. At such times the only strategy is to pray out our complaints to God, following the Scripture models. But through divine blessings, even as we complain, we will realize our own smallness before almighty God, creator and ruler of the universe, and our own lack of understanding compared with his own omniscient and benevolent wisdom. And so our complaint prayers are not mere self-centered whining that life has not treated us right. Instead, our complaints are those of dependent children, running in fear and in hurt to our almighty Father, who rules all things. God, if he chooses, will relieve our pain. And if, for nurture's sake, he chooses not to do so, even then we are to snuggle and nestle into his arms, knowing that Father God loves us, hears our complaints and will love us now and forever.

Two stanzas, the first and the last, from one of John Newton's homespun hymns thus say all that finally needs saying:

> Be gone, unbelief! My Savior is near,
> And for my relief will surely appear.
> By faith let me wrestle, and he will perform;
> With Christ in the vessel I smile at the storm.
>
> Since all that I meet will turn to my good,
> The bitter is sweet, the medicine food;
> Though painful at present, 'twill cease before long,
> And then, O how pleasant the conqueror's song!

One last thought, as a postscript to the truth that Newton tells. C. S. Lewis's last novel is titled *Till We Have Faces*. Many (including himself) have regarded it as his best, though the very subtlety and skill of the storytelling makes it an elusive piece of reading (you have been warned!). In the long first part, the ugly queen of a pre-Christian pagan kingdom writes her life story as a complaint against the gods.

> I will accuse the gods, especially the god who lives on the Grey Mountain. That is, I will tell all he has done to me from the very beginning, as if I were making my complaint of him before a judge.

Secure in what later will appear as self-centered and self-righteous self-ignorance, she tells how this god robbed her of her beautiful sister, and what came after. Then in the brief second part, she tells of a visionary experience through which she began to see how unsuspected possessiveness had corrupted her love for her sister and for another person too, and to realize how much real unreality there had been in her life thus far. Her cherished feeling of injured innocence dissolves away.

> I saw well why the gods do not speak to us openly, nor let us answer.
> . . . How can they meet us face to face till we have faces?

The true self-knowledge, indeed the real selfhood, that is needed for true, close fellowship with God (so Lewis is indicating) in many cases only comes through the experiences of pain, loss, grief and hurting that initially move us to complain.

> I ended my first book with the words *no answer.* I know now, Lord, why you utter no answer. You are yourself the answer. Before your face questions die away.[3]

The last page of *Till We Have Faces* tells us that the queen was found dead, with the final sentence of her manuscript unfinished. Already, so the wording intimates, she is facing death with equanimity. She now has her face; she is ready to meet her god. (An equivalent Christian story would, of course, spell "god" with a capital *G.*)

Lewis's understanding of how the God who rarely explains himself to us yet works to turn believers into increasingly real persons is, we think, the proper footnote to Newton's simple spiritual song of peace and hope. Beyond the darkness of our complaints light will shine on us at last. As the children's chorus prompts us to put it, we will count our blessings, name them one by one, and it will surprise us what the Lord has done.

---

[3]C. S. Lewis, *Till We Have Faces: A Myth Retold* (London: Geoffrey Bles, 1956), pp. 11, 305, 319.

HANGING ON

I wait for the LORD, my soul waits,
and in his word I hope;
my soul waits for the Lord
more than watchmen for the morning,
more than watchmen for the morning.

PSALM 130:5-6

The phrase "hanging on" makes me (J. I.) think of the time many years ago when my wife Kit and I were taking a little-used path to see a waterfall. The path had not been well-maintained. Kit did not have any problem with it because she has always been very agile; she is like a mountain goat on unstable terrain. I am different. I was always clumsy, and besides I have a high center of gravity; at least, those are the excuses I give for losing my balance more quickly than some. The path became a badly cambered slope, tilting sideways on the right side toward a steep bank down into a stream. To steady myself, I put one hand up and gripped a small branch of a tree that overhung the path. Then my foot slipped! As I began to descend streamward rather ungracefully on my backside, Kit yelled, "Hang on!" She meant, I suppose that I should hang on to the branch because it would arrest my descent. But, alas, the branch had broken. Nevertheless, when my wife yells for me to do something, I ordinarily do it, so as I slipped ever more awkwardly down the bank, I held on firmly the entire time to this bit of broken branch. I'm glad to say that I didn't end up in the stream; a tree root stopped me a little distance down the bank, and I scrabbled back to the path. I remember the laughter on Kit's face as I held up my tiny twig of supposed safety. But I had indeed hung on.

The opposite of hanging on is letting go, which in terms of attitude means "giving up." It is said, whether truly or not, that right at the end of his life Winston Churchill was asked to speak at a "Prize Day" at his old school. When the moment came, he toddled up to the microphone and simply said (this was the beginning and also the end of his speech) "Never, never, never, never, never give up." Then he sat down. Very Churchillian, even if it never happened! It chimes in with a cartoon hanging on the corkboard in J. I.'s college office. Pictured is a pelican that has in its great beak the head of a frog. But the rest of the frog is outside of the beak, in fact the frog's front legs are splayed wide gripping and squeezing the pelican's narrow neck. The legend that goes with the picture is a version of the same formula that Churchill is alleged to have used: "Never, never, never give up."

When J. I. was a student, the president of the InterVarsity chapter that was nurturing him had a phrase that he constantly used for encouragement: "Keep on keeping on." The phrase called for what in Britain was termed "stickability," for which the North American's equivalent is "stick-to-itiveness." Spiritual stick-to-itiveness in the face of discouragements of all sorts was what this chapter president was asking for when he used those words. Hanging on, as J. I. hung on to his little branch, is a phrase that means the same thing.

Hanging on to God in praying is often hard. Life is full of forces that tug us away from prayer. Disappointment in some project in which we have invested much of ourselves will take the wind right out of our sails, so that we now find it hard to pray, especially if we had prayed much for God's blessing on the project when it started. Health troubles can make us feel that the effort to keep on praying is too much for us and so we stop. Broken relationships and breakdowns in the family exhaust our souls, creating a sense of discouragement that makes us feel that prayer simply does not work, and that if God has let us down in this all-important matter, why should we pray about anything at all. Clinical depression can become a blight on prayer: our body chemistry combines with circumstances to color our whole world gray and make everything seem hopeless—including our efforts at praying. Hanging on in prayer during such circumstances is the specific problem area that the present chapter addresses.

My (Carolyn) friend Maggie for many years served as a confidant to a mutual friend who suffered from depression—and for reasons that none of us could fix. Our depressed friend often found it difficult to pray or even to believe in a loving God. Maggie prayed with her from time to time, encouraging her to sit in silence save for adding a simple amen to prayers on her behalf. One day Maggie gave her a "pocket rock," carefully chosen from her garden for its smooth shape, subtle colors and perfect size. "Keep this rock in your pocket," Maggie told her friend. "When you can't believe, when you can't pray, hold onto this rock. It is a reminder that God is your rock, and that (for now) I am believing for you." I am glad to say that our friend survived those difficult years and continues today as a woman faithful in prayer—often now on behalf of others. For someone clinically depressed, praying alone may simply be impossible—temporarily anyway. Hanging on to God in prayer may mean for such a person praying with others for a time, listening in to their prayers, trusting their faith, until God through the mercy of medicine, counseling and shifted circumstances brings healing.

Hanging on in prayer is often, then, difficult for us. But deciding not to pray because of lost projects, lost health, lost relationships, lost family or lost peace of mind is not at all a rational decision. Patience and persistence and perseverance in praying are real Christian virtues that we are sometimes required to work hard to maintain. Much of this effort is inner and hidden, like hand-carved gargoyles under the roofline of some Gothic cathedral, never seen by anyone but God. But prayer is truly the inside story of the Christian's life, and keeping it going is therefore very important. Earlier in this book we made quite a point of saying that "Help" is regularly the best prayer we can make (see pp. 53). To ask the Lord to help us to keep going (to hang on) in fellowship with him, in spite of every circumstance that discourages us, is always an excellent prayer.

How does God help us to be persistent in praying? By leading our minds to dwell on four things: (1) the *relationship* that calls for and undergirds persistent praying, (2) the *records* of persistent praying in Scripture, (3) the *reasons* why persistent praying becomes necessary, and (4) (conversely) the *resistance* to persistent praying that we have to overcome.

This kind of help works like a spiral tunnel on the railroad. (There are a number in Switzerland, and a famous one on the Canadian Pacific line through the Rockies.) The train enters by the bottom portal, gains height by spiraling up within the mountain, and exits above, sometimes directly above, where it went in. When you look down, therefore, you may see the entry point right below you, and in any case, being higher up, you will see more as you look around than you could see before. In the same way, dwelling on the four realities we will review may, with God's blessing, enlarge our vision of God and his ways (for, when we are under strain or living with depression, our vision of God easily grows narrow and cramped), and thus hope, strength, and resolve will be brought back into the heart. All truth enters the heart via the head, that is, the understanding, said the Puritans, following Thomas Aquinas. That statement is just as true when we are in low spirits as it is at other times, when we are in a calmer and more cheerful state of mind. May God help us all toward enlarged vision and firmer determination in our praying as we tunnel our way (excuse our whimsy!) through the thoughts we are now to deploy.

RELATIONSHIP

Earlier on, we looked at two of Jesus' parables that must have had his disciples scratching their heads. In one, a friend comes knocking on the door at midnight in order to borrow some bread and is at first roundly rebuffed, though he gets the bread in the end through what we would call sheer cheek. In the other an unjust judge gives in, cynically and resentfully, to the persistent visits of a widow (the widow is a regular biblical figure for the underprivileged person). "This widow troubles me," he said, "so I'll give her what she wants in order to get rid of her." Did Jesus tell these stories to give us an image of God our heavenly Father as a reluctant donor of things we badly need? No! Jesus showed in many other settings that God the Father is loving and generous and righteous and faithful and *wants* to give good gifts to his children. But Jesus told these stories to encourage us "always to pray and not to lose heart," which is exactly how Luke introduces the story of the unjust judge (Lk 18:1), to make sure it will not be misunderstood. Persistent, insistent petitioning, according to our Lord Jesus, is most certainly appropriate when the pressure is on. But why is this if God is truly our loving heavenly Father and truly wants to give us good gifts?

Here is a question that is not always well answered. It is not, as some seem to suppose, that passionate petition twists God's arm, so to speak, and thereby coaxes out of him what he had not originally wished to give. Nor is it that passionate petition, working itself up to an inner certainty that the gift requested will be given, induces God to give what he would not have given had it been asked for in a more low-key style. "One parable illustrates one point" is the usual rule in Jesus' teaching, and the one point of the stories just referred to is that we should pray insistently and persistently about crucial needs, not *because* God will not meet them unless we do but *as if* he would not. Why does Jesus teach us, and therefore clearly want us, to do this? Four reasons, at least, may be given.

First, God the Father loves to be petitioned in a way that shows he is appreciated as the source of all that is good. This glorifies him.

Second, the Father wants to see that we are taking both our acuteness of need and his greatness as the one who can meet it with absolute seriousness. This takes us beyond superficiality in the way we think, feel and live, and binds us closer to him because of the clarity with which we realize that he is really our only hope.

Third, the Father knows that the more earnestly we have asked for a particular gift and the longer we have waited for it, the more we will value it when it is given, and the more wholeheartedly we will thank him for it. This will lead to increased joy.

Fourth, the Father's larger plans for blessing us and others may require him to delay giving us what we ask for until the best time and circumstances for its bestowal are reached. To keep asking with patient persistence and to wait with expectation for the answer is thus sometimes necessary, and is always the reverent way to go. This strengthens the muscles of our faith, as constant walking strengthens the muscles of heart and legs.

The fact to focus on for encouragement, however, when we seek to express the persistence of our faith in the prayers we go on making as we face short-term disappointment and desolation, is that there is a covenanted family bond that unites us to God the Father, God the Son and God the Holy Spirit, and unites the Three-in-One to us forever and ever. Paul describes universal Christian experience when he writes: "The Spirit himself bears witness with our spirit that we are children of God, and if children then heirs—heirs of God and fellow heirs with Christ" (Rom 8:16-17). Professed Christians who neither testify to this testimony nor rejoice in the identity that it confirms are, to say the least, very much out of sorts. Being children of God is our supreme privilege and security—and is at all times the supreme incentive to us to pray.

The Christian's sonship to God the Father is both by adoption, which bestows the family status, and by regeneration, which is the work of the Holy Spirit renewing the heart and thereby bestowing in embryo the family likeness. Adoptive sonship in Paul's world was regularly a wealthy childless citizen's choice of someone to be his heir and carry the family name into the future, and that is the analogy that God through Paul uses here. In contrast, regeneration of heart has no secular analogy: it is a creative change effected in union with Christ, instilling in us a God-centered, God-exalting cast of mind that is inexplicable in terms of anything that was there before, just as the source and destination of the wind are more than any observer can know (Jn 3:8). Regeneration is an outgoing of the same power that brought this world into being (through a big bang?) when previously there was nothing there at all (nothing to go bang, therefore)—absolutely nothing in existence besides God. The twin blessings of adoption and regeneration, while not shielding us from any of life's grimmer experiences, do turn us into unique people with unique privileges and a unique destiny, and when the bad experiences come it is vital that we do not forget who and what we are.

Luther is reported to have said that religion is a matter of personal pronouns, and indeed it is. Marriage illustrates this, for marriage is a covenantal bond by virtue of which the parties can say "*my* husband" and "*my* wife." Childhood illustrates it too: the child's sense of identity grows directly out of being able to say "*my* dad, *my* mom." So also God's covenant with us enables us to say "*my* God," and the covenantal reality of our adoption enables us to say "*my* Father." By the same token, each of us may speak of the Lord Jesus, in whom we put our faith, not only as, in Thomas's words, "*My* Lord and *my* God" (Jn 20:28)—though that is where our faith must start—but also as "*my* brother"—older brother, as reverence moves us to say—for, wonder of wonders, he calls us all his brothers. "Go to my brothers [the whole band of disciples]," said the risen Lord to Mary Magdalene (Jn 20:17), and Hebrews 2:11-12 says, "He is not ashamed to call them [believers] brothers, saying, 'I will tell of your name to my brothers' " (the quote is from Psalm 22:22). ("Brothers" in these texts is the generic masculine; "brothers and sisters" explicates the meaning.) To realize that we are in solidarity with Jesus as siblings, if we may so put it, in the Father's family is a huge support in times of inner distress and the self-belittling thoughts that depression and harsh circumstances bring on, and that is why we highlight the matter here.

The Holy Spirit ministers as the agent of the Father and the Son, so in light of what has been said it should be no surprise to us to read: "You [believers] have received the Spirit of adoption as sons, by whom we cry, 'Abba! Father!'" (Rom 8:15)—that is, who has imparted and now sustains our filial instinct for affirming and addressing the Father of our Lord Jesus as our Father too. Nor should it surprise us to find Paul stating the gospel like this: "When the fullness of the time had come, God sent forth his Son, born of woman, born under the law, to redeem those who were under the law, so that we might receive adoption as sons. And because you are sons, God has sent the Spirit of his Son into our hearts crying, 'Abba! Father!' " (Gal 4:4-6). So Paul teaches us to be aware that the Spirit of God is prompting us to cry for ourselves in certainty and confidence, "*My* Father, *my* God." That is the privilege of Christ's people.

Constantly in the Gospels the Lord Jesus presents the Christian life as, to borrow a phrase, "life with Father." In Matthew 6, the central chapter of the Sermon on the Mount, where Jesus shows his disciples how to pray and give, and where he speaks of amassing eternal treasures, and where he tells them not to be anxious about daily needs, God is "your heavenly Father" throughout. The same is true in much of chapter 7, where he warns them against censorious judgment of their brothers and encourages them to pray expectantly for what they need. Each teaching is grounded on their relationship with God as their loving, listening, providing, righteous, powerful, generous Father. Throughout this sermon God's Fatherhood is seen as yielding a basic moral structure for Christian living.

The business of a father is to protect and look after his children, as well as to nurture them in the way in which he wants them to go when they are grown. Within that frame of the covenanted family relationship between us believers and our God, we see in Scripture his promises to answer prayer, promises that remain permanently valid, for God is always faithful to his own word. Feelings have their ups and their downs, but whether the sun is shining or whether the clouds are down and the rain is falling, the promises of God still stand. We touched on them in previous chapters, and here we simply underline the certainty of their fulfillment when duly invoked. In the Sermon on the Mount, Jesus says, "Ask, and it will be given you; seek, and you will find; knock, and it will be opened to you" (Mt 7:7). He is talking about persistent praying. All three verbs in the Greek are in the present tense, which express continuous action, keeping on keeping on doing what we do. Jesus says, "Keep asking, keep seeking, keep knocking." Then he gives the reason why: "For everyone who asks receives, and the one who seeks finds, and to the one who knocks it will be opened" (Mt 7:8). Amazing! But that is what Jesus says, and all his words are true.

So according to Jesus, there is no such thing as unanswered prayer when a faithful child of God brings requests to his or her heavenly Father. The prayer will be taken notice of. As we have seen, it may not be answered in the form in which we offer it. It may be answered by God making us aware that there are things in our life that have got to be changed before he can give us what we have asked for. It may be that he will answer our prayer in a way which makes us realize that we were not asking for precisely the right thing in the first place. So God answers the prayer we *ought* to have made rather than the prayer we *did* make. But that is not unanswered prayer.

Jesus must have known that his disciples drew a breath when he spoke the promise "Everyone who asks receives, and the one who seeks finds, and to the one who knocks it will be opened." It sounds too good to be true. So he adds, in order to make sure that they take his point, "Which one of you, if his son asks him for bread, will give him a stone? Or if he asks for a fish, will give him a serpent? If you then, who are evil, know how to give good gifts to your children, how much more will your Father who is in heaven give good things to those who ask him!" (Mt 7:9-11). This line of thought is a tremendous incentive to bold and persistent prayer.

The promises of God, made as an expression of his family-covenant relationship with his people, give us incentives and directives that encourage us to pray persistently, hanging on to the words that our God has spoken, never mind how discouraging the immediate circumstances and how exhausted our inner feelings. Given the encouragements that are ours within our relationship with the Lord, we cannot wonder that the apostle Paul should direct us to "pray without ceasing" (1 Thess 5:17). Exactly! That is what we must learn to do.

RECORDS THAT ENCOURAGE

We can take records of persistent praying in the Bible as object lessons for us, and so we look here at two categories of these object lessons. One is persistent praying in the Psalms; the other is examples of persistent praying by three of God's servants: Nehemiah, Hannah and Zechariah.

God gave us the 150 psalms of the Psalter to be our prayer book as well as our hymn book. They establish perspectives and lines of vision and patterns of communion between ourselves and the Lord that all our praying, praising, hymnology and liturgy ought to follow as a guide. The psalms have a technical term for persistent praying, usually translated "Wait." We wait *on* or wait *for* the Lord. In ordinary secular use waiting sounds like inactivity, but in the psalms waiting on and for the Lord is just the opposite of inactivity; it is a sustained effort of keeping on keeping on in prayer and expectation. It involves focusing on the Lord, attending to the Lord, asking the Lord to help us to hang on until the time for his action comes. "Wait for the LORD; / be strong, and let your heart take courage; / wait for the LORD!" (Ps 27:14). Dogs in training must learn to stand motionless, unmoving and unmovable when the owner or trainer says "Stay." One wonders if Eugene Peterson had this in mind when, in *The Message,* he paraphrased "Wait for the LORD" in that verse as, "Stay with GOD."

"Be still before the LORD and wait patiently for him; / fret not yourself. . . . / Wait for the LORD and keep his way, / and he will exalt you to inherit the land," says David in Psalm 37:7, 34. Here *The Message* says, "Quiet down before GOD . . ." (no panicking, no diminishing of desire for God to show his hand), but "wait passionately for GOD." These words go far to describe the resolute hanging on that persistent prayer becomes.

Psalm 40, also from David, is a testimony of God's response to this kind of praying:

> I waited patiently for the LORD;
>> he inclined to me and heard my cry.
> He drew me up from the pit of destruction,
>> out of the miry bog,
> and set my feet upon a rock,
>> making my steps secure." (Ps 40:1-2).

That opening phrase in *The Message* is "I waited and waited and waited for GOD." The Hebrew expression thus rendered is, literally, "Waiting, I waited." "I waited patiently" is one attempt to capture the thought that "I kept on waiting until . . . and then at last God moved."

Psalm 62, another psalm from David, is striking in that it adds the ingredient of silence to this hanging on in prayer. In verse 1 we read the following, "For God alone my soul waits in silence; from him comes my salvation." The term "in silence" expresses the thought of having got beyond complaining, and no longer rushing to and fro making a noise as people in trouble tend to do. "I am waiting in silence; I know that God has heard my prayer. I am waiting now for him to rescue me." In verse 5, David admonishes himself: "For God alone, O my soul, wait in silence." He reminds himself that "my hope is from [God]." *The Message,* in both verses, gives us a broken sentence, "God, the One and Only—I'll wait as long as he says." How succinct! How directly to the point of hanging on in quiet prayer—for however long it takes. Here, as in the other psalms quoted, we find an encouraging example for imitation.

One of the songs of ascents depicts most vividly the longing and the hope that goes with this kind of waiting prayer. As pilgrims ascended on their long-wearing trek to their thrice-annual worship in the temple at

Jerusalem, they sang these psalms to express their hopes. Psalm 130 pictures the patience of a night watchman assigned to guard the walls of a city, perhaps Jerusalem itself. He works every night, no doubt slowly pacing atop the wall, watching for signs of movement in the darkness below, guarding, listening, doing his job. But he knows that every night his task is completed when sunlight creeps into the eastern sky. The sun has made this appearance after every night of his life. It has signaled the end of his shift; he will go home to rest. His hope in God is as well-founded as is the predictability of dawn. Dawn *always* comes. So as the pilgrims climbed on their journey, right up to Jerusalem's guarded walls, they reminded themselves, through prayer, of their hope in God.

> I wait for the LORD, my soul waits,
>   and in his word I hope;
> my soul waits for the Lord
>   more than watchmen for the morning,
>   more than watchmen for the morning. (Ps 130:5-6)

The repeated last line with its footstep-type rhythm signals, even to our ears, the faithful plodding of the watchman on his rounds—in hope, as he watches for dawn. And so we hang on to God in hopeful prayer, as watchmen wait for the morning, as watchmen wait for the morning.

Now we turn to two biblical stories of persistent praying, one about a man, the other about a woman. Here first is Nehemiah, whose book is a public figure's personal memoir, like a politician's autobiography today. We have met Nehemiah before, in passing; now we must focus in detail on the first stage of his recorded testimony. The book starts with a date, then records a prayer, then gives another date. "It happened in the month Chislev, in the twentieth year, as I was in Susa the capital, that Hanani . . . came with certain men from Judah" (Neh 1:1-2). These men brought bad news: the walls of Jerusalem, those walls that watchmen had once guarded so carefully were flattened; even the gates in the walls had been burned. Hostile forces occupied the surrounding territory, and the few Hebrews remaining within the circle of crumbled walls were in "great trouble and shame" (v. 3).

Burdened by this news, Nehemiah fasts and prays for the restoration of Israel in Jerusalem, and he works up to praying thus: "Oh, Lord, let your ear be attentive to the prayer of your servant, and to the prayer of your servants who delight to fear your name." (From his sidelong reference we can see that Nehemiah has not been praying alone; he has enlisted others who have been praying with him about the need in Jerusalem.) Here is the final request of his prayer: "And give success to your servant today, and grant him mercy in the sight of this man" (Neh 1:11).

Who is "this man"? In the last words of the chapter we find that it is King Artaxerxes, monarch of Persia. What is the mercy that Nehemiah asks for? His friends from Jerusalem, and others too perhaps, must have told him, and he must have agreed with them, that if he were put in charge in Jerusalem he had what it would take to put everything right there. But Nehemiah is not free to go. His position is that of a high-class slave. "Now I was cupbearer to the king" (v. 11), he says. This means that every day, seven days a week, 365 days a year, he has to be at the palace to taste in advance the food and drink being prepared for the banquet that evening, at which he will keep an eye on all aspects of the food service and personally hand the king the royal goblet. It was high-risk employment, because in those days political opponents would on occasion poison the royal food and drink in order to get rid of the monarch. The cupbearer's ministry was primarily to detect any poison; this he would do by getting sick and maybe dying in the king's place. If that happened, the king could of course easily get another cupbearer the next day. High-risk employment, indeed! No wonder slaves or aliens were usually selected for it. But that was Nehemiah's job. Actually, it was a position of great dignity while it lasted, for it gave constant intimacy with the king. Cupbearers often became influential people in ancient palaces, and we may suppose that this very able man Nehemiah was one such already. But at the same time this was a job that tied him down. Royal retainers had no statutory holidays, and in any case there could be no time off for the cupbearer. The king ate and drank every day! So when Nehemiah says, "I was cupbearer to the king," it was an indication of impossible circumstances. Going to Jerusalem for long enough to repair and resettle its ruins seemed to be ruled out from the start. Nonetheless Nehemiah and his friends give themselves to prayer that somehow or other Nehemiah will be enabled to go to Jerusalem and do the job.

In the opening verse of chapter 2 we find another date: the month of Nisan in the twentieth year of King Artaxerxes. Nehemiah then tells us exactly how in that month, in an amazing way, he was appointed on the spot as the king's special commissioner (soon it was governor, and it may have been that from the start) to go to Jerusalem to rebuild it. How far apart were these dates? Nine months. Each day, one supposes, the group had prayed, "Give success to Nehemiah *today;* grant him mercy in the sight of the king"; and they had had to wait. Persistent waiting—what we have called hanging on to God—had marked their praying, just as it should mark ours when the needs will not go away; and God answered their prayer at the right time, as he always does. So at last Nehemiah was off on the most challenging task of his life, in which, as we know, with God's constant help, he succeeded brilliantly.

Hannah too was a person willing to hang on in prayer. In the first chapter of 1 Samuel we hear about Hannah praying for a child, and it is clear that she has been praying for a long time. Hannah and her husband, Elkanah, and his other wife (along with the other wife's children) travel every year to Shiloh, where the ark is, to make their annual sacrifices. Hannah is mocked by her rival wife, comforted by her husband with extra food (which she refuses to eat) and remains brokenhearted that the Lord "had closed her womb" (v. 5). Elkanah, a warm-hearted, unimaginative man, cannot empathize with her ongoing distress. ("Am I not more to you than ten sons?" [v. 8].) Still she prays that she may have a baby. Her prayers are so intense that she sways back and forth, putting her whole body into her praying; her prayers are so private that she says them only in her mind, though her voiceless lips keep moving; the family circumstances are so painful that she weeps as she prays. She promises that if God gives her a son, he will be a special servant of God all of his life (v. 11).

Eli the priest, taking it easy, leaning in his chair against the doorpost, was evidently not accustomed to such prolonged and intense praying, particularly by a woman. He thinks she is drunk—and says so (v. 13). Most women in Hannah's distress about this embarrassing problem of infertility would have simply slunk away and let him think what he wanted, but Hannah did not do that. She recalls him to his priestly duties, duties that events surrounding Hannah's part in the story suggest that old Eli has been sadly neglecting. Hannah tells Eli exactly what is wrong. "I have been pouring out my soul before the LORD" (v. 15). Eli has seen this woman come to the temple year after year; now he knows the source of her grief and the subject of her prayers. Through Hannah, Eli rises to his calling as priest and pronounces a blessing prayer—which God honors: "Go in peace, and the God of Israel grant your petition that you have made to him" (v. 17).

Four years later, Hannah presents young Samuel, now age two or three, to Eli to be a lifelong servant of God, which Samuel in fact became throughout his life in his role as Israel's prophet, priest and anointer of kings. Hannah could not have known, during her years of painful prayers, how and when God would bring about his response. We, however, with our privilege of New Testament hindsight, can see how important those prayers were and how God used them at the right time for the spiritual welfare of his people and for the glory of his own name.

Similarly in Luke 1, we read about the elderly priest Zechariah, who also was childless. It is clear that he and his wife had been praying about that, probably throughout their marriage, but with no results so far. Luke introduces their story by saying, "They had no child, because Elizabeth was barren, and both were advanced in years" (Lk 1:7). Then an angel appears and says, "Do not be afraid, Zechariah, for your prayer has been heard, and your wife Elizabeth will bear a son, and you shall call his name John. And you will have joy and gladness . . ." (Lk 1:13-14). How many years had Elizabeth and Zechariah been praying for what the lawyers call "issue"? We don't know. But what a marvelous work of God is now announced by the angel: God has heard your prayers—and Elizabeth will bear a son. The son is to be named John. You both will have joy at his birth, and he will have a supremely important ministry preparing people for the coming of the Lord. What a wonderful assurance for these aging parents to hold on to during the anxious months prior to John the Baptist's arrival! Once again we see the wisdom and goodness of God, answering sustained faithful prayer at the strategic moment and in the way that gives the answer maximum significance in the larger divine plan.

PERSISTENT PRAYER: THE REASONS WHY

Earlier in this chapter we gave brief reasons why our praying about matters of weight and urgency, short- or long-term, ought to be sharply focused, deeply serious and—to use the overworked contemporary word—passionate in style. Here we glance with similar brevity at the related, indeed overlapping, question, why does God require us and regularly make it necessary for us to be patient, persistent and persevering as we ask for specific blessings and then wait on him for the answers? As the two questions overlap, so may our responses to them.

First, by compelling us to wait patiently for him to act, *God purges our motives.* Often our first formulation of a request is more self-centered and self-serving than it ought to be, just because of the many layers of egocentricity that encase our sinful selves, like the successive skins that encase the heart of an onion. As we wait on God, repeatedly renewing our requests, he leads us to see that the initial motivations of our asking, heartfelt as it doubtless was, were more concerned with comfort, convenience and glory for ourselves, and less with his honor, praise and glory than was right. Thus, by showing us how he sees our praying, our heavenly Father peels off us some of those layers of self-absorption, so that we reangle and reshape our requests, and our motives become more pure in his sight. These repeated and repeatedly revised petitions are not the "vain repetitions" that Jesus warns his disciples against but are our progressively distilled longings that God will glorify himself by the way that he enriches us his servants. Through the waiting process God is attuning us more directly to himself.

Second, by compelling us to wait for him, *God shapes his giving in a natural way.* Though arresting answers to prayer, quick and spectacular, are sometimes given, it is not God's way to multiply miracles indiscriminately. The significant clusters of miracles furthering the exodus, establishing the political ministry of Elijah, Elisha and their successors, vindicating Daniel as a man of God, and verifying the messiahship of Jesus and the new creational kingdom proclamation of the apostles are often celebrated, but it is not so often noted that miracles are always the exception, never the rule, and that God's evident will for most of his servants a great deal of the time is that they live wisely, obediently and reverently within the ordinary processes of ordinary life.

Look again at how God answered Nehemiah's prayer. He kept Nehemiah and his friends, who prayed constantly for miraculous mercy from the king "today," waiting for nine months—250-plus days. During that time, as was inevitable and, as we see, part of God's intention, Nehemiah's downcast look as he gloomed about Jerusalem became more and more part of him, to an extent that doubtless he did not realize, for he knew that looking sad in the presence of a Persian monarch was regarded as a form of treason and was punishable by death. (That is why he was "very much afraid" [Neh 2:2] when the king finally commented on his haggard and glum appearance.) In that age of beards and poor-quality metal mirrors, however, a man could easily miss being aware of how he looked. When the king, who evidently liked and respected Nehemiah, spotted and spoke of his appearance, correctly diagnosing the trouble as "sadness of the heart," it gave Nehemiah opportunity to speak frankly, without disrespect, of the ruin of Jerusalem and how it had affected him. Nehemiah, as we said, could not have raised the subject of a leave of absence himself, but now with friendly and solicitous goodwill the king himself raised it. Interested in the problem of Jerusalem because of his concern for Nehemiah personally, he asked what Nehemiah would like him to do about it. Here, at last, casually arising as part of a personal chat, was the moment that the praying posse had been seeking each day from God throughout the previous nine months! What the Jewish cupbearer-slave was in no position to make happen by any form of conventional engineering, his tragic face—marked and lined by nine months of grieving and now evoking kindly concern rather than the expected anger—had brought about for him. Nehemiah fired off an arrow prayer to God, made his request, and was soon on his way. Prayers answered? Yes! By miracle? No, by a natural flow of events—which took time. Ordering a natural flow is God's habitual way of answering prayer, and it very often takes time, so we have to be willing to wait.

A third reason why persistent prayer is necessary is that *God's nurturing strategy sometimes rules out immediate answers.* Children say to parents, "I can't wait." And all of us who are parents have from time to time said to our children, "You've got to learn to wait." The ability to wait is one of the differences between childishness and maturity. Mature people are, among other things, persons who have learned to wait. God is in the business of maturing us in Christ, and this lesson is integral to adult Christianity. Babies are not born with "wait buttons," as any nursing mother is well aware. But by toddler stage patient parents begin teaching their child to wait. Slowly a healthy child matures and begins to recognize priorities, even that some priorities are more important than his or her own. They learn patience; they learn to curb impulses; they learn to observe priorities; they learn to endure. This is what the writer of Hebrews describes as the path to spiritual maturity: "It is for discipline that you have to endure" (Heb 12:7). Sometimes God uses delayed responses to prayer to discipline and train our spiritual muscles. We hang on in prayer, and our faith muscles grow stronger. We learn to curb our impulse to doubt, to blow up in anger, to grab whatever we can get. We learn to trust God—and to keep on praying.

Discipline means training. In what and for what is God training us by obliging us to wait on him for answers to prayers? Paul answers this in part when he makes the absurd-sounding claim that we Christians, who are justified by faith and know peace with God, can "rejoice" in suffering. How so? "We rejoice in our sufferings, knowing that suffering produces endurance, and endurance produces character, and character produces hope, and hope does not put us to shame, because God's love has been poured into our hearts through the Holy Spirit who has been given to us" (Rom 5:3-5). Did Nehemiah and Hannah and Job and Paul suffer in their times of waiting for God as they prayed over and over their troubles in ignorance of what God's timing for action might be? If we define suffering broadly, to cover all forms of not getting what you like while not liking what you get, the answer is, of course they did. We suffer similarly when our prayers seem to be achieving nothing.

So what can we do in the meantime, besides (of course) keep on praying? We can allow this suffering and waiting to move us along the sequence that Paul so vividly describes: allowing suffering to produce endurance, the quality of "keeping on keeping on," which in turn builds our character, which then produces hope, confidence, that is, that God will keep us going, as he has done so far, until we reach our final glory. And our hope is reinforced by assurance that God loves us, now and forever (see Rom 8:38-39); knowledge of this love of God has been poured into us by the indwelling Holy Spirit—whether or not our prayer is being answered in the time or the way we most wanted. Through this continuing process of all-round progress, we can become content to let God choose the best time to give his best gifts.

OVERCOMING RESISTANCE TO PERSISTENT PRAYER

We have now looked at a series of reasons why we should hang on to God in prayer, but anyone who has walked with God for any length of time will know that this is much easier said than done. Why is persistent prayitng so difficult? And now we come back to the jeremiad with which this book started. Let's be honest, persistent prayer *is* difficult. And though we keep up appearances, perhaps very successfully, we all wish in our hearts that we were steadier and better altogether at keeping up communion with God, praying with sustained concentration, persistently, about situations of need, and praising with persistence too as we go along. Why do we find such persistence so hard? It is because the *world,* the *flesh* and the *devil* combine to oppose all forms of the life of prayer and to resist all our efforts to live it. Limits of space rule out any attempt to deal with this resistance in anything like an adequate way, but a few quick comments may be made.

The *world,* meaning community life organized without and against God, will seek to distract and derail us from our praying by implying that this is a weird and pointless way to behave. The broad way of the world, namely, living without regard for God, is a way that it has always been tempting to lapse into. We want to do what other people do, and they do not pray constantly, so why should we? They fill their lives with this-worldly activities and involvements, so that in any case prayer is ruled out for lack of time, and why should we not do the same? Any number of things seem to them more important than making prayer a habit, and are they not perhaps right? Thus, insidiously, the world works all the time to keep us from praying.

The *flesh,* meaning the inner dynamics of our human hearts as twisted by still-present indwelling sin and not yet fully reordered by grace, is weak, as we can see from what took place in Gethsemane. When the disciples ought to have been praying with and for Jesus as he had wanted them to do while he himself prayed for strength to go through with what was coming that very night, he found them asleep. "The spirit [that is the regenerate heart] indeed is willing," said the Lord Jesus sadly, "but the flesh is weak" (Mk 14:38). Again and again, when we have something spiritually significant to do (and that includes prayer, every time), desire, motivation, strength of heart (that is, of mind and will), zeal and single-minded concern for God's service and glory will be lacking, and we will need to ask our Lord to reenergize us through the Holy Spirit to keep us from total collapse. When Jesus said: "Watch and pray that you may not enter into temptation" (Mk 14:38), this was undoubtedly what he had in mind.

And then, of course, there is the *devil,* "your adversary," as Peter calls him, who "prowls around like a roaring lion, seeking someone to devour" (1 Pet 5:8). Satan is not a creator but a destroyer; wrecking God's plans and ruining human souls is all he wants to do. At the close of Paul's letter to the church at Ephesus, he directs: "Put on the whole armor of God, that you may be able to stand against the schemes of the devil" (Eph 6:11). Part of that armor appears in verse 16, where Paul talks about taking the shield of faith with which to "extinguish all the flaming darts of the evil one." What Paul is referring to is what we would call dirty warfare as practiced in the first century A.D. "Flaming darts," or "projectiles," were spears or arrows or javelins with burning cloths, dipped in oil, tied to their points so that when they hit they would burn as well as pierce, and so do double damage. "You will need the shield of faith," says Paul "to quench those fiery assault weapons." The metal shield of a Roman soldier would deflect all projectiles and be impenetrable by flames. Similarly, Paul means, active faith that calls on the Father, the Son and the Spirit for strength to stand firm against all distortions of revealed truth, all discouragements from faithfulness to it and all temptations to despair, will make you invulnerable to Satan's frontal attacks. Nothing changes that.

God-given faith, then, will quench all the fiery darts of the wicked one, all those assaults that take the form of reasons to stop praying and throw our hands in, in relation to our fellowship with God, temporarily if not permanently. We find ourselves telling ourselves that resistance is hopeless; we can't hold out against the temptation any longer, and that's that. The blazing arrows are wishful harmful thoughts of that kind,

which damage our souls as water dripping through our ceilings damages
the carpets and furniture, and faith must take action to quench them.

The supreme example in Scripture of the kind of wishful, harmful
thinking that we, following Paul, have in mind is Eve's thinking when
Satan tempted her and deceived her into eating the forbidden fruit. "The
woman saw that the tree was good for food, and that it was a delight to
the eyes, and that the tree was to be desired to make one wise" (Gen 3:6).
With these thoughts in her mind, realization that eating would be unbe-
lieving disobedience, on which she had been clear a moment before, escaped her. Unbelief regularly begins as thoughtlessness of this sort. Satan
put ideas into Eve's head, and she didn't think, didn't make herself remember, what God had said to Adam. Unbelief will begin for us with
similar thoughtlessness if we give it half a chance. Should we ever forget
God's redeeming love in Christ and our holy calling as servants of Christ
and our hope of heavenly happiness through Christ, it would be a lowering of the shield of faith, and then Satan's next flaming arrow would,
spiritually speaking, strike us square in the face.

But faith will keep us going in obedience; pray always. Faith will keep
us in expectation; hope always. Faith will keep us hanging on to God in
prayer despite all the discouragements that we feel; grip God's promises
always. There are tricks that we can use; different tricks help different
people. If you find that your thoughts wander when you are praying silently, pray aloud. If you find that once the day gets going you can never
find time to pray, get up earlier and pray before you do anything else. If
you find that your thoughts and words simply won't come together,
write out the petition that you are seeking to get into focus and use your
own written prayer to present the matter to God. You may find that
keeping a journal in which you record the prayers that you've been looking to God to answer is a great help; some do. Take note of whatever dis-
tracts you from prayer and try to avoid it. These are just commonsense
tools of help. They will not make hanging on in prayer easy; but they
may help to make it possible.

Get real then in prayer. Get serious and keep going. It matters that we keep going because of the relationship with our God that we are called to maintain and move along in. Follow the advice of the motto of Oak Hill College in London, England: "Be right and persist."

It may bring clarity and realism here to declare explicitly that all the modes of prayer that we have reviewed, petitioning, praising, meditating and maintaining each of these under pressure, are acts of war—defensive and counterattacking warfare against the supernatural being who is God's sworn enemy and ours too. The massive topic of spiritual warfare and the place of prayer in it is more than we can open up here, but what was said above tells us what is essential for us to know. In all our communion with God, Satan and his hosts are opposing us every step of the way, constantly seeking to weaken us and drain our strength by indirect means in addition to the direct attacks that they periodically mount against us. With regard to this aspect of our Christian lives, however Luther's classic hymn has it right.

A mighty fortress is our God,
A bulwark never failing;
Our helper he amid the flood
Of mortal ills prevailing.
For still our ancient foe
Doth seek to work us woe;
His craft and power are great,
And armed with cruel hate,
On earth is not his equal.

Did we in our own strength confide,
Our striving would be losing;
Were not the right Man on our side,
The Man of God's own choosing.
Dost ask who that may be?
Christ Jesus, it is he,
Lord Sabaoth, his name,

From age to age the same,
And he must win the battle.

And though this world, with devils filled,
Should threaten to undo us,
We will not fear, for God has willed
His truth to triumph through us.
The prince of darkness grim—
We tremble not for him;
His rage we can endure,
For lo! His doom is sure;
One little word shall fell him.

It is always in the place of persistent prayer, as we call out to our heavenly Father and call in Christ the risen Lord to help us, that each victory in this war begins to be won. So, God help us to persist in our praying. God help us, then, to be found hanging on.

JOINING IN

I will bless the LORD at all times;
his praise shall continually be in my mouth.
My soul makes its boast in the LORD,
let the humble hear and be glad.
Oh, magnify the LORD with me,
and let us exalt his name together!

PSALM 34:1-3

Actors are cattle," the great Alfred Hitchcock is reported to have once said, and it is well known that on the set he insisted on getting exactly what he wanted, even putting actors at risk in order to do so. J. I. locked horns with a Hitchcocky director one time when he was enlisted to do a spot for a video. The director thought the script J. I. had brought with him was flat and dull; dismissing it, therefore, he showed J. I. off the cuff what he wanted him to say and how he was to say it. J. I. meekly gave it a try, but to no satisfaction. The director's words were not what he naturally would have said; they would not flow together on J. I.'s tongue, for the memory of his own script kept derailing them. Tension grew as he tried it again, and again and again, and again and again and again, till the moment when he had to leave to catch a plane. Whether any of his efforts were used he never found out; he only knows that the director disliked them all. "I don't think you could have a career in films," said the latter as they shook hands. J. I. assured him that no such career was planned, and they parted Christians, though hardly more. Whatever the director had known about J. I. in advance, he clearly had not known that, for better or for worse (J. I.'s friends differ sharply on this), in role play and communication J. I. only has it in him to be himself, and he gets stubborn and uptight if you try to push him into being anything different. The good man's abstract notion of J. I. had not included this concrete fact.

The necessity of being oneself, J. I.'s stumbling block in that studio, is by contrast foundational to the Christian life. "Be what you are"; "live out what God has wrought within"; "express your new nature, which is now the real you"; " 'be holy' means 'be natural in Christ' "—all of these maxims express the basic principle on which all we have said so far about praying has rested. Praying, however hard in practice, is a natural, instinctive, authentically personal action on the part of all who are born again. We struggle to pray, not just because we know we should but because deep down we want to. The urge to pray is natural to every believer, and we are never more truly ourselves than when we are making the attempt.

So far in this book our focus has been almost entirely on individual prayer, the kind of praying that we do when we are alone, following Jesus' admonition to "go to your room and shut the door and pray to your Father who is in secret" (Mt 6:6). This private communication between each of us and the Father has been the center of our attention, and in that solo setting we have looked at petition, which in Scripture is the heart of personal prayer; we have explored meditation, the contemplating of God and his glory; we have looked at the voicing of praise and of complaint, the expressing of urgency and pain as we ask God to help us; and in the previous chapter we have highlighted the importance of hanging on to God in persistent prayer that expresses persistent faith and persistent hope, because we know for certain that God is not going to abandon us, however grim things feel at this moment.

All of these modes of prayer develop our selfhood and individuality in Christ, which throughout our Christian lives is a work in progress, one dimension of our growing toward what we will be when our glorifying transformation is complete and we see Christ as he is. (In saying this we echo Paul and John; see 2 Cor 3:18 and 1 Jn 3:2.) The gospel of our Lord Jesus Christ does continually individualize, making us more and more into real individual persons than we have been hitherto. It makes us realize that here we stand (one-by-one-by-one) in the presence of the God of creation, the God who runs this world, the God whose greatness is infinite, and each one of us has to deal with him individually; nobody can do it for us. The gospel teaches us to say to ourselves, *I may not any more drift along with the crowd, even the Christian crowd, nor may I any more get absorbed in serving the great god Self; henceforth I must acknowledge that I live my life under God's eye and must answer to him for whatever I do. I have to be the person who exercises faith in his Son, Jesus Christ, the Savior of the world, my personal Savior and Lord. Show me, then, Lord Jesus, how I am to be your disciple and please you in everything I do.* That is God in Christ individualizing us, making us realize and develop our own individuality in his presence, thus making us *serious*, which is the way that evangelicals of two hundred years ago in Britain used to express the real-life quality of being a believer.

This emphasis on deepened personhood and intensified individuality is integral to understanding and living our life of faith and hope and love and prayer. But it is not the whole story, either about our praying or about our discipleship or about our identity in Christ or about our Christian existence as such. The idea of the life of fellowship with God as—to borrow a well-used phrase, "the flight of the alone to the Alone"— an entirely private affair in which others have no place, is a mistaken abstraction, leaving out one major aspect of reality, just as was the film director's abstract idea of J. I. There is a further concrete fact to be taken account of, namely, the *churchly* quality of biblical Christian selfhood, which God forms through his Word and Spirit in all the regenerate. This is something that the thrust of this chapter requires us now to explain.

THE TOGETHERNESS OF THE CHURCH

Starting from where we are, there is some ground-clearing that must first be done. For many, the word *church* signifies just a building. William Ewart Gladstone, sometime prime minister of England, who dominated British politics through the second half of the nineteenth century, was a high Anglican, much exercised in mind over church questions. "What is the Church of England?" he once asked his cab driver. "It's that big building on the corner, with the spire," was the answer he got. To many today, a church is a small white (or in Britain, gray stone) building with a high steeple in a rural setting pictured on a Christmas card. They might be surprised to find that Scripture says virtually nothing about church buildings, speaking only of churches meeting in people's houses (see Rom 16:5; 1 Cor 16:19; Col 4:15, Philem 2).

For others the word *church* is a label for a denomination, that is, an association of congregations with a distinctive heritage and theology within the global Christian community: the Church of England or the Assemblies of God, for example. But this is not the biblical usage either, though the associations of congregations that we call denominations, just like the individual congregations that make them up, may and should embody the church as it is defined and displayed in Scripture. Scripture, we find, describes the church, whether local, global or cosmic, embodying saints in glory along with saints on earth, as people connected to each other in complex ways so as to become a single unit. The Bible uses various images to describe this collection of people. Together they become a building, a family, a temple, a planted field, a body, a flock, a branching vine. All of these images picture in different ways distinct and varied items linked up and firmly connected to each other as parts of a single whole, something more valuable than any of them could be on their own. A doorknob is useless unless attached to a lock on the door of a building. There, however, it becomes quite important. Single objects like a doorknob, a stone, a head of wheat, a toenail become valuable because of their *connections* as part of a building, a temple, a crop or a human body. Without this *togetherness* the single parts lack the significance they would otherwise have, and likewise the entity composed of them is not complete. So it is with the church. And we, God's people, are within this unity.

The biblical images of the church reveal two kinds of connection within the same body: *associational* and *organic*, the latter implying that a single flow of life and energy is being shared. Clearly, the latter term goes deeper into this reality than the former, for while associations are, so to speak, horizontal, oriented to other people, the organic concept points vertically, as it were, to the life of the living Christ, which we share not only with him but with all others who, like ourselves, are alive in him. United inseparably to him, we are inseparably united to them too. We are each linked with every other Christian everywhere as intimately as conjoined twins are linked, yet not in any way to our disadvantage but entirely for our benefit. Two images stand out here, Christ's picture of himself as the vine of which believers are branches (Jn 15:1-17) and Paul's image of the body, of which Christ is both the head and the animating life, and each Christian is a functioning body part.

This powerful image of the church as a body is treated extensively in Romans 12, 1 Corinthians 12 and Ephesians 4. In 1 Corinthians 12, we read:

> For just as the body is one and has many members, and all the members of the body, though many, are one body, so it is with Christ. For in one Spirit we were all baptized into one body—Jews or Greeks, slaves or free—and all were made to drink of one Spirit.
>
> For the body does not consist of one member but of many. . . . If the whole body were an eye, where would be the sense of hearing? . . . The eye cannot say to the hand, 'I have no need of you,' . . . Now you are the body of Christ and individually members of it. (1 Cor 12:12-14, 17, 21, 27)

So we are "members one of another" (Eph 4:25)—"all parts of the same body," as the second edition of the NLT renders the phrase.

What does this mean? Let us illustrate Paul's illustration. Think of a bicycle wheel. The spokes are joined both to the hub and to the outer rim. Each spoke gives strength to the rim, and extra strength comes from the fact that near the hub each spoke overlaps or crosses over another. Christ, our risen Lord, is like the hub, and we who believe are like the spokes, linked both to Christ and to the rim. The rim corresponds to the church's organized outreaching life; it is the place where, metaphorically for the church and literally for the bicycle, the rubber hits the road. To this life each of us must ever be a contributor, a part that strengthens the wheel as a whole, and the precise crossover of each spoke should remind us that we are each providentially placed in Christ's body to serve and strengthen, and to be served and strengthened by, other individuals whom the Lord will send our way.

Or think of how in the human body one eye or ear appears to take on extra duty to compensate when the other eye or ear is out of action, so that we seem to ourselves to see and hear almost as well as we would if both eyes and ears were working. Or again, think of how arm and shoulder muscles (under continuous use) grow hugely strong to serve their paraplegic owners, who must spend their days propelling a wheelchair. The point to be grasped is that within the body of Christ it belongs to our identity, first to be sharing a common life with Christ and in and through Christ with, quite literally, every other Christian that there is; and second, as a consequence, to be giving ourselves to love, serve and strengthen our fellow participants in Christ's body. To duck out of this commitment is not an option. And not to see the reality of this given bond that links us not only with Christ but also with all Christians right from the start of our Christian lives is to be bedeviled (in the most literal sense) by an abstract individualistic notion of the Christian life that ignores an enormously significant, truly fundamental, elephant-size concrete fact.

This organic connection with one another in Christ goes far beyond Sunday morning worship, though it should powerfully affect that worship, requiring us every time to run a thorough check on our thoughts, motives and movements. It is important to ask such questions as "Am I avoiding sitting near David in row five, and making eye contact with him, because I secretly wish that he was not here?" Yet David is a member of Christ's body along with me, as I am along with him. Christian love regularly requires of us good will to persons we do not particularly like. More positively, if Janet and Arthur have announced their intended marriage, am I almost as joyful as they? If sent an invitation, will I attend their wedding as a visual support of their vows? If Rosemary and I have a major disagreement about church policy or about the color of the roses on the altar, for that matter, do I quickly seek her out and make peace as Matthew 18:15 directs and as Matthew 5:23-25 confirms, and thereby protect our church from being infected with our division? If I learn that John is engaged in an unfair business practice, do I humbly confront him about his sin and ask that he return to honesty—even if that conversation is uncomfortable (Jas 5:19-20)? Do I invite to my home Sue the single mom and Pete the college student and Mario the businessman and Grandma Francis who uses a wheelchair and Edgar who seems homeless and Anna whose husband is sick with cancer and Julie who makes me laugh and Audrey who is so terribly awkward in social settings and Gino who speaks another language; do I invite all of these people into my home? Why should I? Because we, all of us, belong together shaping a single body and that body has one head: my Savior and theirs, Jesus Christ (Eph 4:15). We are all connected to him and thus cemented to each other by his grace in a body whose visible shape is "church." This is the only kind of behavior that befits those who really believe they are members one of another, forming together the body of Christ. And we *need* each other! God has called us together to be this body on earth, and that means that by our very relationship with each other, we are to testify to his redeeming power.

How? By the togetherness that we seek to unpack in this chapter.

Self-sufficiency, like self-absorption, is a no-no in the body of Christ; God will not prosper the pride of those who think they can get along without other Christians' help. Spiritual isolationism is in his eyes not a virtue but a vice; only through mutuality of dependence, ministry and pastoral care do Christians really grow and churches really go forward. The New Testament concept, plain in Paul but implicit everywhere, is that the one universal church is manifested in miniature whenever and wherever people band together to be the church—that is, to do the things that the church does: learn the faith from Scripture; praise, adore and pray to the Father and the Son through the Spirit; maintain the sacraments of the gospel; establish pastoral leadership; and practice care, correction and encouragement of each other, deploying all the endowments for service that the Holy Spirit gives. These are the essentials of local church life. Even beyond the local church, this sense of belonging to one another (though less intense) extends to others of like faith within the denominations and even in principle to all Christian believers throughout the world.

The togetherness of the church, particularly the church at prayer, can wonderfully attract those who need to know the love of Jesus. Society's emphasis on individuality has created a vast emptiness, a loneliness that hungers for genuine connection. Clubs, committees and social networks based on common interests no doubt go some way toward filling the gap, but it takes Christ's love, expressed by and experienced through Christians, and specifically Christians in the fellowship of local churches, to achieve connections that satisfy the lonely heart. It is no accident that Paul's great teaching in 1 Corinthians 12 on the church as body of Christ is immediately followed by the famous love chapter, 1 Corinthians 13. Only to the extent that we teach and preach and sing and pray and live the love of Jesus, both toward each other and toward those who do not yet know him, will the church fulfill its mission to draw others to Christ. But loving connectedness within the church sends a powerful invitation as, for a moment, we drop our linked hands with each other to draw someone else into our circle of belonging—belonging, that is, to each other, just because we all belong to Jesus Christ. Within the arms of the church this unbeliever can hear in Scripture, in song, in sermon, in prayer and most importantly in the love-shaped lives and words of welcome and witness on the part of the Lord's people, that Jesus loves this person and is inviting this sinner into the fellowship of the body, where he or she too can find and celebrate salvation.

Much of our praying is solo work—direct conversation between each of us and God. But in the church we unite our hearts and our voices in what we may call *joined* praying. Scripture repeatedly emphasizes that God places great value on these prayers from godly people whose hearts unite with each other in seeking common goals. Most of what happens in Christian worship is a form of prayer. Hymns, songs, prayers from a prayer book, extemporaneous prayers of the pastor and the people, guided prayers, many Scriptures recited, invocations, confessions, intercessions, benedictions—all address God. As the people of God at worship together, we join our hearts and often our voices in all of these, with God as our target audience. Ideally the church at worship is diverse individuals purposely and conscientiously uniting to express shared thoughts and desires for the glory of God and for the good of each other, their joined voices revealing a unity in fellowship and focus that only God can create. A thousand years before the formation of the Christian church, David the psalmist pictured something of the unity that God's people can experience within the church.

> Behold, how good and pleasant it is
> > when brothers dwell in unity!
> It is like the precious oil on the head, . . .
> of Aaron. . . .
>
> It is like the dew of Hermon
> > which falls on the mountains of Zion!

For there the LORD has commanded the blessing,
   life forevermore. (Ps 133)

All churches are flawed, but even through those flaws, God uses the church to sand off the rough edges of our characters, to reveal his love through the diversity of his bonded people, to teach us about himself through Scripture read and preached, to energize us as we each develop our unique skills in his service, to purify us through the vulnerability of confession, to inspire us through those who have walked God's path further than we, to spur us toward love and good works, and to draw us closer to himself and each other through our united prayers, all of this for the praise of his own glory, which he displays in and through the togetherness of his church.

This chapter will examine in close-up the topic of "joining in." Using what we have just said about Christ, the Christian and the church as our launch pad, we will develop the togetherness aspect of prayer by a threefold emphasis: God *wills* togetherness in prayer; God *uses* togetherness in prayer; God helps us to learn and even *love* togetherness in prayer.

GOD WILLS OUR TOGETHERNESS

We "serious Christians" constantly stress individuality of discipleship. We don't always stress in the same way our unity with fellow believers, which, well-experienced, is a foretaste of (even as we ventured earlier, a rehearsal for) the togetherness of heaven. In Hebrews 12, at the end of a long exposition of the supremacy and glory of the Lord Jesus Christ as our Redeemer King, our great High Priest and the founder and perfecter of our faith, the writer speaks of faithfulness and hope in our discipleship to him, and among other things he says:

> You have come to Mount Zion and to the city of the living God, the heavenly Jerusalem, and to innumerable angels in festal gathering, and to the assembly of the firstborn who are enrolled in heaven, and to God, the judge of all, and to the spirits of the righteous made per-

fect, and to Jesus, the mediator of a new covenant. (Heb 12:22-24)

Here is defined for us our ultimate togetherness in a great company that includes countless angels, the gathering of the firstborn (Christians now departed?), God the Father, spirits of the righteous made perfect (Old Testament saints?) and Jesus himself. The verb is "you have come." Obviously we who are at this moment writing or reading are not yet in heaven in the full sense. But we do in some way already participate in the togetherness of that final gathering through our corporate worship. "With Angels and Archangels, and all the company of heaven, we laud and magnify thy glorious Name," says the Anglican Prayer Book.

The book of Revelation consists of seven letters of encouragement from the living Lord to seven churches, followed by a long visionary appendix from chapter 4 to the end of the book. The appendix reinforces God's summons to faithfulness and his promise that those who overcome as they face life's pain and grief and discouragement and evil powers and circumstances and all kinds of pressure to throw in the towel will enjoy great and unimaginable glory in consequence. That glory will essentially be a matter of togetherness around the throne of God in praise and adoration, a supreme joy for all who are there. Punctuating the nightmare visions of dreadfulness in this world, all through this appendix, we see shafts of sunlight, visions of the final glory of heaven, and hear throughout a drumbeat of emphasis on togetherness. Read, preferably aloud, the passages that follow.

> I looked, and I heard around the throne and the living creatures and the elders the voice of many angels, numbering myriads of myriads and thousands of thousands, saying with a loud voice, "Worthy is the Lamb who was slain, to receive power and wealth and wisdom and might and honor and glory and blessing!" And I heard every creature in heaven and on earth and under the earth and in the sea, and all that is in them, saying, "To him who sits on the throne and to the Lamb be blessing and glory and honor and might forever and ever!" (Rev 5:11-13)

I looked, and behold, a great multitude that no one could number, from every nation, from all tribes and peoples and languages, standing before the throne and before the Lamb, clothed in white robes, with palm branches in their hands, and crying out with a loud voice, "Salvation belongs to our God who sits on the throne, and to the Lamb!" And all the angels were standing around the throne and around the elders and the four living creatures, and they fell on their faces before the throne and worshiped God, saying, "Amen! Blessing and glory and wisdom and thanksgiving and honor and power and might be to our God forever and ever." (Rev 7:9-12)

I looked, and behold, on Mount Zion stood the Lamb, and with him 144,000 who had his name and his Father's name written on their foreheads. And I heard a voice from heaven like the roar of many waters and like the sound of loud thunder. The voice I heard was like the sound of harpists playing on their harps, and they were singing a new song before the throne and before the four living creatures and before the elders. No one could learn that song except the 144,000 who had been redeemed from the earth. (Rev 14:1-3)

I saw . . . those who had conquered the beast and its image and the number of its name, standing beside the sea of glass with harps of God in their hands. And they sing the song of Moses, the servant of God, and the song of the Lamb, saying,

> "Great and amazing are your deeds,
>   O Lord God the Almighty!" (Rev 15:2-4)

After this I heard what seemed to be the loud voice of a great multitude in heaven, crying out,

> "Hallelujah!
> Salvation and glory and power belong to our God,
>   for his judgments are true and just." . . .

Once more they cried out,
"Hallelujah! . . .

And the twenty-four elders and the four living creatures fell down and worshiped God who was seated on the throne, saying, "Amen. Hallelujah!" And from the throne came a voice saying,

"Praise our God,
    all you His servants,
you who fear him,
    small and great." (Rev 19:1-5)

The city has no need of sun or moon to shine on it, for the glory of God gives it light, and its lamp is the Lamb. By its light will the nations walk, and the kings of the earth will bring their glory into it, and its gates will never be shut by day—and there will be no night there. They will bring into it the glory and the honor of the nations. (Rev 21:23-26)

The throne of God and of the Lamb will be in it, and his servants will worship him. They will see his face, and his name will be on their foreheads. And night will be no more. They will need no light of lamp or sun, for the Lord God will be their light, and they will reign forever and ever. (Rev 22:3-5)

How many images and sounds of togetherness appear in these scenes of gathered praise in John's revelation? Too many to absorb! After reading these visions of heaven and its worship, we cannot doubt that the togetherness of all unfallen angels with all godly humans, uniting in praise before God's throne, is central in God's purpose. This is, perhaps, the surest thing we know about heaven. Heaven is the goal of our earthly pilgrimage, the destination where through the mercy of Christ every single one of God's people will spend eternity. Heaven is a place, a state, a condition and an experience of togetherness. What will heaven look like? The silence of Scripture on the details allows our imagination the pleasure of whimsy.

Three summers ago I (Carolyn) was hiking in the woods of southern Wisconsin with a group of high school students. We tramped the bottom of a ravine, crisscrossed a sparkling creek on wet stones (a few soggy feet here), threaded our way up a path tracing the side of cliff walls, while misty sunlight etched lacy shadows on mossy tree trunks. It was an "off" day. The cliffs were too slippery for our planned rock climbing with ropes, so we hiked. Moss, stream, birdcalls, scuttering furry things in the brush, cool rain-washed air: not surprisingly, we began to speak of heaven. I declared that "my heaven" was just this kind of place. Right here was as perfect as I could imagine. Amanda, who is fine with rural hiking but much prefers the noise and activity of city life, insisted that "her heaven" was a city—and besides that's the way the Bible describes it. Liz, who thinks of herself as "the typical compromising middle child" said she liked both me and Amanda, and would like to spend her eternity in both of our heavens, perhaps alternating weekends. We all laughed at our silly attempts to picture what is indescribable and to schedule what is timeless. Conversations about heaven tend to end that way, joyfully so.

In the time of the Roman Empire, cities were thought of as places of safety, refuge and prosperity. In today's society, urban blight, poverty and crime can trigger a different feeling about cities. Is heaven a literal city? It seems clear that God used the term *city* in the book of Revelation to picture, within the limits of human language, the safety and opportunity and richness that our eternity with him will provide. And at the minimum Revelation's description of heaven as a city illustrates an all-encompassing joining in of God's people.

Of this, then, we can be certain: heaven will be an unending enjoyment of togetherness in worship, where every person present joins in. And this will be the full realization of an ideal that God is already working toward here on earth. The heart of God's prescription for the life of his people, right from the time of the exodus onward, has been their regular togetherness, as an assembly of people coming together to worship their common Lord. That is why every gathering of believers on earth for worship (whether in Old or New Testament times, or this very week) may properly be thought of as a rehearsal for the glory that is to come.

God implants in all regenerate hearts an instinctive urge toward the togetherness in fellowship that is his goal. So the psalmist cries: "Oh, magnify the LORD with me, / and let us exalt His name together!" (Ps 34:3). When on Pentecost morning the Spirit came down and a new human community was formed, the Acts narrative tells us that all of these people were together in very intense and joyful worship and service of the Lord. Writes Luke:

> They devoted themselves to the apostles' teaching and *fellowship*, to the breaking of bread and the *prayers* And all who believed were *together*. . . . And day by day, attending the temple *together* and breaking bread in their homes, they received their food with glad and generous hearts, *praising God* and having favor with all the people. (Acts 2:42, 44, 46-47, emphasis added)

When they heard that their leaders Peter and John had been arrested and told to stop their preaching:

> They lifted their voices together to God, and said, "Sovereign Lord, who made the heaven and the earth and the sea and everything in them, who through the mouth of our father David, your servant, said by the Holy Spirit,
>
> > 'Why do the Gentiles rage,
> > and the peoples plot in vain?
> > The kings of the earth set themselves . . .
> > against the Lord and against his Anointed'—
>
> for truly in this city there were gathered together against your holy servant Jesus, whom you anointed, both Herod and Pontius Pilate, along with the Gentiles and the peoples of Israel." (Acts 4:24-27)

They were saying in effect, "Yes, Lord, your word has been fulfilled. We invoke you as the God who predicted what happened in the death and the resurrection of Jesus, and what is happening now in the opposition being shown to us who are servants of Jesus." And then, still very much together, they asked for help. Most of us would have begged for protection and peace. Not them; they were too mission-minded for that; they prayed in line with what God had already designated as their own future work. "Now, Lord, look upon their threats and grant to your servants to continue to speak your word with all boldness" (Acts 4:29). Their petition was corporate; they addressed God as members one of another; they were all praying in these courageous terms *together.* They *joined* in prayer. And God used their joined prayers to continue his work of protecting and empowering the spread of Christianity throughout the known world in a single generation—as the remainder of the book of Acts indicates.

In Hebrews 10:25 the writer tells his readers how to prepare for eternity: Don't neglect "to meet together, as is the habit of some." Failure to gather together, or nonattendance at the announced meetings, might seem the wise course when persecutors are targeting Christ's people, as was apparently the case here, but it is not a good move. The writer warns us that attempts at solo faith, undercover and unnoticed, are the wrong way to go. Togetherness, in one form or another must remain the essence of our practice of discipleship, come hell or high water. This is the will of God, and the one highway of spiritual well-being. It is by our togetherness in worship here, foreshadowing our togetherness hereafter, that we are to express the reality of being members one of another in Christ.

GOD USES OUR TOGETHERNESS

The Father, the Son and the Holy Spirit work to draw all Christians into active habitual togetherness, not only because this expresses the truth of our oneness in Christ but also because the divine plan is to use our togetherness as a means of our mutual blessing, as we each share what we have received through Christ. Think of the triune God as an artist and the world as a studio and display area, and the perfecting of the church through the perfecting of all who belong to it as the complex artwork that is continually on the go there: a vast enterprise, no doubt, but one that is not beyond the artist's power. In Ephesians 4 Paul analyzes what is involved. Through persons and leadership gifts for evangelism and nurture, he says, God works

> to equip the saints for the work of ministry, for building up the body of Christ, . . . to the measure of the stature of the fullness of Christ. . . . [S]peaking the truth in love, we are to grow up in every way into him who is the head, into Christ, from whom the whole body, joined and held together by every joint with which it is equipped, when each part is working properly, makes the body grow so that it builds itself up in love. (Eph 4.12-16)

There are three things in particular to notice here. First, "speaking the truth" is an unavoidable undertranslation, for the Greek word means expressing and living out the truth in every way possible, and there is no single English word for that. John Stott, following some older commentators, gave "truthing it" as a rendering, coining a new verb to catch this breadth of meaning.[1]

Second, "the measure of the stature of the fullness of Christ" is a single corporate destiny in which all Christians will share, rather than an individual transformation that will be reproduced in millions of other separate lives. The word *fullness* is the key. No one of us can embody and exhibit so much. The fullness of Christ will not be actualized until all the millions of the Lord's people are all together in glory, each with our own story of how the Lord has shown us mercy, each as the personal evidence of the re-creating and transforming power of God that has been working in our lives ever since we became believers through the artistry of our heavenly Father and our Savior and the Holy Spirit doing this terrific job of individual renewal for each of us. That state of glorified togetherness will constitute "the measure of the stature of the fullness of Christ" of which we will one day be part. Such is the corporate destiny within which all of us "grow up in every way into him who is the head, into

---

[1]John R. W. Stott, *The Message of Ephesians*, The Bible Speaks Today (Downers Grove, Ill.: InterVarsity Press, 1979), p. 172.

Christ." We are each one a work in progress by the grace of God, but the Bible looks ahead to this transcendent reality of united togetherness with each other in, with, facing and alongside Jesus our Lord, and therefore tells us in no uncertain terms that joining together with other believers should be our continued aim and priority throughout life. Togetherness should be our goal here because we know that it will be our ultimate fulfillment in glory. We should live, then, in Christian fellowship conscious that in our togetherness we are preparing for heaven and being prepared for heaven. All of our prayers to God, whether on our own or in company with others, should be made with that future clear in our minds.

As alliterations to aid our memory, we may properly say that God uses our togetherness here and now for *enlightenment,* for *enlargement* and for *encouragement.* We can learn this from Psalm 107, which begins:

> Oh give thanks to the LORD, for he is good,
>> his steadfast love endures forever!
> Let the redeemed of the LORD say so,
>> whom he has redeemed from trouble
> and gathered in from the lands,
>> from the east and from the west,
>> from the north and from the south. (Ps 107:1-3)

After this comprehensive invitation to all recipients of saving mercy to give thanks, the psalm continues with a series of testimonies. We can catch the rhythms of a pattern (trouble, prayer, rescue, thanks) as one by one the people of God testify of his great goodness toward them.

> Some wandered in desert wastes,
>> finding no way to a city to dwell in;
> hungry and thirsty,
>> their soul fainted within them.
> They cried to the LORD in their trouble,
>> and he delivered them out of their distress. . . .
> Let them thank the LORD for his steadfast love,

> for his wondrous works to the children of men! (Ps 107:4-6, 8)

Some sat in darkness and in the shadow of death,
prisoners in affliction and in irons,
for they had rebelled against the words of God. . . .
Then they cried to the LORD in their trouble,
and he delivered them from their distress. . . .
Let them thank the LORD for his steadfast love,
for his wondrous works to the children of men! (Ps 107 10-11, 13,
15)

Some were fools through their sinful ways,
and because of their iniquities suffered affliction; . . .
Then they cried to the LORD in their trouble,
and he delivered them from their distress. . . .
Let them thank the LORD for his steadfast love,
for his wondrous works to the children of men! (Ps 107:17, 19, 21)

Some went down to the sea in ships,
doing business on the great waters; . . .
[God] commanded and raised the stormy wind,
which lifted up the waves of the sea. . . .
Then they cried to the LORD in their trouble,
and he delivered them from their distress. . . .
Let them thank the LORD for his steadfast love,
for his wondrous works to the children of men! (Ps 107:23, 25, 28,
31)

These vignettes of God's mercy toward forlorn and undeserving folk whose very enterprise has landed them in trouble—fainting, hopeless, foolish, endangered souls—leads to closing generalizations about the lost, the just and the wise.

[God] raises up the needy out of affliction
and makes their families like flocks.

The upright see it and are glad, . . .

Whoever is wise, let him attend to these things;
  let them consider the steadfast love of the LORD. (Ps 107:41-42)

The psalm shows us that testimonies like these yield *enlightenment*. Wise people learn from the experience of other believers how rich, varied and inexhaustible are God's resources of rescuing love, which he deploys when those in trouble, little as they merit mercy and much as they realize that, humble themselves before him and cry out for help. God, who is faithful to his promises, heeds their praying and comes to save them accordingly. The sharing of such experiences in fellowship today has the same happy effect of making the wise wiser in their understanding of God's steadfast divine love.

From psalms like this the godly also gain *enlargement*, as their hearts are drawn out to join in the thanks and praise of those who have been thus blessed. The effect of testimonies such as those contained in Psalm 107 is to deepen our realization of how good and great the Lord is, and hereby again and again he shows us how God works in us and what he pulls out of us in a way that we could not have envisioned until it happens. Then comes a measure of joy, delight, praise and energy for his service that focuses our heart on him, fills our heart with him and anchors our heart in him with quite a new intensity. The psalmist in Psalm 119:32 pictures this energized state as *running:* "I will run in the way of your commandments when you enlarge my heart!" This enlarged heart is not a case for the cardiologist, but a spiritual process at the core of our being whereby we gain energy to serve God and lose our inhibitions and restraints about doing so. The sharing of experiences of God's goodness, other things being equal, will have a similar enlivening effect in our circles of fellowship today and tomorrow.

That *encouragement* is received as we read or hear stories of people in extremity whom God in mercy rescued from final disaster is obvious, too obvious to need discussing. What may need discussing is whether what we call our fellowship with other Christians, both in the flesh and in our reading, is bringing such stories our way. But that is a question that we, the writers, and each of our readers, must answer for ourselves.

RELUCTANT JOINERS: LEARNING AND
LOVING TOGETHERNESS

This is a book about praying, and this chapter bears the title "Joining In," and its theme is making the most of prayer together—and our readers may by now be wondering whether their authors have gone off track. But no; what we have been trying to do is to prepare our readers to get the message on our topic at the proper deep level. Our reason for writing about our given togetherness in Christ's body and our ideal of regular sought-out fellowship with each other is that we all need to be fully aware that these are integral elements in God's plan for us, the second being dictated by the first. We are squaring up to a state of affairs that we think is widespread and that if not challenged and transcended will keep us from seeing our togetherness as the deep-level necessity that it is, and also from embracing it as the deep-level benefit that it is; and that, we think, is something that will keep us from practicing prayer together the way God wills. Our pages so far have had as their aim the raising of consciousness about this; we want to induce an awareness that will correct an imbalance and clear a blind spot, so that we may adjust our mindset to God's full purpose for us in Christ.

The personal lopsidedness that we want to challenge is sometimes labeled pietism—an unfair use of a noble word. True pietism is piety, godliness and devotion anchored in the truth that my individual relationship with God is the most important thing in my life, and so must ever be my top priority. The popular form of pietism that we now face, found among evangelicals as well as others, is this priority of "personal relationship with God" pulled out of shape by this modern, secular, Enlightenment-bred type of individualism that teaches us to see ourselves as distinct from, if not actually against, all existing forms of society (family, school, political consensus, cultural consensus, church, whatever). In secular contexts this individualism glorifies the rebel; in Christian contexts it makes recognition of churchly identity as part of our Christian identity difficult, even when we have learned to distinguish between the one universal church that God sees and knows and the many local, denominational, building-housed or home-based churches that we see and know. The popular pietist way is to value church services and parachurch gatherings as we value gas stations and parties and maybe college lectures too: we show up in order (in one sense or another) to fill up and then go on our way without any sense of continuing commitment to the source of the filling.

Thinking this way, evangelicals, with a whole smorgasbord of Bible-based Protestant worship places to choose from, often become inveterate church-hoppers, not settling anywhere. Roman Catholics and Orthodox of similar bent move around less, but failure to realize that maintaining the deepest possible togetherness with fellow believers is integral to maintaining the deepest possible faith fellowship with Christ is widespread among them as well. These spiritual individualists appreciate the good sermons, good pastoral care and good friendship that organized churches offer, but they do not appreciate that full commitment to Christ's church body is integral to full commitment to Christ the Head himself. Not until we get past this blockage point in our too-individualistic view of discipleship will we be able to join in prayer with other Christians as we should.

Healthy Christian togetherness does not usurp the place of our individuality; instead our togetherness is the frame for expression of that individuality. John Wesley with great wisdom said somewhere, "There is nothing more unchristian than the solitary Christian." Persons who practice what may be called "Lone Ranger Christianity" cannot share in the fellowship of Christian brothers and sisters where real spiritual growth takes place. Their kind of Christianity is inevitably stunted; it is, indeed, more than a little perverse. We grow in the sense of our own individual identity with the Lord as we grow in realization and expression of our brotherhood and sisterhood with all the rest of the saints who are also marching to Zion as we are. As we cultivate personal fellowship with the Savior, so we must cultivate, as a matter of conscience, this full-scale kind of togetherness with his people, who with us are his body. This is the churchliness of faithful discipleship.

Acting out that churchliness is far easier for some than for others. Some of us are naturally gregarious people, happiest in a roomful of talkers or at least with two or three good friends. We bare our souls with relative ease. Others of us are intensely private people who love solitude and for whom the most casual conversation is a strain, if not actually a pain. Yet God calls us all to grow as we learn to pray and to worship *together*. Those who find this kind of togetherness a natural joy must exercise sensitivity toward brothers and sisters who find it difficult. Conversely, Christians for whom it is difficult should see this building of connection with kindred souls as a spiritual discipline at which they must exert themselves both for their own spiritual well-being and that of others as well as for the sake of worshiping God as he desires. They can find camaraderie with C. S. Lewis, a spiritual giant, who (though he enjoyed spiritual friendships) never found public worship to his liking, as we have already noticed. Still, he disciplined himself to attend and participate as regularly as the church door opened and closed, and so must we.

Our claim is that all Christians can *love* togetherness in praise and prayer, and that all Christians are called to *learn* the practice of that togetherness, which is more than just being alongside each other when God is addressed. But some of us, if we opened our hearts with perfect honesty, would have to admit that we do this with an inner detachment that is instinctive to us, not by reason of our cultural conditioning but because, fundamentally, we are loners, even at prayer, and we are never happier than when we are out on our own with the Lord. In the rest of life's tasks we find that loneliness is comfortable, and the idea of togetherness is something of a threat. Most of us have a measure of this in our makeup, at least during certain periods of our lives. How then will we respond to this inner reserve, whether it is an every hour, every day condition or one that comes upon us during times of, for instance, grief or loss or strain or insecurity?

A day or two of self-indulgence will not hurt us in this area. A week of solitude and privacy—call it a retreat—is all to the good, particularly if part of that time is spent deliberately communicating with God. But if isolation and privacy becomes a pattern of life, spiritual growth in critical areas is all but impossible—and we deprive the community of faith of all that God could give them through our presence. Worst of all, we stifle expression of our oneness in Christ and thereby displease God. Those of us who are naturally inclined loners may need to grab ourselves by the shirt collar and give ourselves a stern scolding, something along the line of: *My true identity before God is marred if I indulge this attitude of emotional withdrawal and keeping my relational distance. It does not allow me to be fulfilled; I am not growing in grace as long as I indulge myself in inner detachment in this way; my children and friends are not benefiting as they should from my example of shared faith. My call from God as one of his people is to be transparently close to others in fellowship, ready to open my heart to share my own testimony, just as I need to receive the testimony of others, and I should be as ready to pray with them as they are to pray with me.* This kind of self-given shoulder-shaking lecture from time to time can help us to accept our God-given responsibility of joining with others in praise and prayer to God, and (perhaps) eventually even to enjoy it.

Polite reserve, so commonly viewed as a virtue among those of us bred north of the fortieth parallel, has got to be overcome—for our own spiritual health and for the glory of God. The Scriptures speak of Christian believing as *corporate,* Christian worship as *corporate* and Christian growth as *corporate.* Christianity, as is often said, is body life, and body life is life together in the intimacy and trust of open sharing of ourselves with the good of others always in view. None of us may contract out of that.

Nor may what we see as some Christians' personal quirks hold us back. A *Peanuts* cartoon character once declared: "I love the human race. It's people I can't stand." We are called to grow past the "can't stand" view of people and begin to grow alongside our flawed brothers and sisters in Christ. Our readers may know this well-worn anonymous ditty:

> To live above with the saints we love,
> Oh, that will be glory!
> But to live below with the saints we know?
> Now that's a different story! [2]

But we can and often must love people (that is, seek their good) without, at first anyway, being able to like them; to stand apart from a needy or exasperating believer on the ground that we do not like them is simply sinful.

Thus—at last!—we reach the point where we can speak directly about joining in praise and prayer with others who are in Christ with us, and with whom by the grace of God we who believe are already one. The blockage we have to transcend is that of being alongside others physically while not entering into full togetherness with them spiritually—a sin of omission that is very easy indeed to commit. As a clergyman I (J. I.) face congregations during hymns, and it is not hard to see who is not singing. (There are always some, usually men. Why? I can guess, though I do not really know.) When the congregation is praying, however, only God can tell who is not joining in, for all hunch or kneel with eyes shut in the same way, and many suppose that by simply being there and listening to prayers, they are actually joining in when in fact they are not. Some guidance is needed here.

There are two distinct modes of corporate prayer, and we all need to learn to join in both. The first is the informal, unscripted type of prayer that is natural and usual in the family, between friends and in the prayer

---

[2]Attempts to find the source of this "ditty" have been unsuccessful—except that it was an old Irish toast.

meetings that take place both in and outside the organized life of churches. The second is prayer in the church service, whether liturgical in the sense that it follows a set text or extempore in the sense that the leader addresses God as spokesperson for the congregation in words that are partially, perhaps wholly, unwritten and, to use an old word, *conceived* at the moment of speaking. This puts leading in prayer at a service and at a prayer meeting essentially on a par. When another person is praying aloud, the temptation is to do no more than passively listen, but the proper task is actively to think and pray in our heart along with the leader, making the petitions our own as we hear them spoken. To form and maintain this habit takes effort, but we are not joining in according to the will of God, save as we labor to do this.

We would add that all who lead in prayer, whether liturgical or extempore, should strive to be clear and orderly in what they say, to make this participatory thinking and desiring as straightforward as possible. It should be recognized that neither rhapsodic incoherence in "conceived" prayer nor dreary unexpressive droning when reading "set" prayers is ordinarily a sign of the presence and power of the Holy Spirit.

As, in Richard Baxter's words, God in conversion "breaketh not all Men's hearts alike,"[3] so in teaching us the togetherness dimension of Christian living God does not always work the same way but adapts to each person's temperament. He teaches some, who naturally warm to public gatherings, properly to value public worship and rallies and prayer meetings by using these events to enrich their personal alone times with God, giving them songs, insights and models of devotion to animate what previously seemed to them a barren routine. And he teaches others, who temperamentally find any form of joining in hard, properly to value these gatherings by thinking of their personal prayer (where they are much more comfortable) as preparation of heart for the corporate reality of praise and prayer in company and as part of that company.

---

[3]Richard Baxter, *Reliquiae Baxterianae* (1696), 1.7.

Carol Wimber said of the early Vineyard days, "We learned that what happens when we are alone with the Lord determines how intimate and deep the worship will be when we come together."[4] Since the Lord wills that worship should truly be intimate and deep when we come together, we who belong to the cool, withdrawn, shy and introverted brigade, who by instinct prefer privacy to intimacy and distance to close relationships, might well begin by adding a hymnal or book of Christian songs to our regular private prayers. We need not be skilled singers to do this. Many songs and hymns are really prayers for people together to address to God. Other songs are confessions of faith and expressions of God's greatness that we can readily adopt as our own prayers of commitment. During our times alone with God we can read these words as part of our communication with him, even when we cannot bring ourselves actually to sing them. Weeks later, perhaps, when those same songs come into our public worship, we will have already voiced them alone to God and so will be better able to unselfconsciously join other believers singing them in church. We will, after all, have practiced them at home.

Similarly, all of us may well draw on last Sunday's printed order of worship or the prayer book used in our faith tradition as we practice our alone time with God. We can pray the prayers aloud to God, read the set Scriptures and reflect on them, and remind ourselves of their truths throughout the day. Gradually the regular patterns of worship and the nuances of liturgical prayers and responses will become a natural part of our ongoing conversation with God. As we invite God's Spirit to teach us, small phrases will become loaded for us with significance we had never before discerned. In this way our private time with God will gain deeper meaning—and we will bring that meaning with us when we gather for corporate worship.

The bottom line for us all is: *Choose* togetherness, the radical togetherness of those who know they are inseparably and eternally one in

---

[4]Carol Wimber, cited in John Wimber, "Worship: Intimacy with God" <www.pastornet.net.au/renewal/journal6/wimber.html>.

Christ and whose relationship is rooted in praise and prayer together. *Choose* not to be held back by shyness, embarrassment, social convention or any form of personal inhibition (attitudes anchored not in concern for dignity and good taste, as some make themselves believe, but in a panicky fear of vulnerability). *Choose* to give and receive love on a basis of humble and mutual openness. *Choose* to commit yourself to a congregation long term, to identify as fully as you can with its goals and members, to open your life and your home to your fellow believers, and to give help wherever help is needed. In short, choose *togetherness,* and choose wholehearted, closely bound involvement in the congregation's worshiping life of prayer and praise as the central element of that togetherness. For this and nothing less than this is the will of God.

❧10❧

WITH MY WHOLE HEART

*Of what concernment unto the glory of God, and in our living unto him,
prayer is, will be owned by all. It is that only single duty
wherein every grace is acted, every sin opposed, every good thing obtained,
and the whole of our obedience in every instance of it is concerned.
What difficulties lie in the way of its due performance, what
discouragements rise up against it, how unable we are ourselves in a due
manner to discharge it, what aversion there is in a corrupted
nature unto it, what distractions and weariness are apt to befall us under
it, are generally known also unto them who are any way exercised in
these things. Yet doth the blessedness of our present and
future condition much depend thereon.*

JOHN OWEN, 1681

*Take my heart; it is thine own;
It shall be thy royal throne.*

FRANCES RIDLEY HAVERGAL, 1874

*Almighty God, unto whom all hearts be open,
all desires known, and from whom no secrets are hid:
Cleanse the thoughts of our hearts by the inspiration of thy Holy Spirit,
that we may perfectly love thee, and worthily magnify thy holy name,
through Jesus Christ our Lord.*

ANGLICAN BOOK OF COMMON PRAYER

Nothing, they say, is now so sure as that which we once doubted, and we affirm nothing so strongly now as that which we once did not believe. J. I. can testify to this with regard to the psalms. As a cradle Anglican, he said and sang them in church from his earliest days. As the converted and convictional Anglican that he became at eighteen, it took him some twenty years to believe in his heart that what everyone had told him about the psalms was true, namely, that they were models of praying. Why this blockage? At the time, he ascribed it to two facts. First, the psalmists, being poets, jumped around logically, presenting their thoughts more like flowers in a bunch than like links in a chain, and since J. I. has a linear, lawyerlike mind, this bothered him. Second, the psalms show a concentrated, uninhibited, almost ferocious intensity in the way that they say—shout, rather—their "Help!" and their "Thanks!" This was something that J. I.'s cool inner restraint could not cope with. Forty years on from the time when the psalms began to open up to him, he now sees the problem he had rather differently. The truth was, so he now thinks, that until that time, despite having gained some competence in explaining things (including prayer!) to other people, he still hardly knew experientially what praying with his whole heart really meant.

What he was missing was something of which the psalms themselves speak clearly and pointedly. Psalm 86:11 reads: *"Unite* my heart to fear your name"; then the next verse, assuming an answer to this prayer, declares: "I give thanks to you, O Lord my God, with my *whole* heart" (a sentiment also found in Psalm 9:1; 111:1; 138:1). Psalm 119, the 176-verse colossus of the Psalter, speaks of seeking God (vv. 2, 10), of keeping his law (vv. 34, 69) and crying out to him "with my *whole* heart" (v. 145). What point exactly, now, was this phrase making? What were the psalmists telling us about themselves when they used it?

In this book we have been exploring the key moods and modes of personal praying, with constant appeal to the Psalter for illustration and confirmation of what we say. We begin this closing chapter by observing that in all these modes and moods praying with our whole heart is what the psalms actually model. Now, therefore, we will focus on questions that arise once we see this—questions, be it said, that neither theological expertise nor knowledge of how others have prayed nor collections of composed prayers nor mastery of any verbalizing technique can answer for us. The questions that spring to mind are: How should we comprehend the reality of praying with our whole heart? How can we tell if we are doing it? And what might be keeping us from wholeness of heart in our praying—that is, from "praying in the Holy Spirit" (Eph 6:18; Jude 20), which phrase evidently expresses, in New Testament theological terms, just the same thought? To answer these questions we must look again at what the Bible says about the heart—in other words, what God himself tells us about our human condition.

The Human Heart

In the past, writes Os Guinness:

> Character was . . . understood as the inner form that makes anyone or anything what it is. . . . Character was the deep selfhood, the essential stuff a person is made of, the core reality in which thoughts, words, decisions, behavior and relationships are rooted. As such, character determined behavior just as behavior demonstrated character. Character was *who we are when no one sees us but God.*[1]

Guinness's last sentence moves the viewpoint beyond the world of empirical observation, in which the philosophical-psychological-sociological concept of character was distilled, into the world of spiritual reality and divine revelation. In that world personal character, as described, is diagnosed as the evidence and expression of the indiscernible reality called the *heart*—"the hidden person of the heart," as Peter puts it (1 Pet 3:4)—which we may properly define as you and me as we really

---

[1] Os Guinness, *Time for Truth* (Grand Rapids: Baker, 2000), p. 46.

are in the sight of God, the seer and searcher of our hearts. Bible writers may not have known about the circulation of the blood, but clearly they knew that as the physical heart, with its pumping beat, sustains bodily life so the metaphorical heart, the dynamic inner self, energizes every aspect of our personal, relational life. All our desires, motivations, purposes and plans, good or bad; all our inner urges and powers, our relational attitudes and intentions; all our judgments, doubts, suspicions and certainties; all loves, hates, hopes, fears, rejoicings and sorrowings; all our imaginings and our creativity; all proceed from our soul or spirit or heart (these biblical terms are virtual synonyms). In the biblical sense of the word, my heart, for better or for worse, is the essence of the real living person that is me.

So our *thoughts, words* and *imaginations* come out of our hearts. Scripture assumes this throughout. When David prays, "Let the words of my mouth and the meditations of my *heart* / be acceptable in your sight, / O LORD, my rock and my redeemer" (Ps 19:14), his two phrases link up to express a single reality, the voicing of the thoughts that flow out of the heart. The two halves of Psalm 139:23, "Search me, O God, and know my *heart!* / Try me and know my thoughts!" similarly show that thoughts spring from and so reveal the heart. And when the psalmist declares, "My *heart* overflows with a pleasing theme; / I address my verses to the king; / my tongue is like the pen of a ready scribe" (Ps 45:1), he is telling us that all his poetic imaginings and celebratory utterances are products of his heart. He is writing his poem, apparently, for a royal wedding, in which the king marries his princess bride; Christians use it to celebrate the glory of the Lord Jesus taking his church into the fullness of his fellowship. All forms of exuberance issue from the heart.

So too *motives, purposes* and *plans* are rooted in our hearts. Motive, for instance, appears as God's focus of attention in Psalm 66:18, where the psalmist comments on his own praying: "If I had cherished iniquity in my *heart*"—that is formed and clung to a purpose of doing what would displease God—"the Lord would not have listened." A very different motivation is revealed in Psalm 40:8: "I desire to do your will, O my God; / your law is within my *heart.*" As for plans and purposes, note Solomon's words at the dedicating of the temple: "The LORD said to David my father, 'Whereas it was in your *heart* to build a house for my name, you did well that it was in your *heart'* " (2 Chron 6:8); and contrast Peter's admonition to Simon the sorcerer, who wanted to purchase the power to confer manifestations of the Holy Spirit at will: "Pray to the Lord that, if possible, the intent of your *heart* may be forgiven you" (Acts 8:22). Note too Jesus' devastating diagnosis of the source of the vices that foul our lives: "From within, out of the *heart* of man, come evil thoughts, sexual immorality, theft, murder, adultery, coveting, wickedness, deceit, sensuality, envy, slander, pride, foolishness" (Mk 7:21-22).

As all the blood in our body is pumped out into circulation by our physical heart, so all our hopes, dreams, brilliancies, follies, virtues and vices, all that we are and say and do, flows out of the inner essence of the real me and the real you, which the Bible calls the *heart* in this transferred, metaphorical sense.

Two things must now be underlined before we go further. First, *biblical religion is essentially heart religion;* real Christianity, as the Puritan Richard Baxter constantly insisted, is "heart-work." Observance of what Puritans called "duties"—prescribed behavioral procedures, like the practice of prayer—only please God when done for his honor and glory, done, that is, out of what Jesus called "an honest and good *heart*" (Lk 8:15), meaning a God-centered motivation, humble, thankful and adoring. Jesus taught that keeping the great commandment starts with the heart—"you shall love the Lord your God with all your *heart* and with all your soul and with all your mind and with all your strength" (Mk 12:30)—and he designates the supreme blessing of seeing God for the pure in *heart* (Mt 5:8), while castigating the Pharisees for formal religiosity without a God-attuned heart, and assuring them that "God knows your *hearts*. . . . [W]hat is exalted among men is an abomination in the sight of God" (Lk 16:15). All is wrong if the heart is not right.

This shows us why theologian John Calvin chose for the emblem on his personal seal the image of a heart held—squeezed, rather—by a giant hand, circled by the Latin words *Prompte et Sincere* (Quickly and Honestly), which told what quality of obedience to God, from his God-gripped heart, Calvin always aimed at. And it shows us why the heart figures so prominently in Cranmer's classic sixteenth-century Anglican Prayer Book, and how it is that Cranmer's prayers can be so powerful a devotional aid today. In the Holy Communion service, the Prayer Book teaches us to pray "cleanse our hearts" and "write . . . thy laws in our hearts," then to acknowledge ourselves "heartily sorry" for our sins, then to "lift up your hearts" in thanksgiving, and then, as we receive the bread, to "feed on [Christ] in our hearts by faith with thanksgiving," while the final prayer is that the peace of God may "keep your hearts in the knowledge and love of God, and of his Son, Jesus Christ our Lord." The daily service (twice-daily, on Cranmer's ordering) calls on us to confess our sins "with an humble, lowly, penitent and obedient heart . . . with a pure heart and humble voice," and asks God to "make clean our hearts within us." Other Prayer Book prayers ask for "hearts . . . mortified from all worldly and carnal lusts," for "new and contrite hearts," that God's Holy Spirit may "in all things direct and rule our hearts," and that God will "pour into our hearts such love toward thee, that we, loving thee above all things, may obtain thy promises, which exceed all that we can desire."[2] These prayers (to look no further) are samples of heart religion as it is surely meant to be.

Second, *the unrenewed human heart is fundamentally in bad shape.* An oracle from God declares: "The heart is deceitful above all things, / and desperately sick"—the NRSV renders this as "devious above all else; it is perverse"—"who can understand it? / I the LORD search the heart /

---

[2]The Book of Common Prayer is available in its 1662 English, 1928 American, and 1962 Canadian versions. The above quotations are from the Canadian text. The "other prayers" (collects) quoted are from New Year's Day, Ash Wednesday and all Lent, and the sixth and nineteenth Sundays after Trinity.

and test the mind, / to give every man according to his ways" (Jer 17:9-
10). Many times in this book the conventional assumption that people
are all naturally good (good at heart, as we say) and that only external
influences and deprivations of one sort or another ever make anyone
bad has been shown to be wrong. The truth is that all human beings
are twisted and flawed deep down inside. The human heart is in the
grip of a pernicious anti-God allergy, an inner drive toward self-
centered self-assertion at all times, a chameleon instinct for practical
self-deification that the Bible calls sin and diagnoses as pride. Pride,
thus understood, is a passion always to be in control so that all our desires get satisfied and in all relationships we dominate. So pride makes
impossible a truly respectful attitude to other people, which sees
everyone else as mattering more than oneself (the way Paul says it should
be: see Phil 2:3), and it makes impossible a truly reverent attitude to
God, which sees his glory as all that matters and ourselves as here to
praise and please him in all that we do, starting with our treatment of
others. All God-centeredness is categorically ruled out by the "me-ism"
of pride. If therefore we practice religion, pride in that religion is at the
heart of it, and if we do not practice religion, pride is the seed of our
idea that we do not need God in order to live well. Pride within leads
us to affirm ourselves, feeling that we are the world's most important
people; pride teaches us to justify ourselves, seeing what we have done
and are doing now as essentially good and decent behavior, whatever
those around us may think to the contrary; and pride generates satisfaction with ourselves as we are, with consequent unwillingness to
change or be changed. Such is the bad news about the human heart.

Pride, operating as described, is the reality that Christians call original
sin. "He laughed at original sin" is a biting line from Hilaire Belloc, who
knew, as all believers do, that our sinful pride or prideful sin (call it
whichever you like) is no laughing matter. Pride as described above is
the willing pandemic of the human community. Born in us, it is precisely
that sickness of the heart to which Jeremiah points, and it produces rad-

ical inward malaise and malfunctioning—deformity, indeed—throughout our entire spiritual system. We speak today of tobacco, drinking and
drug habits as addictions, and sin too is an addiction, a habit of the heart
that mars and undermines what might have appeared at first as good
character. And this sinful heart of ours is in its sickness, as Jeremiah tells
us, supremely deceitful—devious, falsifying, fantasizing, self-deceiving,
as addicts' hearts always are: which means that we ourselves by ourselves
can never be fully realistic about ourselves, never discern our own inner
twistedness, until God begins to reveal to us what is really wrong with
us. Only God can show us the root of our addictive denial of reality,
namely, our inescapable awareness, deep down, of our Creator and his
claims, which our heart so obsessively distorts or denies. Only God,
whom we cannot deceive, however much we may wish and try to, can
free us from the self-deceptions that our sinful pride has generated. Today's world is full of bad news, much of it truly horrific, but the bad news
about human hearts and the consequences facing those whose hearts are
not changed is the worst of all.

THE NEW HEART

The Bible proclaims the healing of the heart as a gift of God through the
gospel, an integral aspect of the divine work of saving grace. God through
Ezekiel speaks of it in these terms: "I will give you a new heart, and a new
spirit I will put within you. And I will remove the heart of stone from your
flesh and give you a heart of flesh. And I will put my Spirit within you and
cause you to walk in my statutes" (Ezek 36:26-27). It is natural to suppose
that this passage was in Jesus' mind when he used the two-word parable
"born again" (or, perhaps, "born from above") to describe this change to
Nicodemus (Jn 3:3-8) and when he chided "the teacher of Israel"—the
supposed expert, therefore, on Scripture—for not knowing what the person he had hailed as "a teacher come from God" was talking about (vv. 10,
12). Certainly this was what John had in mind when he spoke of being
"born" of God (see 1 Jn 2:29; 3:9; 4:7; 5:1, 18). Certainly this is what Paul

had in mind when he spoke of believers being co-resurrected in Christ with Christ out of prior spiritual death (Eph 2:1-10; Col 2:9-14), and out of death in Christ with Christ, accepted as the deserved end of one's life to date without God (Rom 6:3-11), and when he spoke of the believer as a new creation in Christ (2 Cor 5:17; Gal 6:15), saved through "the washing [that consists] of regeneration and renewal by the Holy Spirit" (Tit 3:5). Regeneration and new birth, co-resurrection and new creation are four names for the same work of God.

Those who come to living faith in the living Christ as their Savior and Master find themselves radically changed inside, and one mark of the change is that remembering God and looking to him and praying to him as Father (and praying to Jesus also) are now instinctive movements of the soul (see Rom 8:15-16; Gal 4:6). The miracle that we call regeneration has taken place, the heart is new, everything is different and fellowshiping with the Father and the Son through the ongoing ministry of the indwelling Holy Spirit, who maintains our sense of union and communion with and abiding in both of them (see 1 Jn 1:3; 2:20-24; 3:24), become our natural and habitual way of life.

The New Testament shows us three linked qualities that will mark out all those whose hearts have been thus renewed. First, they will be consistently *repentant*. That means more than being rueful, regretful and remorseful. Understanding repentance as turning back from the dark paths of self-service to face, love, thank and serve God, and as forsaking all former practices of disobeying and departing from them, and acknowledging therewith the guilt of those practices and clinging to Christ for forgiveness through his cross, and as resolutely following him into a life of devoted discipleship, they will repeatedly renew their commitment to holiness, and they will constantly reexamine themselves in God's presence to make sure that no ungodly ways have crept back in. This thoroughgoing personal repentance is beautifully focused by Francis Ridley Havergal. Though the following verses are placed in most hymnals and song books in sections on commitment to Christian service, repentance is the reality that Havergal is here spelling out.

Take my life, and let it be
consecrated, Lord to thee.
Take my moments and my days;
let them flow in ceaseless praise.

Take my hands, and let them move
at the impulse of thy love.
Take my feet, and let them be
swift and beautiful for thee.

Take my voice, and let me sing,
always, only, for my King.
Take my lips, and let them be
filled with messages from thee.

Take my silver and my gold;
not a mite would I withhold
Take my intellect, and use
ev'ry pow'r as thou shalt choose

Take my will, and make it thine;
it shall be no longer mine.
Take my heart it is thine own;
it shall be thy royal throne.

Take my love; my Lord, I pour
at the feet its treasure store.
Take myself, and I will be
ever, only, all for thee.[3]

Second, those whose hearts have been changed in the way described will be consciously *returning* to God day by day—traveling home, that is, to their Maker, Defender, Redeemer and Friend, from whom, like the prodigal in Jesus' parable, they had wandered away. This is the larger

[3]Francis Ridley Havergal, "Take My Life and Let It Be" (1874).

frame of understanding within which their repentance and consecration are set. As daily they renew the giving of their lives back to God, so they see themselves coming ever closer to the joy they will know when they are finally home with the Father, the Son and the Spirit in the glory God has prepared, as we are told (1 Cor 2:9), for those who love him. Scottish minister George Matheson expressed some of this when he poeticized his pain at losing the lady who broke her engagement to him because he was blind. What his prayer song voices is not the self-pity we might have expected but the worship and hope of a faithful returner.

O Love that will not let me go,
I rest my weary soul in thee;
I give thee back the life I owe,
that in thine ocean depths its flow
may richer, fuller be.

O Light that follow'st all my way,
I yield my flickering torch to thee;
my heart restores its borrowed ray,
that in thy sunshine's blaze its day
may brighter, fairer be.

O Joy that seekest me through pain,
I cannot close my heart to thee;
I trace the rainbow through the rain,
and feel the promise is not vain
that morn shall tearless be.

O Cross that liftest up my head,
I dare not ask to fly from thee;
I lay in dust life's glory dead
and from the ground there blossoms red
life that shall endless be.[4]

---

[4]George Matheson, "O Love That Will Not Let Me Go" (1882).

The vision of faithful Christian living as returning to God, both as a response to disappointment and pain and as a daily discipline and indeed as a life project, flows from texts like the doxology with which Paul rounds off his doctrinal exposition in Romans: "From [God] and through him and to him are all things. To him be glory forever. Amen" (Rom 11:36). Here, from a mountaintop of theological insight and vision, Paul proclaims that all is *from* God in the sense that he has created it; all is *through* him in the sense that he sustains and overrules all existence and all life, including our own; and all is *to* him in the sense that he is its destination, goal, recipient and inheritor. In other words, all persons, all living things, all created realities, all historical processes and all products of art, science, imagination, ingenuity, and skill are means to his glory, pleasure, and praise; either by reason of the intrinsic quality that is in them through his own giving or by reason of the wisdom, truth, and justice that he has shown and will show in dealing with all forms of sin, all living of lies, all corrupting of beauty into ugliness, and all modes of callousness and cruelty, both human and Satanic. All these evils are due to receive, if they have not already received, the retribution they deserve, and God's love for the goodness he imparts and for all who by his grace learn to cherish it shines forth ever more gloriously as a result. (What a weight of meaning that little word *to*, which of itself signifies simply movement toward some link with something or somebody, is carrying in this verse!)

Persons with renewed hearts see the triune God, in all the majesty that Scripture ascribes to him, as filling their horizon—rather, as being their horizon—at every point. They look at everything in the light of God, and everything becomes a path leading their thoughts to God; and that is because the regenerate heart loves and desires God more intensely and insistently than human lovers ever desire their beloveds.

Whom have I in heaven but you?
And there is nothing on earth that I desire besides you.

My flesh and my heart may fail,
> but God is the strength of my heart and my portion forever.
>> (Ps 73:25-26)

I say to the LORD, "You are my Lord;
> I have no good apart from you.". . .
The LORD is my chosen portion and my cup. . . .
I have set the LORD always before me . . .
> in your presence is fullness of joy;
> at your right hand are pleasures forevermore. (Ps 16:2, 5, 8, 11)

O God, you are my God; earnestly I seek you;
> my soul thirsts for you, . . .
> as in a dry and weary land where there is no water. . . .
Because your steadfast love is better than life,
> my lips will praise you. (Ps 63:1-3)

Starting from where they are at any moment in their life, regenerate persons constantly feel, deep down, that drawing closer to God through Christ and the Spirit in union and communion, prayer and praise is what they most want to do, and this feeling stays with them. In other words, the regenerate are now programmed for that great life-embracing, life-enhancing return, within which all specific acts of repenting and coming back to God find their place. This mindset is exemplified by George Matheson's poignant lyric (see p. 269) and is at least faintly illustrated by the lifting of spirits that all hikers know when they turn and head for home. Homecoming is a joyful affair in ordinary life, and it certainly is so as we travel home to God.

Matheson's words have become a familiar hymn, and all who stand and sing it in worship should be praying it as they do so; thus, please God, we may come to share with Matheson the renewing of light, joy and peace within that flow from knowing we are loved by God as we face up to Christ's cross in relation to our personal hurts, disappointments and distresses.

Third, the desire of the renewed heart for God and for the fullness of life in God moves returners to become *runners*, exerting themselves with a zeal, effort and focus matching that of athletes going flat out to win their race. Racing is in fact a recurring New Testament picture of faithful, purposeful, cutting-edge discipleship (see 1 Cor 9:24, 26; Gal 2:2; Phil 2:16; 2 Tim 4:7; Heb 12:1; cf. Acts 20:24). Paul describes his personal running as follows: "Not that I . . . am already perfect, but I press on to make it [resurrection from the dead] my own, because Christ Jesus has made me his own. . . . [F]orgetting what lies behind and straining forward to what lies ahead, I press on toward the goal for the prize of the upward call of God in Christ Jesus" (Phil 3:12-14). He spells this out, note, for imitation: "Let those of us who are mature think this way" (v. 15). Similarly Hebrews 12:1-2 urges us to "lay aside every weight, and the sin which clings so closely, and let us run with endurance the race that is set before us, looking to Jesus." We will be on the home stretch, with the prize before us; we will be running home.

My (Carolyn) friends Jim and Carol have taken the image of "pilgrim" as a lifelong model. Raised in a missionary family on one continent, schooled in a second, then serving as a missionary in a third continent and finally as assistant director of a large international mission agency, at midlife Carol had trouble thinking of any earthly place as "home." Eventually she realized that her home did not have any earthly address. She and Jim are pilgrims here, sometimes running, sometimes walking, but their home is in eternity with Jesus. All of what happens here, including Jim's one-hundred-page passport, is a journey toward heaven. When they recently returned to Ecuador, where Carol grew up, they were assigned identification tags labeled "Temporary Visitor." They accepted this tag as a badge testifying not only of their trip to Ecuador but of their entire lives—on a journey to eternity. And the smiles on their faces while they continue without fixed abode in this world speak not of the misery of refugees who have left their home behind but of the eager merriment of returners running home, and very much looking forward to arriving there.

THE UNITED HEART

What we have said so far might seem to imply that those who have been inwardly renewed in Christ by the Spirit will always have their hearts united, as Psalm 86:11 puts it, to fear God's name—that is, to honor, revere, love, praise, thank, obey and thus glorify him—with all their energy and powers of concentration all the time. But though it will certainly be like that in heaven, the reality here on earth is not so simple. Before we came to faith, the God-repelling allergic addiction called sin dominated our hearts, and sin continues its effects on us. Motivationally and behaviorally the effects of sin were twofold: first, to keep the true God at a distance while we played God to ourselves, and, second, to disintegrate our focus on life so that in our desires, dreams, actions and habits we became complicated, compartmentalized and inwardly chaotic to a degree, with self-centered passions driving and pulling us in any number of directions at once. When in the course of his journey to faith C. S. Lewis turned at last to serious practical self-examination, "I found," he writes, "what appalled me; a zoo of lusts, a bedlam of ambition, a nursery of fears, a hareem [sic] of fondled hatreds. My name was legion."[5] All unregenerate adults are in fact in the same boat, and though when we come to faith this tangle of self-regarding drives and urges ceases to rule us, many of its components remain with us, marauding inwardly to poison the springs of our new purpose in Christ and to regain as much control of our behavior as they can. This is what Paul refers to when he writes: "the desires of the flesh are against the Spirit, and the desires of the Spirit are against the flesh, for these are opposed to each other, to keep you from doing the things you want to do" (Gal 5:17). The words "the things you want to do" refer to the range of purposeful de-

---

[5]C. S. Lewis, *Surprised by Joy* (London: Fontana, 1959), p. 181.

sires that now dominates our life—the desires, that is, that are aspects and tributaries of the single overmastering desire, to glorify God with our whole heart.

But the desires that constitute the flesh in Paul's sense, though now dethroned, are not yet destroyed, and in many cases remain psychologically potent within us. Perfect accomplishment of what we want most heartily to do is still beyond us: at this point our reach exceeds our grasp. To be sure, we fight moral and spiritual battles with what we find inside us and we win victories; we make progress, cleansing ourselves "from every defilement of body and spirit, bringing holiness to completion in the fear of God" (2 Cor 7:1). But here on earth the task is never finished. Everything we do appears in retrospect as something we could and should have done better, and whenever we measure our actual performance by Scripture, shortcomings stand out.

In Romans 7:7-25 Paul offers a personal analysis of this to bring out and ram home his larger gospel theme of deliverance in Christ from law religion to life in the Spirit (see Rom 7:6; 8:2). Paul's point is that for himself as a sample Christian, just as it had been for him in his pre-Christian days, the law, which spells out God's standard of righteousness, gives no power against the lapses it forbids, exposes and condemns. Playing with the word *law,* Paul speaks of a "law" in his human system that wars against the "law" of his mind and takes him captive against his will. His analysis ends with a rhetorical summary: "So then, I myself serve the law of God with my mind, but with my flesh I serve the law of sin" (v. 25). The first half of the statement refers to the voluntary service of the renewed heart, expressed in a thoughtful purpose of law-keeping obedience to God; the second half refers to the involuntary down drag of indwelling sin in its myriad forms, obstructing, distracting, dissembling, deceiving and keeping us from doing, properly and purely, the things that we most want to do. Things our hearts know we should not do—little things, maybe, but grievous—repeatedly fool us into thinking we want to do them just this once or into doing them with-

Santa Clara County Library District

408-293-2326

Checked Out Items 8/18/2016 17:46
XXXXXXXXXX4886

Item Title	Due Date
1. Praying : finding our way through duty to delight 33305211386432	9/8/2016

No of Items: 1

24/7 Telecirc: 800-471-0991
www.sccl.org
Thank you for visiting our library.

out thinking at all, and then we wake up to the fact that we have done, not the good we should have done, but things that were poor quality, much less than the best, and often downright bad. This is an ongoing aspect of every Christian's experience as long as we are in this world.

So Christian living involves a permanent element of conflict and struggle, not only with temptations that come from outside but with impulses, urges, attitudes, moods and mental states that bubble up around the heart and to some extent block and derail our purpose of obeying and honoring God with perfect purity of heart and perfect precision of action. We do not want to be less than perfect in serving God, but in practice we always are. So when Scripture speaks of praying with our whole heart, the focus is on intention rather than accomplishment, and the wholeness of heart referred to is comparative rather than absolute. The desire expressed is that our praying here and now may fully reflect God's work of uniting our heart (one aspect of ongoing sanctification) as far as it has gone.

To be sure, refreshing moments are given us when our heart feels utterly fixed on God and completely united and absorbed in loving response to him, but these do not last, nor are they ever the whole story. There is always more going on inside us motivationally and temperamentally than we are aware of at any moment, as professional counselors, helping us to look back, are often in retrospect able to show us. Meanwhile, as we persevere in prayer, we can count on God's work of uniting our heart to progress.

Just how much does it mean then to ask for and receive, on a moment-by-moment basis, both for our praying and for our private and public living, a heart united to fear God? Comparing translations of the Hebrew verb in Psalm 86:11 points us to the answer. *Unite* is in KJV, RSV, NASB and ESV. The classic Anglican Prayer Book has "knit my heart unto thee." "Give me an undivided heart" is the NIV, TNIV and NRSV rendering. Among the paraphrases, TEV offers "train me to serve you with complete devotion"; NLT has "grant me purity of heart"; and *The Message* from and perhaps most luminous of the lot, gives us "Put me together, one heart and mind; / then undivided, I'll worship in joyful fear." This is then followed in the next verse by "from the bottom of my heart" for the Hebrew "with my whole heart," which catches the nuance beautifully. "Unite my heart" is thus revealed as a prayer that all Christians frustrated by the Romans 7:14-25 experience would and should naturally make. (Several psalmists evidently knew this experience, even if they had no words for it, and every real Christian knows it.) The prayer is for an increase of inner integration that will show itself in an ever deeper and more intense concentration on God himself, the light and joy of the psalmists' life and ideally of ours too.

Four tests will tell us how far our own hearts are united Godward in this sense. We note them now before we go further. First, how far are our *heads* right? All renewed hearts have an instinct for embracing Bible doctrine as God's truth and for interpreting and assessing all life by it, and for sensing God's presence and gift in all that is good everywhere. A bleak alternative to this, of course, is the all-too-familiar reality of compartmental living, whereby religion is viewed as a distinct department of our existence, and prayer is one of the due tasks in that department, but this religiosity has no link with the rest of our life, where sick fancies and porn or envy and hate or power-hungry ambition and greed may still be in full control. This, however, is a version of the hypocritical role play that Jesus condemned in the Pharisees and that we should condemn too. It is an evil to be avoided. So, what should we say of our own head—the life of our own mind?

Second, how far are our *hands* right?—used, that is, with a purpose of pleasing God? "Take my hands, and let them move / at the impulse of thy love," wrote Frances Havergal. Hands stand for our life activities, all the many things we actually do. The question is, are they engaged to please God or just to please ourselves or those around us? Pleasing others is a trap we must learn to avoid. So, what should we say of our own hands—the actions and enterprises of our own life?

Third, how far are our *habits* right? What of our routines? Our favorite ways of spending time not otherwise committed? Our cherished ways of thinking and subjects of thought? Our hobby and sports interests, even? Things that are not good or that are overdone can become so routine that our conscience ceases to complain with regard to them, and thus moral sores can become part of our being without our realizing it. That often happens when bad habits get hold of us. So, are our own habits holy? Are we concerned that they should be? Are we trying to make them so? What should we say of our habits, the formed and formative regularities of our own life?

Fourth, how far are our *hopes* right? Human beings live very much in their personal hopes, and it is of things hoped for that Jesus speaks when he tells us to lay up treasure in heaven, since where our treasure is there our heart will be (Mt 6:20-21). What do we save for, plan for, scheme for, pray for? Is it for the joy of ever-closer fellowship with the Father and the Son, here and hereafter, that we hope most of all? Does the hope of giving our gracious God pleasure unify what we do with our lives? And will it be to God's honor if the hopes we most ardently cherish at this moment are fulfilled? So, what should we say of our hopes—the focus so largely of our own present life?

From these necessary questions it can be seen that we need to watch like hawks what it is that we take into our hearts, for what we take in will always seek to take over. We are what we are at heart, no more, no less. The heart becomes the inside story of everyone's life, and we do not understand ourselves, or anyone else for that matter, until we are in touch with what goes on in us and in them at heart level. So we cannot wonder that in the book of Proverbs, where the literary form is a wise man instructing his son, there are constant admonitions to guard our hearts and seek to harness them in obedient trust Godward. "Trust in the LORD with all your *heart*, / and do not lean to your own understanding" (Prov 3:5). "Let your *heart* hold fast my words; / keep my commandments and live" (Prov 4:4).

My son, be attentive to my words;
   incline your ear to my sayings.
Let them not escape from your sight;
   keep them within your *heart*. . . .
Keep your *heart* with all vigilance,
   for from it flow the springs of life. (Prov 4:20-21, 23)

We are to aim at avoiding what pollutes the springs, says the wise man; that is wisdom and anything else is folly.

PRAYING IN THE SPIRIT WITH THE WHOLE HEART

We have gone into detail about the human heart, in the biblical sense of that phrase, because it is so little understood by Christians today. We referred earlier to J. I.'s longstanding failure to appreciate the whole-heart praying of the psalmists because, as he now sees, his personal piety, such as it was and marked as it was by a good deal of surface-level passion, was still too cerebral, and his heart, deep down, was still too much in a "frozen-chosen" mold, needing to be loosened up and indeed warmed up. We do not think he is the only modern Western Christian who has had a problem here. Our individualistic culture in the West naturally spawns a sense of identity in isolation, and many instinctively guard their sense of distance in all their commerce with people and things outside themselves; and this makes openhearted, uninhibited, self-surrendering Christian transparency, both Godward and manward, difficult and at first unwelcome.

Now please be clear: what we are talking about at this point is not just achieving wholeheartedness in the everyday sense of warm, unhesitating, enthusiastic and robust commitment to something or someone, desirable though that sort of wholeheartedness so often is. The biblical reality that we have in view is the spiritual, supernatural wholeness of heart that springs from realizing two overwhelming truths. Truth one is that without the Father, the Lord Jesus and the Holy Spirit we would be lost in darkness and discontent forever. Truth two is that, through the love of the holy Three who have rescued us from ruin, we are already enjoying a new life of acceptance, fellowship and security with God, the life of joy, peace, praise and happiness in holiness that will be ours in much greater fullness to all eternity. As we realize these realities more deeply, our hearts become freer, lighter, more God-entranced and thus constantly closer to the psalmists' hearts as expressed in their recorded verbal praying. That is the matter of fact that we aim to unpack now.

The New Testament twice directs us to pray in the Holy Spirit. What, we ask, does that mean? Not, we think, praying in tongues, though some may experience that. Nor is praying in the Holy Spirit praying out of some kind of ecstatic inner experience every time. In our view, praying in the Spirit means conversing responsively with God on the basis of a triple awareness, each element of which flows out of the teachings of Scripture and is imparted to us by the indwelling Holy Spirit of God.

The first awareness is a panoramic understanding of the new-created, new covenantal, Christ-centered order of things that now overlays and augments the ongoing life of this planet and its inhabitants. The focal point of the new order is God's gift of eternal life to believers, the life of fellowship with God that will go on through eternity and never end. This new life is a present reality for all those who through faith know, trust, love and serve Jesus Christ as their Savior King. The resulting global awareness of God's salvation purposes, which the Holy Spirit writes in their hearts via Holy Scripture, may be pulled together and schematized in order as follows:

• Believers know themselves to be new creatures, born again, each blessed with a new heart that draws and drives them to a constant exercising of faith in the biblical Christ and of repentant obedience to the Bible's God, and to praising, honoring, and seeking to please and glorify their Maker as their life's purpose.

• Believers know themselves to be ransomed, healed, restored, forgiven and adopted into God's family through the atoning death of Jesus Christ the Mediator, whose personal presence with them through the Holy Spirit is now a permanent fact.

- Believers know themselves to be indwelt by the Holy Spirit, who out of Scripture shows them God's ways, work and will, who united them to Christ as limbs in his body so that they share his endless risen life, and who gives them direction and confidence in their praying, along with discernment to see how God is answering their requests.

- Believers know themselves to be traveling home to heaven's glory along a very up-and-down, sometimes very rough and rocky road, and they are continually having to learn to accept its hardships.

- Believers know themselves committed, as limbs in Christ's one universal church body, to serve God and others both in a Christian congregation and in Christian fellowship between and across congregations, giving themselves unstintingly to meet needs, to maintain unity, to support all that makes for church growth, both qualitative and quantitative, and to do everything they can to extend Christ's kingdom in this world.

- Believers know themselves to be up against Satanic opposition to the Savior, the gospel, the church and themselves personally as Christ's loyalists, and they accept that faithfulness to Christ in face of anti-God influences all around inescapably involves them in spiritual warfare, in overt opposition to much that they meet, and in countercultural gestures, strategies and stances of many kinds.

- Believers know that God's church, of which they are part, is his task force, now on mission in the world to make Christ known everywhere, to practice neighbor-loving Samaritanship everywhere, and to use all available means of witness and channels of influence to further Christian forms of family life, education, commerce, politics, entertainment and artistic culture.

- Believers know that holiness is their personal priority, that evil must not be done even as a means to a good end, that where no option is free from unhappy side effects the least evil is to be chosen, that the merely good (or not bad) must never become the enemy of the best, and that justice with peace is the goal to aim at in all community clashes of whatever kind.

Such, in brief, is the panoramic, comprehensive, big-picture view of the Christian calling that the Holy Spirit communicates to all God's people. What it involves in detail is something that all of us go on discovering all our days, but the convictional outline remains as above, shaping both our behavior and our prayers.

The second awareness is a progressive, intensifying realization of the glory of our Lord Jesus Christ as our Savior, Master and Friend, our prophet, priest, and king, our Lord and our God. The Spirit leads us to dwell on his wisdom, power and love as the Shepherd whose sheep we are, as the Vine whose branches we are, and as the Redeemer whose ransomed trophies we are: the Redeemer who in love gave himself up to die on the cross in order to rescue each of us personally from hell, and who in love will keep us close to himself forever. It was Jesus' promise that when the Spirit should come to fulfill what we may properly call his Pentecostal ministry: "He will glorify me, for he will take what is mine and declare it to you" (Jn 16:14). What then is it that the Spirit makes increasingly vivid to us? Jesus' person and work, his preeminence and power; his identity and dignity as the enthroned Son of God; his past, present and future deeds; his love, faithfulness, promises and gifts to us and care for us—in short, everything about him. Thus the Spirit glorifies Jesus, making him glorious in our eyes, so that he fills the horizon and becomes the central reference point of our existence. And the Spirit has been doing this for all believers ever since that momentous Pentecost morning that Luke in Acts 2 describes.

Our part is to be careful lest by any means we resist, obstruct, grieve and so quench the Holy Spirit so that we miss the full benefit of this ministry (see Acts 7:51; Eph 4:30; 1 Thess 5:19). On the contrary, we should constantly be praying that the Spirit will open the eyes of our minds and hearts wider so that we may see more of what he is showing us—specifically, the Son's role as the channel to us of every good thing God gives us, starting with our very existence and moving on to every aspect of the grace and mercy that saves and transforms us sinners. (See and study in detail how Paul spells all this out in one brief letter, Col 1:13-22; 2:6-15; 3:1-17.)

Paul, who began as a hater of Jesus' name and a hammerer of his disciples, became a man for whom Jesus Christ truly was all in all (see Phil 1:20-23), filling the entire horizon of his life as the lover and Lord of his soul (Gal 2:20). The love of Christ, he says, meaning the love Christ has shown to him, was the driving, directing, captivating, controlling, compulsive and propulsive force of his life, animating and energizing all his years of selfless service as a church planter and pastor (2 Cor 5:14; cf. 2 Cor 11:23-33). Certainly Paul was a driven man, but it was his sense of the hugeness of Christ's love and mercy to him that drove him. He could never get Christ out of his mind, nor did he want to. He never ceased to be thrilled and thunderstruck by the way Jesus had laid hold of him in the midst of his vendetta against the church and turned him right around. Henceforth Christ was his reference point in everything, and no one could ever more truly take on their lips John Newton's words of address to Jesus: "My Lord, my life, my way, my end."[6] The apostle was permanently humbled, dazzled, entranced and overjoyed at Christ's "love beyond degree," as Isaac Watts phrased it,[7] and it is no surprise to find him writing to his friends at Philippi:

> Whatever gain I had, I counted as loss for the sake of Christ. Indeed, I count everything as loss because of the surpassing worth of knowing Christ Jesus my Lord. For his sake I have suffered the loss of all things and count them as rubbish, in order that I may gain Christ and be

---

[6]John Newton, "How Sweet the Name of Jesus Sounds" (1779).
[7]Isaac Watts, "Alas! And Did My Savior Bleed" (1707).

found in him, . . . that I may know him. (Phil 3:7-10)

At the end of this passage of testimony he declares that his own Christ-centeredness is a model for all believers. "Let those of us who are mature think this way" (v. 15). For the Spirit is given us to lead us all along the path.

That is made explicit by Paul's prayer in Ephesians 3:14-19. Look at the cumulative sequence of petitions for his readers that he spells out.

- That the Holy Spirit will give power and energy to "the hidden person of the heart" (1 Pet 3:4). "That . . . he may grant you to be strengthened with power through his Spirit in your inner being" (v. 16).

- That Christ will reside in the Ephesians' hearts as their faith, spurred to action by the Spirit, reaches out to him in adoration and communion. "That Christ may dwell in your hearts through faith" (v. 17).

- That they will receive an enlarged and enlarging realization of Christ's saving love, in which as believers they are already anchored as their life-foundation. "That you, being rooted and grounded in love, may have strength [not the same word as in v. 15 but a synonym] to comprehend with all the saints what is the breadth and length and height and depth, and to know the love of Christ that surpasses knowledge" (vv. 17-19). Paul's wording seems to express the thought that the more adequately we are enabled to discern the love of Christ and to measure it by what he has done for us already, plus what he promises to do for us in the future, the less adequate to the reality do we feel our perception to be. As when through clearing fog we see the beginning of an overwhelming view and are thereby made more eager to see the rest of it as the fog retreats further, so it is with the love of Christ. As more and more of its selflessness, beauty and power emerges, we find ourselves breathless, mesmerized and, as we put it, carried away.

Samuel Francis catches something of this when he sings:

> O the deep, deep love of Jesus!
> Vast, unmeasured, boundless, free,
> Rolling, as a mighty ocean
> In its fullness over me.
> Underneath me, all around me,
> Is the current of thy love,
> Leading onward, leading homeward,
> To my glorious rest above.[8]

- That an enriching transformation of personal being and moral character from one degree of glory to another, into the likeness of Christ, who as the image of God is being formed within, may be the ongoing reality of their lives. "That you may be filled with all the fullness of God" (v. 19).

For Paul himself and for the Ephesians, and for us, a twofold knowledge is involved here. Realization of the insuperable strength, determination and tenacity of Christ's love for us grows with increasing awareness of the seemingly unfathomable perversity, fertility, futility, nastiness, guilt and shame of our own sinfulness. It has often been observed that Paul's way of referring to his unworthiness, extravagant-sounding to start with, became yet more extravagant as he went along. In 1 Corinthians 15:9 (53 A.D., perhaps) he is "the least of the apostles, unworthy to be called an apostle, because I persecuted the church of God." In Ephesians 3:8 (61 A.D., perhaps) he is "the very least of all the saints." In 1 Timothy 1:15 (63 A.D., perhaps) he refers to "sinners, of whom I am the foremost." It is natural to see this progression down as direct evidence of the Spirit's ongoing exaltation of Christ in his heart by making the Savior's love ever more vivid and precious to him. It is certain that the more clearly the Spirit makes persons appreciate the grandeur of Christ's self-giving love for them, the more they will depreciate them-

---

[8]Samuel Francis, "O the Deep, Deep Love of Jesus" (1875).

selves for the perceived defects of their past and present lives. And in every case the love of Christ is the centerpiece of the glory of Christ of which the Spirit works to make each of us increasingly conscious.

The third reality is the beauty, wisdom and power of the Father, the Son and the Spirit as displayed in the order of creation and natural providence. What to unbelievers is just the way things work is for Christians the endlessly fascinating display area of an endlessly resourceful God, endlessly to be adored for the wonders of nature as well as those of redemption. That takes us back to the world of Job 38—41, Proverbs 8 and many of the psalms. This aspect of the Spirit's ministry is important, more so than is often realized, but this is not the place where we can discuss it in full.

Our present point, the point on which we close, is that praying in the Holy Spirit means opening ourselves continually to the Holy Spirit's ministry of leading us to contemplate and rejoice in the various facets of the glory of our Lord Jesus Christ, and to respond to them in a way that becomes the frame and foundation for the rest of our praying lifelong. What is affirmed here is that this is what constitutes for Christians the reality of praying with our whole heart: Christians pray with a single commanding and controlling focus on the glory of the Lord. And we are told further to affirm that all who pray clearheadedly in terms of the guidelines that this formula provides will find a new fruitfulness in their praying; for God's promise, given to very imperfect Israelites long ago, still stands, so we believe, as a word to us Christians: "When you seek me with all your heart, I will be found by you" (Jer 29:13-14).

Such, then, is true praying in the Holy Spirit, who always glorifies Christ; praying as those who truly know God through Christ praying out of a true, whole, united heart; praying according to the revealed will of God; praying in terms of the pattern set by the Psalter and modeled by the many whose prayings are recorded in the biblical narrative. We who write, like you who read, dare not claim to be more than beginners in God's school of prayer; so—Lord, teach us to pray! Amen.

POSTSCRIPT TO CHRISTIANS BECALMED IN THEIR PRAYING

We began this book in hope of helping Christians who want and try to pray, but who feel that their praying is somehow stuck and that they need some form of jump-start. The image of a sailing ship with no wind in its sails illustrates their feeling exactly. What causes this feeling may have no direct relation to prayer as such: the sense of getting nowhere in prayer may be a byproduct and thus a sign and symptom of some physical or mental or circumstantial condition that strikes at the life and balance of the mind; or from a trough of emotional exhaustion after a high of some kind, sustained perhaps over some length of time; or from long neglecting the sabbath principle of programming periodic variety, regular rest, and sufficient sleep into one's life, all of which conditions make our hearts unfit for prayer just as having pneumonia unfits our bodies for playing hockey. When we feel stuck in prayer, all these possible reasons why should be checked out first. It may be medication rather than spiritual discipline that is needed to remove the blockage. But if the problem really is as it feels, then we would like to offer here some practical suggestions that may help.

Prepare to pray by first thinking over who it is that you will be addressing, what he has done to give you access to himself and a permanent claim on his attention, how you stand related to him at this moment, and how little you deserved the gifts of forgiveness, freedom and a place in the Father's family that you enjoy now. Think of the truly breathtaking fact that through his Word and Spirit the Lord Jesus is building a friendship with you, sinful though you are, and that he is looking to you to be building a friendship of love, trust and obedience with him through your responsive words to him in prayer. Then start talking to your Father and your Savior in terms of the thoughts that are now in your mind.

Pray aloud, at least in a whisper. Speaking your words, even if under your breath, "lipping" your prayers as some call it, helps you to concentrate on what you are doing and guards you against wandering thoughts. In the sixteenth through nineteenth centuries (to look no further), praying Christians regularly spoke their private prayers aloud, and the idea that private prayer should always be made in total silence is quite recent, just as it is quite silly. Moreover, when you are on your own, it will ordinarily help you if you punctuate your out-loud praying by singing or reading aloud favorite hymns and songs of praise. The older Methodist way was to take a hymn book as well as a Bible into their place of private prayer and to use both, and their example, we believe, remains one to follow.

If ever you find yourself lost for words, especially when you contemplate God's holy majesty at the start of a prayer time (and who has not known that experience?) but also at any other point when your heart feels blocked and in need of uncorking, turn to the Lord's Prayer (a model for disciples, Jesus said, as well as a set form: see Mt 6:9; Lk 11:2), and use each clause of this prayer as a hook on which to hang amplifying thoughts of your own. Martin Luther, who used and taught others to use the prayer this way every day, recommended making "a garland of four twisted strands"—first, a celebration of the gracious truth(s) that each clause displays; then, words of thanks to God for all the good gifts from him of which the clause reminds you; then, a confession of your failures, of whatever sort, to take those words seriously as a guide to life; and finally, a voicing of whatever specific petitions the clause might prompt.[1] C. S. Lewis had a similar routine, which he called *festooning* the clauses.[2]

---

[1]See Walter Trobisch, "Martin Luther's Quiet Time," in *The Complete Works of Walter Trobisch* (Downers Grove, Ill.: InterVarsity Press, 1987), pp. 705-13.

[2]C. S. Lewis, *Letters to Malcolm: Chiefly on Prayer* (London: Geoffrey Bles, 1964), pp. 38-44.

Doing this gets your thoughts going, and where thoughts go words will follow.

Have handy secondary sources of help, such as the original Anglican Book of Common Prayer (an enormous help, being so closely attuned to Scripture, sin, grace and the heart). Use prayers composed by others, not as mantras to repeat as if they were spells (a common mistake) but as launchpads for your own thinking about whether this is what you want or need or ought to be saying to God. When you are clear on this, write out your thoughts as your own prayer, which you then actually pray, and you will find that that gets you going in thoughtful personal praying about other things.

Listen for God as you pray your way through the Lord's Prayer. Continue listening as you precede or follow your moments of prayer with the reading of Scripture. What Luther said about listening in prayer is as fruitful as and perhaps more fruitful than anything that has been said on the subject since his day. For Luther:

> It often happens that I lose myself . . . [literally, "that my thoughts go for a walk"] in one petition of the Lord's Prayer, and then I let all the other six petitions go. When such rich good thoughts come, one should . . . listen to them in silence and by no means suppress them. For here the Holy Spirit himself is preaching and one word of his sermon is better than thousands of our own prayers. . . .
>
> If the Holy Spirit should come and begin to preach to your heart, giving you rich and enlightened thoughts, . . . be quiet and listen to him who can talk better than you; and note what he proclaims and *write it down*; so will you experience miracles as David says: "Open my eyes that I may behold wondrous things out of thy law" (Ps 119:18).[3]

Writing what you hear from God as you read and pray remains wisdom: it takes you beyond the monotonous ruts of generalized piety to a variety of insights, realism about both God and yourself, and deepening

---

[3]Martin Luther, cited in Trobisch, "Martin Luther's Quiet Time," pp. 710, 712.

discovery of God's holy ways, leaving you with more than enough to pray about every day.

Form a prayer partnership with someone whose concerns match your own, and share with each other what God shows you as you experiment with some of these suggestions, or maybe along other lines or even as you work your way through the questions and exercises appended to the end of this book.

Find what works for you; if you experiment, you will! And then stay with it. What your heavenly Friend has in mind for you is not unending frustration in prayer but that you should latch on to the way of praying that makes for the closest, most honest and most enriching fellowship between you and him. It will not be quite the same for everyone, yet it will always be similar. We must never forget that our God will not allow us to let the good become the enemy of the best, or the comfortable obstruct the profitable, or what captivates the head insulate us against what activates the heart, or what gives ease get in the way of what brings growth. That explains some of the rough places in our pilgrimage and the dry places in our praying, which even the most faithful Christians experience from time to time: it is our heavenly Friend doing his job unflinchingly well. In character as the Great Physician he is leading us on with himself into perfect health, and he knows what will do us most good at each stage.

So let the last word be Paul's in 1 Thessalonians 5:17: "Pray without ceasing" (KJV); "Keep on praying" (NLT); "Pray all the time" (*The Message);* "Pray on" (J. I. and Carolyn). And see what God will do.

FOR DISCUSSION
AND REFLECTION

CHAPTER 1. THE GOD WE PRAY TO

Study

1. Bishop Ryle wrote, "If I know anything of a Christian's heart, you are often sick of your own prayers" (p. 17). How does this connect, or not connect, with your own experience?

2. Look again at the opening paragraphs of this chapter, which speaks of differing kinds of praying at different life stages (pp. 12-13). What are some significant changes you have seen in your own praying?

3. Study Moses' encounters with God in Exodus 3:1-6, 13-14; 34:5-8. What do these passages reveal about God's nature?

4. How could God's nature, as revealed in the Exodus passages, inform your praying?

5. This chapter warns that if our praying becomes so routine that it is like cleaning our teeth, we may be creating a false sense of spiritual security. On the other hand we can also find great value in some kinds of routine praying (pp. 13-15). What do you find in these paragraphs that speaks an appropriate warning to you? What do you find that you would like to implement in your praying?

6. Look again through the long quotation from Bishop Ryle on pages 16-18. Find one statement that you agree with, one that challenges you, and one that is like your own experience. If you could speak

personally to Ryle, what would you want to say or ask?

7. Pages 21-33 outline eight "sweet P's." "God is *personal, plural, perfect, powerful, purposeful, promise-keeping, paternal* and *praiseworthy.*" Select one of these qualities that you would like to study further and meditate on. Reread the section about it. Look up any biblical passages cited and read their contexts. Note questions that this characteristic of God raises in your mind. Consider reasons why you are thankful that God is this kind of God. How would you like your understanding of this characteristic of God to influence the way you pray?

8. Read John 15:15-16. How does this passage help define your relationship with God?

   In what ways do these words from Jesus encourage you to pray?

9. The final paragraphs of this chapter describe the book as less a how-to book than a to-whom book. The focus is on God and being God's person in this matter of praying. As you begin studying prayer from this standpoint, what hopes and expectations does this statement raise?

Pray

- First Thessalonians 5:17 assigns us to "pray without ceasing" (keep on praying). Set as a goal that for one complete day you will attempt to be in an attitude of prayer during your waking hours, constantly practicing the presence of God, looking for reminders of his work in every setting, turning your thoughts constantly toward him, sending out constant "arrow prayers." For example, the striated shadows of bark on a tree might remind you of the texture of God's creation and you thank him, an ambulance siren reminds you to ask God's mercy for all involved in that emergency, a worrisome phone call invites you to pray a release of those worries to God, a surge of anger triggers an instant prayer of confession. Even at the end of the day, allow a prayer to be your closing thought as you fall asleep into the arms of God.

- "Many who pray meaningfully have found it a wonderful help to schedule times with God and to plan in advance how they are going to use that time" (p. 14). Set a time (perhaps half a day) on your calendar or date book to spend alone with God. If you are able, choose a special setting. Outline what you will read, think about, pray about and meditate on during that time.

Write

Psalm 97 begins "The LORD reigns." Write a song, psalm or paragraph as a prayer of praise that begins and ends with those words.

CHAPTER 2. THE PATH AND THE BY-PATHS

Study

1. As you think of the subject of prayer and various ways you have practiced it, what are some paths to good praying that you would recommend to another pilgrim?

2. What are some prayer by-paths you have tried but would now post with a warning sign?

3. Look through the seven-scene summary of Bunyan's *Pilgrim's Progress* (pp. 42-47). Select one of poems that you find true in some personal sense. What makes this bit of poetry particularly significant?

4. If the life of a Christian is a hike (or a pilgrimage) as Bunyan and we agree, what does this metaphor suggest about what it means to live and grow as a Christian?

5. "The single word *help* is the best ingredient of prayer" (p. 53). To what extent do you agree with this definition? What do you find limiting about it?

6. See Jesus' instructions about making prayerful requests of God in Mat-

thew 7:7-11 (p. 55). Also review the poem on pages 58-59. How could you pray in a way that heeds both of these teachings about prayer?

7. Briefly scan "Unanswered Prayer" on pages 55-59, then study Paul's narrative about his thorn in the flesh in 2 Corinthians 12:7-10, and Jesus' prayer in Gethsemane in Luke 22:42. How do these biblical examples of a true path of prayer help you deal with the problem of Christian prayers, prayed in faith, that God appears to ignore?

8. Prayer by-paths (routes leading to boggy swamps, cliff walls and dead ends) fall into several categories. One of these is a failure to recognize that God is one who is "maximizing good in this fallen world" (pp. 62-63). How might accepting this truth about God affect the way you pray? Whom you pray for? What you ask? How you respond if a prayer appears unanswered?

9. Page 64 suggests another by-path away from good praying, based on God's omniscience (possessing all knowledge). In other words, if God has no needs and he knows our needs already, why pray? How do you respond to this argument?

10. As you think about your current place on the paths and by-paths of prayer, what are some of your current challenges? What steps can you can take to meet them?

Pray

- "Teach me your way, O LORD, and lead me on a level path because of my enemies" (Ps 27:11). Spend time thinking about this passage from the psalms. Try focusing on one or two words in the text at a time as you consider what this verse says about God and your relationship to him. After a time of meditation on this text, pray, talking honestly with God, who is your friend and walks your path beside you.

- Slowly read aloud John 15:12-17, noticing what this passage reveals about the relationship between you and Jesus. Pray to God who reveals himself in this way.

Write

Dr. Packer says that he has found that *"Pilgrim's Progress . . .* pictures the journey of life from the beginning of spiritual awareness right through to glory" (p. 42). Create a maze drawing your life story as a Christian "pilgrim in progress." Show your paths, by-paths, companions, detractors, battles, successes and your ultimate goal. Show where you began and where you are now. Illustrate your maze with symbols, words and short prayers. Present this whole scheme to God, thanking him for his constant presence.

CHAPTER 3. BROODING

Study

1. Brooding is often thought a negative or unpleasant frame of mind, something akin to worry. How has this chapter led you to see brooding in a different light?

2. What do you find worrisome or objectionable in this kind of praying?

3. What is the difference between allowing random thoughts to drift through our minds and brooding prayer (pp. 69-71)?

4. "The usual thing is that matters become clear after prayerful meditation, informed by praying over what we read in Scripture" (p. 77). Under what circumstances have you found this to be true in your own experience?

5. What do you find hard about brooding meditative prayer?

6. Reread the quoted excerpts from Psalm 119 on pages 81-82. What do you find here that encourages you to overcome the difficulty of brooding prayer?

7. Review the seven *l*s of imaginative frames for meditation (pp. 86-89). Which seem most natural for you? Why?

   Which method would you like to challenge yourself by trying? How?

8. Pages 89-94 speak of meditating on Scripture as both a quick and a slow march. What value do you see in each?

9. "We must remember that God (not self) is the center of our universe" (p. 92). Why is this important to keep in mind during brooding prayer? What are some specific ways that this truth should shape your praying?

10. "Whatever is just, whatever is pure, whatever is lovely, whatever is commendable, if there is any excellence, if there is anything worthy of praise, think about these things" (Phil 4:8). How can you best incorporate this admonition into your praying?

Pray

- I will remember the deeds of the LORD;
    yes, I will remember your wonders of old.
  I will ponder all your work
    and meditate on your mighty deeds. (Ps 77:11-12)

  Prayerfully brood on the works of God. If your mind begins to wander, begin to journal these mighty works and your meditative thoughts about them. Turn this meditation into prayer.

- "Meditation is something that you can do well in more than one way" (p. 85). Scan this chapter again noting more than a dozen ways to practice brooding prayerful focus on Scripture. Select one method to practice throughout the coming month.

Write

Select one of the biblical prayers listed on pages 93-94. Write out this prayer, personalizing it for one person by writing his or her name and appropriate pronouns wherever needed. Pray God's Word back to him on behalf of this person.

CHAPTER 4. PRAISING

Study

1. Early in his Christian walk C. S. Lewis asked several difficult questions about praise prayer (see pp. 98-101). What are some of your own questions about how and why God's people ought to praise him?

2. Read aloud Psalm 42 using voice inflections to express the various moods of the psalm. Where do you most connect with this psalm? Why?

3. Which phrases are repeated? What is the effect of these repetitions?

4. How does the psalmist's longing, remembering and thirst contribute to his prayer?

5. What elements of praise do you find in his prayer?

6. How are your own hopes similar to or different from the hope of the psalmist?

7. Review the six Ds of praise praying (pp. 101-10). Which comes most naturally to you? Which do you most need to work on? How?

8. What strikes you as significant about corporate praise (pp. 107, 110-15)?

9. What connections do you see between praising God and proclaiming him to others? What tensions do you find between praise prayer and proclamation?

10. How do you respond to the eternal aspects of praise prayer (pp. 109-10, 115-19)?

Pray

• Make an honest evaluation of your inclination and your practice of praise prayer. Talk to God about what you find, and what you hope to become.

- Give yourself three minutes to write as many names for God as you can recall. Enter into a time of prayer in which you meditate on each name and praise God for what each of those names implies.

Write

Study the pattern of Psalm 136, noticing repeated lines and repeated phrases along with one new subject in each verse. Create one or two significant lines or phrases expressing your own praise of God. Then use them to write your own patterned prayer of praise.

CHAPTER 5. PRAYER CHECKUP

Study

1. If you were anticipating a "soul checkup" by God, how would you most likely prepare for it?
2. On pages 126-33, we find that God's checkups are likely to include the state of our faith, repentance, love, humility, wisdom and focus. Select one of these areas where God has begun his strengthening work in you. What avenues has he used?
3. Select one of the six areas above where you know that you need God's continued work. How might you begin to grow more spiritually healthy in that area?
4. What do you appreciate about God's omniscience (Ps 139:1-6)? What makes you uneasy about this kind of knowledge?
5. What do you appreciate about God's omnipresence (Ps 139:7-12)? When have you wished, even for a moment, that you could hide from God?
6. What do you appreciate about God's omnipotence (Ps 139:13-16)? What questions do you continue to have about God's power?
7. If you were preaching a sermon or writing an essay about Psalm 139:19-22, how would you explain these harsh words as part of a prayer?

8. What connection can you find between the fierce words of stanza 5 (vv. 19-22) and the supplication of stanza 6 (vv. 23-24)?

9. "Go into your chamber, shut the door" begins P. T. Forsyth's paragraph of challenge toward good praying (pp. 144-45). What phrase in this paragraph could you draw on to improve your own praying at this current time? How?

10. Why might you want to invite God to search your hidden self, the part of you known only to him and to you?

Pray

• Begin your prayer with a time of silence. Meditate on the nature of God: his omniscience, his omnipresence, his omnipotence. If you are able to do so with honesty, slowly pray the words of Psalm 139:23-24. Invite God to search your inner being. Wait in God's presence as he gently guides you through his search.

• C. S. Lewis writes that we might well begin each prayer with the words "May it be the real I who speaks. May it be the real Thou that I speak to" (p. 144). Invite God to show you what his search has revealed. Ask him to lead you into the way everlasting. Wait quietly in his presence, absorbing what that means.

Write

P. T. Forsyth says, "Write prayers and burn them" (pp. 144-45). Write a paragraph (or a page) about what this time of searching with God has revealed. Use this piece of writing to pray to God as honestly as you are able. Then destroy your paper.

CHAPTER 6. ASKING

Study

1. When you reflect on your own patterns of petitionary prayer, what do you see as a current challenge?

2. Review the section "What Should We Ask For?" (pp. 153-61). What concept or paragraph do you find here that encourages you to pray?

3. What specific challenges do you find in these pages that you would like to work on in order to better pray within God's will?

4. Review the section "Why Should We Ask?" (pp. 161-64). How does this section help you look at your own motives? What do you find there?

5. Review "On What Basis Do We Ask?" (pp. 164-73). What encouragement and what challenge do you find in the three-legged stool outlined in the first paragraph and described throughout this section?

6. Review the final section "How Does God Answer Our Prayers?" (pp. 173-79). How do you think that you could best acknowledge the difference between human and divine perspective when you make requests of God?

7. If a friend complained to you that God had not granted a longstanding prayer, what encouragement could you offer that person? (See pages 177-78 for ideas.)

8. Return to page 166, the paragraph beginning "The promises of God are trustworthy." What do you find in this paragraph that draws you toward better praying?

9. Glance through the chapter one more time, looking for each quotation of Scripture. What passage is most helpful to your current situation? Why?

10. All of us are likely to benefit from talking over with our heavenly Father from time to time how we should order our personal intercessory prayers. What has God brought most strongly to your mind as you worked with the implications of this chapter? How can you best act on that knowledge?

Pray

- Review questions and answers 100-103 of the Westminster Shorter Catechism (pp. 151-52). Select one of the answers that seems particularly significant to you at this point. Spend ten minutes in meditation and prayer based on that single phrase from the Lord's Prayer.

- Select one of the apostle Paul's prayers for the churches at Ephesus, Colossae or Thessalonica quoted on pages 156-57. Pray this prayer for a church, a Christian group or church leader.

Write

Compose a paragraph (or a page) beginning with the following sentence: Believing that God loves me and invites me to present my needs to him in prayer, I hope to improve my praying in the coming month by . . .

CHAPTER 7. COMPLAINING

Study

1. When someone speaks of "complaining to God," what are some of your first concerns?

2. Focus on one of the complaint prayers of this chapter. In what ways is that particular prayer of complaint also a prayer of faith?

3. Why do you think that God never explained to Job why he was suffering?

4. What do *you* gain by Job's final encounter with God?

5. If you were in Jeremiah's sandals (pp. 184-86), what would you complain about?

6. In what ways is "Weeping Prophet" an appropriate title for Jeremiah?

7. Why is a lifelong walk with God likely to include prayers of complaint (pp. 186-90)?

8. "Regenerate people feel through their minds and think through their feelings" (p. 192). If this is true, how would it affect the way you talk to God about the harsh realities of your life?

9. What do you find helpful about Paul's experience with complaining to God about a "thorn" (pp. 201-2)?

10. "Small . . . is healthy in the presence of God" (p. 204). How might this statement help you to *prepare* to bring your complaints to God?

Pray

- Job's friends sat in silence with him for seven days—and that was the best part of their ministry to him. Bring to God in wordless prayer one of your major areas of suffering. For several minutes sit silently in God's presence allowing his love to absorb your pain. Close your time of wordless prayer by reading God's encouragement from the Psalms:

Cast your burden on the LORD,
 and he will sustain you;
he will never permit
 the righteous to be moved. (Ps 55:22)

Pray (with words) your response to him.

- Scan several of the prayers of complaint recorded in Scripture. Select one that seems to touch your own current pain. Using insights you have gained from reading this chapter, pray your own prayer of complaint using a pattern or idea you find in the biblical prayer.

Write

Bring to mind a Christian friend who is currently enduring suffering. Write what you might want to say to that person about complaining to God.

CHAPTER 8. HANGING ON

Study

1. This chapter opens with several pictures of what it means to persist. What is one of your own favorite images of "hanging on"?

2. What circumstances have made it difficult for you to hang on in prayer? (For examples, see pp. 208-10.)

3. How would you describe the New Testament concept of "sonship"? (Feel free to draw on or expand on what you find on pp. 212-16.)

4. What encouragement to pray do you find in this kind of relationship with God?

5. Read through the psalms quoted on pages 216-18. What do you find here that encourages you to hang on in prayer?

6. Select either Nehemiah's or Hannah's example of persistent praying (pp. 219-22). Which do you most identify with? How and why?

7. "By compelling us to wait patiently for him to act, *God purges our motives*" (p. 222). What do you find thought-provoking about this statement?

8. "By compelling us to wait for him, *God shapes his giving in a natural way*" (p. 222). Scan pages 223-24. Why do you think God often uses natural order as he brings answers to our prayers?

9. "It is for discipline that you have to endure" (Heb 12:7). When have you found that God's delay helped to bring maturity in yourself or in someone else? (See also pages 224-25.)

10. Go back to one sentence or one Scripture passage from this chapter that you want to hang on to as you continue to pray. Why and how is this significant?

Pray

• Slowly and prayerfully read aloud Romans 8:15-17, allowing the full weight of its meaning to be absorbed into your soul. Pray your response to God.

- Bring to mind one of your "hanging on" prayers, perhaps a desire you have expressed for months or years to God. Once again, bring this request to God, this time incorporating into your prayer some of the insights you have gained from this chapter.

Write

Journal your honest thoughts about what it means for you to hang on in prayer. At the end of your composition, record in writing the words of Psalm 130:5-6.

CHAPTER 9. JOINING IN

Study

1. What do you find naturally attractive or naturally challenging about joining in with other Christians?

2. Study Hebrews 10:24-25. What all do you find here that encourages you to join in with other believers? What would you likely contribute; what would you likely receive?

3. Review the paragraph on pages 237-38 ending with "And we *need* each other! God has called us together to be his body on earth, and that means that by our very relationship with each other, we are to testify to his redeeming power." When have you been thankful for some of the forms of connections within the church described in this paragraph?

4. Groups of people, even in church, who join in with some can also "close out" others, perhaps those most needing a sense of belonging among God's people. How can you guide your church to better extend the love of Jesus to those who do not yet know him?

5. Read again the heavenly scene from Revelation 7 (p. 242). Picture yourself among the diverse people in that scene. Are you comfortable or uncomfortable? Why? How could you begin now to connect with the kinds of people with whom you will someday live forever?

6. "Heaven is the goal of our pilgrimage, the place where through the mercy of Christ every single one of God's people will spend eternity" (p. 243). "Every gathering of believers on earth for worship may be properly thought of as a rehearsal for glory that is to come" (p. 244). When and how have you seen glimpses of heaven in your various "rehearsals" here?

7. What do you find insightful or challenging about the "personal lopsidedness" described in the paragraph opening with that term (pp. 251-52)?

8. John Wesley is quoted as saying, "There is nothing more unchristian than the solitary Christian" (p. 252). If John Wesley were sitting next to you, what would you like to say in response?

9. What relationship have you found between your personal prayers and your worship with other believers? How could you use one to improve the other?

10. What counsel about prayer would you offer to a "Reluctant Joiner" (pp. 252-58)?

Pray

- Review the "ditty" on page 255. As you come to the line "To live below with the saints we know," does any particular person come to mind? If so, bring your relationship with that person to God in prayer.

- Reread and pray Psalm 34:1-3, which opens this chapter. Bring to God your personal reflections on each line of the psalm.

Write

Once again read aloud the selected passages from the book of Revelation on pages 240-43, allowing your heart and voice and mind to join in that scene. Write your impressions.

CHAPTER 10. WITH MY WHOLE HEART (AND POSTSCRIPT)

Study

1. Do you find it more natural to pray with your heart or only with your head? For example . . .

2. According to Os Guinness, character is "who we are when no one sees us but God" (p. 261). What do you think your patterns of praying (talking with God) reveal about the condition of your heart?

3. How have you seen pride become a hindrance to prayer? (See pp. 264-66 for ideas.)

4. "I will give you a new heart, and a new spirit I will put within you. And I will remove the heart of stone from your flesh and give you a heart of flesh" (Ezek 36:26). How has this new heart affected your relationship with God? What do you see as your current "growth edge" as God continues to develop your new heart? (You may find ideas in pages 266-73.)

5. In David's prayer of Psalm 86, he asks God to "unite my heart" (v. 11). What would it mean for you to make that same request of God? (Various translations of that verse listed on pp. 275-76 may help you think of possible consequences of that prayer.)

6. Review the four tests of a united heart (pp. 276-77). If you were issuing yourself a progress report on those tests, what would that report say?

7. How has God's Spirit aided your praying? (For ideas see the section beginning on p. 278.)

8. Eight bulleted paragraphs on pages 279-81 begin with the phrase,

"Believers know . . ." What encouragements to better praying do you find here?

9. From the "Postscript" beginning on page 286, select an idea that seems just right for you.

10. Read as a prayer of thanks Samuel Francis's hymn "O the Deep, Deep Love of Jesus" (p. 284). Sit or kneel silently for a period of time, allowing yourself to rest in his love. When you are ready pray your response to God.

Pray

- Pray, asking God to direct your thoughts toward some section of this book that may be of value in your next step toward maturing in prayer.

- "You will seek me and find me. When you seek me with all your heart, I will be found by you, declares the LORD." Slowly read aloud these words of Jeremiah 29:13-14, as God's words to you. Respond in prayer to him.

Write

Read again the section titled "Postscript to Christians Becalmed in Their Praying" (pp. 286-89). Using some of the ideas there as a basis, create a one-week outline for your praying. What will you pray about on Monday, Tuesday and so on. What Scripture will you pray from? Which hymnal or songbook will you use? What area will be the major focus of your prayers? For whom will you intercede? What aspect of God's nature will you meditate on?

One plan could be to select a different phrase from the Lord's Prayer for each day of the week and use that phrase as a heading for all other aspects of your praying. For example, "Give us this day our daily bread" could lead to prayers of thanks for all that God has given you, prayers of praise for his all-bountiful nature, prayers of release from the sin of coveting what you do not have and do not need, prayers of confession for any wasteful habits, prayers for a specific impoverished country and its leaders, prayers for needy families, prayers for a nameless homeless person you saw on the street last week, prayers for those people and agencies who serve the needy, prayers searching for the place God wants you to take in helping to provide for others "daily bread."

Use something in this section to create a daily prayer plan for the week ahead. Afterward, consider if you want to make something like this a continued practice.

FURTHER READING

Good books on prayer magnify God and make you want to pray more than you do. Here is a selection of books that to our minds pass this test with flying colors and are all worth rereading from time to time.

BEGINNER READING

Bunyan, John. *Prayer.* Edinburgh: Banner of Truth. The sense of God's greatness and graciousness that Bunyan communicates across more than three centuries simultaneously knocks you down, lifts you up and urges you into active praying.

Kreeft, Peter. *Prayer: The Great Conversation.* San Francisco: Ignatius Press, 1991. Kreeft's racy, down-to-earth dialogues yield clarity and vision and awaken desire to pray.

Hallesby, O. *Prayer.* Minneapolis: Augsburg, 1975. An invitation to pray as plain and simple as it is profound and searching. This book is a real classic.

ADVANCED READING

Bloesch, Donald. *The Struggle of Prayer.* San Francisco: Harper & Row, 1980. Drawing mainly on Augustine, Luther, Calvin, Richard Sibbes (Puritan) and P. T. Forsyth, Bloesch offer a systematic theologian's survey that is very mind-clearing at a deep level.

Calvin, John. *Institutes of the Christian Religion,* 3.20. Philadelphia: Westminster Press, 1960. A classic minitreatise on the proper mindset for praying and the Lord's Prayer as a pattern for so doing.

Forsyth, P. T. *The Soul of Prayer.* Vancouver, B.C.: Regent College Publishing, 1995. While couched in the rhetoric of a century ago, Forsyth's grip on the theological realities of coming to God is masterful and inspiring.

Lewis, C. S. *Letters to Malcolm: Chiefly on Prayer.* London: Geoffrey Bles, 1964.

————. *Reflections on the Psalms.* London: Fontana, 1961. A well-read, independent-minded, humble-hearted man of prayer shares a wide range of helpful insights.

REFRESHER READING

(For all anywhere on the path of prayer.)

Bennett, Arthur. *The Valley of Vision.* Edinburgh: Banner of Truth. A distillation of Puritan petitions. Wonderfully heartwarming.

Boa, Kenneth. *Face to Face: Praying the Scriptures for Intimate Worship.* Grand Rapids: Zondervan, 1997.

————. *Handbook to Prayer: Praying Scripture Back to God.* Atlanta: Trinity House, 1993. Devotionally, Boa's books are very enriching.

Chapell, Bryan. *Praying Backwards.* Grand Rapids: Baker, 2005. An enlivening exploration of praying in the name of Jesus.

Crabb, Larry. *The PAPA Prayer.* Brentwood Tenn.: Integrity, 2006. A ruthless detection of unrecognized, life-draining self-centeredness in prayer.

Jones, Timothy. *The Art of Prayer.* Colorado Springs: Waterbrook, 2005. A most effective allurement into intimacy with God.

Luther, Martin. *A Simple Way to Pray.* Edited by Archie Parrish. 4th ed. Marietta Ga.: Serve International, 2005.

Moore, T. M. *God's Prayer Program.* Tain, U.K.: Christian Focus, 2005. A highway into regular use of the psalms in one's personal prayer life.

————. *The Psalms for Prayer.* Grand Rapids: Baker, 2002.

Subject Index